GENDER IN IRISH WRITING

GENDER IN WRITING

Series Editor: Kate Flint, Senior Tutor,
Mansfield College, Oxford

Difference in language, in subject matter, in form. This series seeks to explore what is distinctive about women's and men's writing, and to examine the theories of sexuality which attempt to explain these differences. Writings of all periods and genres will be looked at from a variety of radical perspectives: some explicitly feminist, others examining masculinity, homosexuality and gender politics as they are constructed through the writing and reading of texts. The series will draw on recent developments in literary theory in order to examine all aspects of gender in writing.

Published Titles:

Writing Differences: Readings from the Seminar of Hélène Cixous
Susan Sellers (ed.)

Writing for Women: The Example of Woman as Reader in Elizabethan Romance
Caroline Lucas

Gender in Irish Writing
Toni O'Brien Johnson and David Cairns (eds)

GENDER IN IRISH WRITING

Edited by
TONI O'BRIEN JOHNSON
AND DAVID CAIRNS

OPEN UNIVERSITY PRESS
MILTON KEYNES · PHILADELPHIA

Open University Press
Celtic Court
22 Ballmoor
Buckingham
MK18 1XW

and
1900 Frost Road, Suite 101
Bristol, PA 19007, US

First Published 1991

British Library Cataloguing in Publication Data

Gender in Irish writing. - (Gender in writing) -
   1. Ireland. English literature : Special subjects :
   Social roles
   I. Johnson, Toni O'Brien   II. Cairns, David 1948–
   820.353

   ISBN 0–335–09281–0
   ISBN 0–335–09282–9(pbk)

Typeset by Inforum Typesetting, Portsmouth
Printed in Great Britain by St Edmundsbury Press,
Bury St Edmunds, Suffolk

Contents

Acknowledgements

The original idea for this collection of essays emerged from a Panel Session on "Women in Irish Drama" at the 1987 Conference of the International Association for the Study of Anglo-Irish Literature at the University of Caen, and we would like to thank Professor Jacqueline Genet, Vice Chancellor of the University and the Conference Organizer for facilitating that. We also appreciate the encouragement and interest of colleagues working in Irish studies, which helped to convince us that this collection would be welcome.

We are grateful for the assistance of Ray Cunningham and his colleagues at Open University Press, as well as for the advice of the Series Editor, Kate Flint. Derek Longhurst of Staffordshire Polytechnic helped us by proofreading the manuscript. The Polytechnic has also contributed financially and technically to the completion of the project and we are pleased to acknowledge its generous support.

Quotations from Seamus Heaney's works *Door into the Dark*, *North*, *Wintering Out*, *Field Work*, and *Station Island* and from Samuel Beckett's works *All That Fall*, *Happy Days*, and *Not I* are reprinted by permission of Faber and Faber Ltd. Quotations from John Montague's works *The Dead Kingdom*, *The Rough Field*, *Poisoned Lands*, *A Slow Dance*, *The Great Cloak*, and *Mount Eagle* are reprinted by permission of Oxford University Press.

Contributors

Elin Ap Hywel is completing her doctoral thesis on the construction of "woman" in Ireland in the late nineteenth and early twentieth centuries in the Department of Humanities, Staffordshire Polytechnic. Her first degree was in Irish and Welsh. She is well-known as a broadcaster on the arts in Wales and as a poet, writing and giving readings of her poetry in Welsh.

Elizabeth Butler Cullingford is Associate Professor in the Department of English at the University of Texas at Austin. She is the author of *Yeats, Ireland and Fascism* and *Yeats: Poems, 1919–1935 A Selection of Critical Essays.* She is currently completing a book on Yeats's love poetry.

David Cairns lectures in Irish and British history in the Department of Humanities, Staffordshire Polytechnic. With Shaun Richards he has written *Writing Ireland: Colonialism, Nationalism and Culture.* He is currently working on contemporary cultural politics in Northern Ireland.

Patricia Coughlan lectures in English at University College Cork. She has edited a volume of essays *Spenser in Ireland*, and is currently completing a volume in a new history of Anglo-Irish literature.

Mary FitzGerald was formerly Head of English at Crewe and Alsager College of Higher Education. She writes on nineteenth-century Anglo-Irish literature and feminist poetics and politics.

Máire Herbert lectures in the Department of Early and Medieval Irish, University College Cork. She is the joint author of a catalogue of Irish manuscripts in Cambridge University Library published in 1986 and author of *Iona Kells and Derry: The History and Hagiography of the Monastic Familia of Columba.* She is also co-editor of *Irish Biblical Apocrypha: Selected Texts in Translation* and *Beatha Adamnain: Life of St Adamnan.*

Toni O'Brien Johnson lectures in the Department of English, University of Lausanne. She is the author of *Synge: The Medieval and the Grotesque*. She is currently working on the relationship of gender and genre in the context of Irish writing.

Shaun Richards lectures in drama in the Department of Humanities, Staffordshire Polytechnic. He is the co-author of *Writing Ireland: Colonialism, Nationalism and Culture*. He is currently working on a study of twentieth-century Irish drama.

Christine St Peter is Assistant Professor of Women's Studies at the University of Victoria, British Columbia. She has published in the fields of women's fiction, feminist theory and Anglo-Irish drama and is currently working on a study of twentieth-century Irish women novelists.

Introduction

Toni O'Brien Johnson
and David Cairns

Interest in gender in Irish society and in its culture and politics has grown in recent years, but even so, studies of Ireland's literatures in which gender has been foregrounded remain few.[1] One explanation for this might be that those concerned with the politics of gender and representation have devoted their energies to the pursuit of more immediate, practical aims.[2] A second explanation for the low visibility of gender issues in literary criticism may lie in the fact that the pivotal positions within Irish institutions are held by people not interested in exercising such interests. But just as important is the variety of theoretical positions those interested in gender issues hold, as well as the rapidity with which they can move to other positions in appropriating new strategies: all of which makes them elusive for the academic hegemony to grasp or engage with.

From among such a variety of approaches only one essay in this collection, *Gender in Irish Writing*, falls into the category called by Elaine Showalter "gynocritics" (247–50), attending to the work of a woman writer: the essay by Christine St Peter on Jennifer Johnston's novels. This was not a deliberate editorial choice, for we believe that it is crucial that serious attention be given to women writers; however, the choices of the majority of our contributors in this respect exemplify a trend among feminist critics in the late 1980s and early 1990s to widen the field of study from femininity-as-repression to the exploration of gender as a cultural construct, to include the masculine and attend to the construction of the dynamics of gender. The operation of the "pleasure principle" partly explains this trend: there is sympathy with Nina Auerbach's refusal "to give up writers I love because my allegiance to women tells me to do so: we have been told for too long that being a woman means giving things up" ("Engorging the Patriarchy" 157; see Elizabeth Butler Cullingford 66, n.2). But this disposition goes hand in hand with Linda Hutcheon's ambition to confront, challenge and debunk masculinist texts (145), for not all male-authored texts inspire love: many call for suspicion. In addition to the desire not to abandon so-called "canonical" texts to the masculinist academy, these essays also exemplify a theoretical awareness of the need to move from deconstruction to production, to shift from "undoing to doing" (Said, "Opponents" 158). In their productive readings, moreover, they deal with a variety of primary texts that extends far beyond the canon they refuse to abandon: they range from mainstream authors of the Irish Literary Revival like Yeats and Synge to little known material from the pages of *Sinn Féin*, from Seamus Heaney to Early Irish material, to a television series, and from Bobby Sands to Samuel Beckett.

The plurality which has been a noticeable feature of feminist critical practice in the 1980s is markedly at work in the essays in this collection, which refuse purism and neat compartmentalization. Here historicism(s) and cultural materialism(s) coalesce with deconstructive, linguistic and psychoanalytic approaches, not only across the collection but within individual essays. Such ease in borrowing and such disregard for the boundaries of "authorized" methodologies has been encouraged by the practice of French writers like Luce Irigaray and Hélène Cixous, who consciously and nonchalantly steal in order to fly (*voler pour voler*), recognizing that suffocating conventions must be disregarded for the sake of producing new insights. In the majority of the essays, the critic can be seen to be entering the text not merely to deconstruct it but to reconstruct it – whether by establishing its historicity and making the conditions of its articulation evident or, through deconstruction, problematizing language and tropes. And in the majority of the essays the critic does both. The plurality and stealing-in-order-to-fly that the essays exemplify enable fusions and borrowings in and from three of the most significant of contemporary analytical approaches: gender, colonialism and post-modernism. In each of these fields a concern with the production and re-production of power is to the fore, power expressed through languages, images and institutions, exercised through "models", prescription or proscription.

It should be no surprise if deconstructing gender in the texts of a culture should meet with resistance from those who are in command and advantaged by the *status quo*. Such resistance to "seeing" is inbuilt in the very dynamics of the construction of gender, where the unconscious plays such a crucial role: it is no accident that the unconscious has been metaphorized as darkness. Since the culture that produced the texts examined in these essays is patriarchal, and since accordingly it is the male and his constructed "masculinity" that dominates (for knowledge of what it is that makes a man "masculine" is assumed to be universal and therefore unquestioned and unquestionable . . .), it is inevitable that the main resistance to showing up the negative of the construction of "masculinity" should come from the male. It sometimes also comes from male-identified women, who have learnt all too well to accept a role that masculinism authorizes, and who resist the uncovering of the personal and psychological price they pay for such role-restriction. So long as one of the genders dominates the other, the dominant is unlikely willingly to forego the privileged position. Since the female is the object on which the masculine subject has been constructed, a hierarchical dynamic is inherent in this structure, and it is understandable that men should be fearful of having their dependence for "masculiniza-tion" on the objectification of the female exposed, and of losing their privileged position.

One historically significant female figure that recurs in the male-authored primary texts dealt with in these essays is a trope that seems to be traceable to the "sovereignty goddess" from native Irish tradition. She occurs in somewhat different guises in what might for convenience be divided into three different phases. First, the documentation suggests that in pre-Christian Ireland the goddess was conceived anthropomorphically as the centre of an elaborate ritual, the *banfheis rígi*, surrounding the validation of the king, in which she represented both the abstract sovereignty and the physical substance of his kingdom. She embodied various contradictory qualities, varying her shape from young and beautiful to old and ugly depending on the adequacy of the king who "married" her, for her primary concern was with the prosperity of the land with which she was associated (see Mac Cana, "Aspects"; Ní Bhrolcháin). In a second, later phase, some scholars claim that in the Irish literature recorded in the medieval period certain female figures are personifications of this goddess, for instance Queen Medbh of Connacht who instigates the central action of *Táin Bó Cuailgne*, and who mates with a series of monarchs. Deirdre is sometimes regarded as another instance of such personification, for her "tragedy" ensues from the unfittingness of the aged Conchubor to be her mate, as well as from her own insistence on the appropriateness of her choice of Naoíse (Máire Herbert, however, in her essay, does *not* support the view of Deirdre as a reflex of the sovereignty goddess). The ultimate phase in the archaeology of this figure, from the seventeenth century on, is the appearance of Ireland allegorized as a woman in literature and song follow-ing the suppression of the indigenous Irish culture. In this final phase, the figure appears both in Irish and, later, in English. This allegorical female is variously named, and she is generically envisioned as a *spéir bhean*, meaning "sky-woman", in the eighteenth-century classical Irish poetic genre called the *aisling*.[3] Her names there and in later uses of this figure include Eriú, Fódla, Banba, Roisín Dubh, Sean Bhean Bhocht (Poor Old Woman) and Caitlín Ní Houlihán.

The notion of using a female figure to embody such contradictory qualities as this sovereignty goddess does is problematic from most feminist viewpoints. Although it can be argued that there is an enabling potential in having a female deity who might suggest to women that they could themselves be active, decisive and potent (and the relatively favourable status of women in Old Irish law accords with this), as well as encouraging them in the idea that they might be the subjects, not the objects of sexual desire, nevertheless the danger remains of using this "authorized" female figure to represent the unrepresentable. In so far as she stands for sovereignty, this is unrepresentable because it is an abstraction; and where she stands for the land, the earth/body analogy becomes the burden of the woman, with an inevitably reductive effect which tends to undermine any notion of the woman being something more than her mere body. Thus the woman is being used to reproduce an idea, the economy of the country and its community. Her role is fixed, and she ultimately becomes the arbiter of death, notably in her use within the sacrificial discourse surrounding certain strands of nationalism (see Dalton).

Use of this figure today would involve an "appeal to a shared, closed system of meaning" and thus be a "mechanism for the reproduction and reinforcement of sharing and closure" within a nationalist community – words used by Ailbhe Smyth in another context, for the in-jokes surrounding the recent sculptural representation of Anna Livia in Dublin ("Floozie" 10). The "floozie in the jacuzzi" embodies the female figure from Joyce's *Finnegans Wake*, and thus, ironically, functions as a representation of a "fluid" female from a non-representational text that works consistently against fixity. Such a public artefact bears witness to a continuing unconscious masculinist drive to invest the female figure with the meaning it favours and fix it. However, it is of some consolation that contemporary use of the *aisling* by a few male poets like Paul Muldoon ("Sky-Woman" and "Aisling", *Quoof* 32, 39) and Michael O'Loughlin ("Medium", *Stalingrad* 26) is vigorously subversive. Perhaps the voices of actual women are, after all, beginning to be heard.[4]

The problem that faces most feminists in relation to the sovereignty goddess, and variations of her, is that like all mythical figures, she is transhistorical, and thus appears to be beyond any comparison with mere historical women.[5] Moreover, the mythical figure of Deirdre in the written medieval tale represents an attempt to create an emblematic woman more identified with male aims (in this case those of Christian monks), and is therefore the product of a markedly reductive process. The notion that psychological phenomena, including myths, are timeless does not relieve the anxiety caused by such mythical female figures to feminists who wish to claim the right to shape/reshape society: who wish to intervene in this apparently timeless reproduction, and put an end to repetitive variations that are reductive of women. The question whether the essentialism of mythically produced figures must *inevitably* be reductive and have disabling effects on mere historical women emerges as an important one, but one not overtly addressed in this collection of essays.

Whereas studies of gender in Irish writing have been so far relatively few, recently there has been an explosion of studies foregrounding the colonial dimension of twentieth-century Ireland's cultural experience. One eminent critic has expressed her weariness with the frequency with which she now encounters references to Matthew Arnold and "Celticism" in writings on the nineteenth and early twentieth centuries (Longley, "Including the North" 19). A less jaundiced opinion might be that references to Arnold and "Celticism" have multiplied because critics have found the connections and the insights that these concepts afford (and others associated with them) productive. For feminist critics, their productivity lies precisely in that they suggest how colonialism and gender might be linked together as expressions of power relations within the specific context of Ireland.

For the critic of Irish writing, acknowledgement of the colonial dimension of Ireland's experience opens opportunities to share materials and insights with others who are analysing analogous experiences in other colonial and post-colonial cultures and literatures. The relevance of their studies lies not only in the accounts writers such as Ashis Nandy have given us of the psycho-social impact of the colonizers on the colonized, but also in the recognition that the process of decolonization extends long after the "acute" phase, or the war of liberation. For cultural-political weapons and procedures developed in that phase to combat the power of the colonizer continue to be used, though now within a notionally post-colonial state, and a need remains to decolonize the mind, to liberate modes of thought from received readings still being reproduced in – and on – texts.

Hence the contemporary concern of feminist historians to trace how the concurrent activities of suffragism and nationalism in the early twentieth century were meshed, and how the triumph of nationalism resulted in the subordination of women by the deployment of decolonizing discourses within Ireland. The weariness of some is offset by the excitement of others who find the specifics of Ireland's gender relations more explicable with the benefit of these and other insights. Take, as an example, the complex relations of colonialism, language and culture in the ruminations of Joyce's Stephen Dedalus on the renowned "tundish". These are frequently used to illustrate the idea that the use of the colonizers' language by the colonized denies them access to their own language and therefore to authentic self-expression (*Portrait of the Artist as A Young Man* 172; Said, *The World* 48). But, in a passage worth quoting in full, Ailbhe Smyth has questioned just *who* is included in Irish post-colonial "liberation":

In post-colonial patriarchal culture, naming strategies have an over-determined role, invested with an irresistible double force and double meaning. The long-denied power to name, to confer meaning and thus (illusion?) to control material reality, is all the more powerfully experienced and pleasurably exercized when finally acquired. It is a treacherous ambivalent power if the paradigm for its exercise remains unchanged. The liberation of the state implies male role-shift from that of Slave to Master, Margin to Centre, Other to Self. Women, power-less under patriarchy, are maintained as Other of the ex-Other, colon-ized of the post-colonized. ("Floozie" 9–10)

To adapt Stephen Dedalus' reflection on the effect of the colonizer's lan-guage on him to this insight: does the soul of the woman not continue to "fret in the shadow of [the man's] language"? (*Portrait* 172).

Questions raised by the intersection of language, gender and colonialism are confronted by the writers of a majority of the essays in this collection; and for some, they form their central concern. Máire Herbert's analysis of the Deirdre tale outlines some of the tale's linguistic transitions. Redacted from the pre-Christian oral form to a written text in Irish in monastic scriptoria, this tale was translated by scholars in the modern period (during the eighteenth and nineteenth centuries) from the Irish, and circulated in popularizations in the colonially dominated world of cultural nationalism. Some of the early texts used in the course of the late nineteenth-century Revival were, even in their scholarly forms, the results of several stages of revision. No simple formula, Máire Herbert insists, can remove the cultural overlay hiding a pre-Christian "original". Nevertheless, her late twentieth-century reading suggests that the thematic core of the early texts offers the possibility of imagining a society with very different ideas from the texts of the Revival about the status of women, and their use as symbols. Perhaps these possibilities are no less confusing, but they are at least less disem-powering for women. She shows that elements of the tale that are identifia-ble as pre-Christian explore the consequences of Conchubor's transgression of a societal code which viewed the complementarity between male and female as part of a larger, cosmic harmony. Such complementarity does not imply a hierarchy in the relationships between the sexes, where communal and individual welfare rest not on domination but on the harmonization of divergent forces. In her archaeology of the tale, Máire Herbert clearly shows how the core events of its early form became refracted through the insertions of its Christian scribes, which shift the blame from a prideful Conchubor to an Eve-influenced Deirdre.

Máire Herbert's focus upon the Deirdre tale is shared in part by Elin Ap Hywel, but the latter's principal concern is to explore the differences be-tween the construction of "femininity" by some of the Abbey Theatre Revival playwrights and in the pages of the nationalist journal *Sinn Féin*. In relation to *Sinn Féin's* conception of "femininity", she demonstrates the energy and determination devoted to fixing "woman" emblematically and spatially as the pure and domestically incarcerated Mother or, more rarely, as a beautiful maiden "of peerless grace", her much asserted purity a denial of her sexuality. In the view of Elin Ap Hywel, this focus on the altar and the hearth produces a nationalist "woman" reduced to a static secular Madonna, denied meaningful opportunities for either political or cultural action. This essay directly validates the currently common view of later nineteenth-century nationalism as reactionary and backward-looking, assuring an archaic integrity that was culture- and language-based.[6]

In her examination of the Abbey playwrights, Elin Ap Hywel draws distinctions between Yeats, Lady Gregory and Synge on the one hand and Hyde on the other, seeing the former group as writing plays in which achieved female desire is the norm while Hyde, in contrast, produces plays and translations which are far closer in their conception of a passive femininity to the positions of the nationalists of *Sinn Féin* than those of the Abbey. In Lady Gregory's *Kincora*, Gormleith appears to possess power, granted that that power comes from her function as the site on which different strands of male power intersect. Her withdrawal of that power from Brian her husband, before his last fatal battle against the Danes at Clontarf, links her to the sovereignty goddess and the idea that sovereignty is withdrawn from a failing king, who must be replaced by one more fitting. Gregory, too, like Hyde and the Nationalists, writes "woman" to signify something else – in her case a queenly, but none the less male-dependent, metonymy of Ireland.

Of the writers Elin Ap Hywel examines, Yeats emerges as the one who contributes most to the construction of a viable version of femininity. Yeats's Deirdre, for instance, conveys a sense of unashamed gratified sexuality, and there is no indication that the tragic outcome owes anything to her having broken the rules of community and convention. But it is above all for his identification of the creative process with the feminine that Elin Ap Hywel can approve of Yeats – for his alignment with the maverick compulsion that enables self-transformation. Recuperating the Abbey plays she discusses for the purposes of decolonization as well as feminism, she sees their heroines as committing adultery against a misalliance of legislative as well as human bodies.

Like Elin Ap Hywel's essay, Mary FitzGerald's examination of the nineteenth-century Gothic text, *Dracula*, is an exercise in revising which focuses on the intersections of sexuality, power and decolonization. For Mary FitzGerald, decolonization and gender meet in their mutual need to negotiate power structures which are inaccessible and inscrutable; and in *Dracula*, via Bram Stoker's Anglo-Irish background, the Gothic links with the experience of Ireland in the century after the Act of Union. She insists, however, that it is more particularly the sexual politics of *Dracula* that accounts for its neo-mythical status. There, female sexuality is shown to be "terrifying, promiscuous, predatory, and subversive of male identity". Like the sanitizing drive of the cultural nationalists disabling the use they could make of early native literature discussed in Elin Ap Hywel's essay, the males in *Dracula* are compelled to sterilize female sexuality. The openness of the sexual desire of the female vampire, being turned to the closed purity of death, parallels the conventional male desire to penetrate the mystery of the woman. Mary FitzGerald proposes the figure of Mina, "scrutinizing her own texts, and those of men, for traces of a knowledge and a power forgotten therein" as a model for the feminist critic.

Sharing Mary FitzGerald's concerns with power and sexuality, Elizabeth Butler Cullingford offers us a movement between a "hermeneutics of suspicion" and recuperation in her reading of Yeats's early love poetry. After Field Day's engagements with Yeats in their first and second pamphlet series, Denis Donoghue's ironic judgement was that if the "man to beat is Yeats" (Field Day Theatre Company 120), then Field Day's "rewriting" and "re-reading" had yet to achieve their objective of debunking Yeats's "spiritual heroics".[7] Eschewing anything as bellicose as "beating" Yeats, Elizabeth Butler Cullingford's encounter with him reveals a poet acutely sensitive to gender. His personal situation, she argues, left him, for psychological, social and historical reasons, with unstable conceptions of the masculine and the feminine, with the result that he was unable to speak from the position of a unitary, phallic self. Thus something different from the forms and themes of tradition gets through in his early love poetry.

Yeats's early love poetry, in this reading, shows him aware of the struggle of the woman, particularly in the person of Maud Gonne, to become an active subject in a male-dominated world. It also shows him subverting the *carpe diem* tradition by refusing to focus solely or even mainly on physical beauty, as well as being aware of – and troubled by – the implications of his celebrations of androgyny which, he realized, while enabling for his poetry and advantageous for his own access to the feminine in himself, could also lead to the masculine moving towards a colonization of the feminine.

The patriarchal order against which Elizabeth Butler Cullingford sees Yeats writing – one in which the autonomous, unified self claims to constitute itself as "sole author of both history and the literary text" – gives rise to Toni O'Brien Johnson's questioning as to where this leaves the female subject. Her readings of three Beckett plays – *Happy Days*, *All that Fall* and *Not I* – offer an examination of the constitution of this female subject in language. While Elizabeth Butler Cullingford observes that "the myth of the phallogocentric self can be maintained only by a female Other who will hear and repeat it", Toni O'Brien Johnson shows that Beckett reveals the constraints and fixity of such repetition for the female characters he creates. Although the three central female characters refuse to remain silent, as the proportionate volume of their words increases, they move progressively towards an alienated discourse, for their scripts in the later plays yield less and less to mere *rational* analysis.

Toni O'Brien Johnson draws on Lacanian considerations of the "mirror-phase" in the constitution of the speaking subject, observing how in the originary mother/child dyad there is "no silent mirroring". This is the starting point for a detailed consideration of the psychological damage suffered by the three women in which they are themselves instrumental – as the Other/object for the constitution of the masculine/subject, trapped thereby into constituting their own subjectivity in "a limited male author-ized version of femininity", echoing patriarchal scripts. The further away from male authorization these women move (the extreme case being the speaker in *Not I*) the less capable they become in their attempts to construct themselves autobiographically through speech – incapable of producing their own "autobiography" as a coherent story – yet the more desperate their need to tell their story becomes. Despite the fact that Beckett's texts are gender-sensitive, nevertheless the dramatist's own unconscious, gender-related problems with distance and attachment are reflected in them. This occurs regardless of his desire to avoid his texts being used for mythologiz-ing purposes, which would foreground the figures and the functions they embody from the unconscious. The essay concludes with a call to refuse, in the light of the evidence in these plays, the inevitability of women's sec-ondary narcissism, through the development of alternative psycholinguistic strategies to the mere echoing of patriarchal scripts for the constitution of the self. It also pleads for a refusal of the silent objectifying gaze, so that the Other, whether female or male, can be *adequately* reflected and enabled in the constitution of the self.

Whereas Beckett's women are garrulous, the women in the male-authored poems considered by Patricia Coughlan are silenced – and appro-priated for masculinist purposes. Here, in the poetry of John Montague and Seamus Heaney, women who are domesticated and compliant are positively endorsed and here, also, we return to the invocation of "allegedly immemorial archetypes of femininity" as metonymic of the land and sov-ereignty of Ireland. Patricia Coughlan's examination deconstructs these "immemorial archetypes", documenting in detail instance after instance in the works of both poets, where gender roles are assigned by reference to stereotypes of the woman fixed in the domestic sphere to the benefit of the male poets' definitions of their own writing activities. As the study pro-gresses, further evidence emerges for the phallic and scopic nature of the language of the poets, leading to the conclusion that the selves of these poets are constructed against the feminine. Patricia Coughlan warns us at the outset that the gendered nature of the poems' insights might be *uncon-scious*, but her accumulation of so many detailed examples of this gendering makes it impossible for it to remain so now. Recuperation will have to wait.

As a result of Patricia Coughlan's reading of Heaney and Montague, the possibility of being flattered only to be deceived is reduced, and the claims to universality of an utterance that continues to deprive the female of mind and voice while insisting on her materiality becomes suspect. The cost of the idealization of rural life, together with the fixed position it has accorded the woman, is revealed. And the denial of autonomous subjectivity to female figures even by such able male poets as these emerges as a reflex of their difficulty in breaking out of the ingrained binary habit of masculine self-formation *against* the feminine.

While Patricia Coughlan's essay shows women who are immobilized and fixed by male poets, Christine St Peter's looks at that always troubling figure for the patriarchal order: the woman writer. This essay gives serious attention to a writer whose eight novels have received relatively little attention from academic critics. Examining the critical reception of the novelist Jennifer Johnston as both Irish and a woman writer, Christine St Peter traces the complementarity between the path of development (in terms of technique and subject matter) of Johnston's writing, and the critical responses to her successive texts. She shows Johnston's approval by male critics like Auberon Waugh and Anthony Burgess for her "perfect art", but this turns out to be yet another instance of flattery to deceive, for they deprive her of both seriousness and scope, and are therefore belittling, if not patronizing. They tend to reduce her to the genteel, or to see her as a male *manqué*, while Christine St Peter shows that her canvas is unusually large for an Irish writer, and her historical scope considerable.

Using a materialist-feminist approach, considering ideology as visible in the gaps, silences and contradictions of the text, Christine St Peter focuses upon some of the many contradictions in Johnston's "Big House Myth". She concludes that Johnston's women characters destroy their husbands and sons, thus recreating the myth of "woman the devourer", but she sees this activity as an effect of the "entrapment" of women. She notes how Johnston, in moving her focus onto the contemporary moment, initially brought with her the tropes and formulae of the Big House genre, so that in a number of her novels, flight or isolation are the only alternatives to the female entrapment that is characteristic of the identification of woman with the house she stewards. In *The Railway Station Man* a third possibility is added: the hesitant assertion of a different future in which human isolation can be broken down. The precondition for this is a determination on the part of the two principal characters to reject Irish orthodoxies and received versions of the past. Here, Christine St Peter emphasizes the need to move beyond merely personal solutions to larger, social ones.

David Cairns and Shaun Richards, in their examination of some twentieth-century Irish drama, also show how resistant the inherited tropes can be to even the most determined attempts at deconstruction. Their initial focus is on the Revival trope of the *Sean Bhean Bhocht*, in its representations of "woman" as devouring Mother Ireland, one of the most disabling representations examined in this collection. Commencing with Yeats's *Cathleen Ní Houlihan*, Cairns and Richards examine the impact of the trope in the early twentieth century – through dramatic imitation, in Maud Gonne MacBride's playlet *Dawn*, and through the use of the *Sean Bhean Bhocht* figure in the works of political activists such as Patrick Pearse and Joseph Mary Plunkett. In relation to this period, and drawing upon recent work by feminist historians, they comment upon the coincidence and implications of representing Ireland as "woman" while denying actual women political and civil liberties.

Cairns and Richards's chief concern is to explore two different responses in contemporary drama to the tropes of the *Sean Bhean Bhocht* and Deirdre: in the play *Bailegangaire* by Thomas Murphy and the television drama series *Lost Belongings* by Stewart Parker. Parker's approach is to use the Deirdre tale to induce horror in the audience at the suffering of his Deirdre, who is presented as a totally innocent victim, with the intention that the audience should be moved to act. Detailed commentary and analysis of Parker's screenplay then raises questions about the text and the medium, showing how resistant the trope is to deconstruction.

In Thomas Murphy's play, however, the unfinished narrative of Mommo is the crux, and the impossibility of moving on, without dealing with it in some way, becomes the central issue to be addressed. In this play, the present is an unending reprise of the past, but the narrative is concluded and, in that sense deconstructed, and so can be abandoned for more relevant action. In *Bailegangaire*, "doing" and "undoing" are concurrent, with the result that a new future can be constructed and entered. It is significant that Murphy's play dramatizes a cultural crisis and its solution, but that his all-woman cast of characters are none the less recognizable women rather than abstractions. Mommo may represent the *Sean Bhean Bhocht* on one level, but her release is not followed by rejuvenation; instead, she is more fittingly restored to an awareness of the love and continuing care of her granddaughters.

In offering critiques of texts that reproduce patriarchal paradigms of gender, together these essays take a step towards unsettling such paradigms. They also invite the withdrawal of projections of certain male fantasies from female figures enfolded in the texts examined, and the discontinuing of the use of "woman" as an empty signifier. They practise different ways of reading texts both old and new, and they interrogate and explore reputedly immemorial and immutable linguistic practices and gender typology. But as a collection, they also offer pointers to the huge space for gender studies in Irish writing that remains almost uncharted. Readers, we hope, will listen to the silences, and hasten to fill them.

Notes

1 The collection of sociological and historical essays *Gender in Irish Society* edited by Chris Curtin *et al.* does not consider gender in writing, and in its focus on gender remains a distinguished but isolated foray into the field.

2 The accounts and analyses by the Irish Women's Movement supply critiques of contemporary Irish society containing many valuable insights, and we are pleased to acknowledge our indebtedness to this work. Among relevant inform- ing publications are the following: Smyth, "Women and Power in Ireland: Problems, Progress, Practice" and *Womens's Rights in Ireland*; John Wilson Foster (ed.), "Critical Forum: Feminism North and South, 15 Years On"; Ní Chuilleanáin; Owens; Beale; Ward; Nulty; and the series of *Lip* pamphlets issued by Attic Press (for instance, Viney; Clodagh Corcoran; Eavan Boland; and Longley "From Cathleen to Anorexia").

3 On the *aisling*, see Gerard Murphy, "Notes on Aisling Poetry"; and Joseph Leerssen 246–87.

4 For a discussion of subversive use of the *aisling*, see Toni O'Brien Johnson, "Making Strange to See Afresh"; and for a warning against the dangers of the habit of thinking in the immutable gender polarities that the trope of Ireland as woman perpetuates, see Butler Cullingford, " 'Thinking of her . . . as . . . Ireland': Yeats, Pearse and Heaney".

5 For a discussion and references in relation to "myth criticism", see Humm 89–103.

6 See in particular the recent comments by Julia Kristeva in *Etrangers à nous mêmes* esp. 261.

7 The Field Day Theatre Company was established in 1980 in Derry by the actor Stephen Rea and the playwright Brian Friel to produce "a new theatre and a new audience" in Ireland. The directors of the Company now also include the poets and critics Seamus Heaney, Seamus Deane and Tom Paulin, the singer and broadcaster David Hammond and the playwright Thomas Kilroy. Each year since 1980 the Company has staged a new production or adaptation, usually specially commissioned. Since 1984 it has also published each year three pamph- lets as interventions in contemporary cultural-political debates. With the excep- tion of one pamphlet in the third series, Field Day has the appearance in its Board and its activities of an all-male enterprise. See Field Day Theatre Com- pany vii–viii; Hadfield and Henderson; Gray; and Heaney, "A Field Day for the Irish".

1

Celtic heroine? The archaeology of the Deirdre story

Máire Herbert

The Irish Literary Revival of the late nineteenth century sought to redefine the country's present by recalling a past world of nobility and bravery. For writers of the period, recovery of the era of legend was "recovery of a heroic Ireland" (John Wilson Foster, *Fictions of the Irish Literary Revival* 10). Early Irish narrative thus became a source to be mined by the littérateurs. They appropriated from the sagas the exemplary figure of Cú Chulainn, the warrior hero for whom honour was more important than life. From the mythic world of male valour, moreover, a female figure was also appropriated – Deirdre, the tragic heroine. She too was celebrated in poetry, prose and drama of the Revival. Yet, in contrast to the clearly defined role of the male in this recreated heroic world, enigma surrounds the female role. Was Deirdre betrayed by love? Or was she a victim of the heroic ethos? Did she submit to fate, or did she influence her own destiny? The evident ambiguity of her portrayal in Anglo-Irish literature raises the question of its source.

Indeed, the source initially appears hydra-headed. In the nineteenth century, the scholarly activity of translating the original Irish texts of heroic legends was matched by that of popularization. Literal, textually based translations appeared in learned publications, but their material was also made accessible to a wider public, refashioned by writers such as Standish James O'Grady and Lady Gregory, in accordance with contemporary literary expectations and nationalist aspirations. These fictional transformations in turn became the source of further literary creation. As far as the Deirdre story is concerned, George Russell's dramatic version drew on O'Grady's work (Kiberd, *Synge and the Irish Language* 176), while the *Deirdre* of Yeats

was based on Lady Gregory's rendition (Jeffares and Knowland 76). Not all
Revival dramatizations of the story were based on secondary adaptations,
however. Synge returned to the primary material in the Irish language for
his *Deirdre of the Sorrows*. Yet his version of the tale is an amalgam based on
published redactions from the early, medieval and modern periods (Kiberd,
Synge 176–95). In fact, the extant Irish material itself was protean, reflecting
the manner in which the theme was constantly reworked throughout the
centuries, to suit the changing circumstances in which it was being recounted (Quin 53–66).

We thus perceive a manifold process of mediation, whereby an early
Irish story was transmitted through successive vernacular cultural eras, and
received into the milieu of a new linguistic community. In literary terms,
each transformation of the Deirdre story has its own significance. Each,
however, derives from a narrative which was originally significant in a
society of heroic values. Is it possible to recover anything of the story's
original significance? Our evidence must be sought in the earliest extant
version, a text written in Early Christian Ireland, probably in the eighth or
ninth century.[1] To what extent does this text enable us to reach back to the
primary cultural setting of the narrative?

The earliest written version of the Deirdre story certainly does not represent the beginning of the story's history. Rather, it recreates in literary
form materials largely originating in the oral tradition of an earlier cultural
era. The social milieu of early Irish heroic narrative parallels, in many
respects, that of Celtic Gaul in the century before Christ (Jackson 28–43).
Comparative studies affirm that the Irish sagas retain many survivals of
ancient Indo-European custom preserved among the Celts (Dillon 245–
64). The story-matter, therefore, has its origins in a universe of considerable
antiquity. Yet access to this universe is only made possible by the fact that
its long-maintained, orally preserved traditions were reshaped as written
literature in Early Christian Ireland.

Writing does not simply transfer oral narrative to a new mode. As Ong
points out, "the condition of words in a text is quite different from their
condition in spoken discourse" (101). The fluid, empathetic and participa-
tory oral story telling becomes fixed, and objectively distanced in its written
form. The change of medium thus undoubtedly influenced the nature of
the early Irish narrative. So also did the cultural environment of the new
medium. Christianity was the prime agent of the establishment of literacy
in Ireland, and the Deirdre tale most probably was redacted in a monastic
scriptorium. Thus, though the prevailing ethos of the narrative seems far
removed from that of Early Christian Ireland, nevertheless, the subject
matter was given literary form in an intellectual milieu which was innova-
tive rather than merely conservative, and which embraced the learned
heritage of the Christian–Latin world as well as the heritage of Ireland's
past.

In assessing the existing tale, therefore, it is evident that there is no simple formula whereby removal of a cultural overlay can disclose a pre-Christian "original". We are dealing with a literary composition, not an unmediated recording of the survivals of the past. Yet narrative was the means whereby a particular presentation of societal and human issues was encoded and transmitted from the Irish pagan period down to Christian times. We must be mindful, then, that what Lévi-Strauss characterizes as an underlying structure of relationships (202–28) may be inherited by the written tale through the thematic core which made the myth more than transitory in the first place (Kirk 280–5). The Deirdre tale, as it now survives, is mainly in prose, but it also incorporates both rhyming syllabic verse, and *rosc*, a compositional form which does not fit neatly into the categories of prose or poetry. The form of the syllabic verse clearly demonstrates that it was composed in the Christian period. Recent study indicates that the passages styled as *rosc* also are to be assigned to this period (Breatnach 452–9). Both *rosc* and syllabic verse relay only speeches, and bear none of the narrative burden. Therefore, though prose, verse and *rosc* now evidently form a unity, and will be treated as such, nevertheless, it has seemed methodologically desirable that analysis should distinguish between the formally Christian rhetorical passages and the main prose narrative.

In the manuscript colophons the tale is styled "The exile of the sons of Uisliu and the exile of Fergus and the death of Deirdre" (Vernam Hull 3–7). This seems to view it retrospectively as a narrative explanatory of past events. However, the function of the myth of preliterate society was, as Dumézil says, "to.express dramatically the ideology under which a society lives" (*Destiny of the Warrior* 3). Does the written narrative of the Deirdre story embody a coherent statement about the outlook and structures of the society which it purports to describe?

The narrative may be read as social drama, following a pattern which Victor Turner sees as cross-cultural and transtemporal (145, 148). Turner distinguishes four main phases of public action in narratives of social drama: a breach of relations, a phase of resultant crisis, redressive action and, finally, either resolution or irreparable schism (146–54). In the Old Irish story, social relations are violated when Deirdre, requisitioned by the king of Ulster, Conchubar, elopes with the king's young warrior, Naoise. There follows crisis, as the pair and their companions are forced to seek refuge from the wrath of Conchubar, first throughout Ireland, then overseas. Subsequently, the Ulstermen attempt to redress the situation, reproaching the king for allowing excellent members of his warrior band to suffer danger abroad on a woman's account. Finally, however, the king reneges on his promise of reconciliation, so that, instead of resolution, there is definitive breach, death for the returned exiles, and further schism within the warrior band, as Fergus and his following abandon the treacherous Conchubar to take service with his enemies.

What was the import of this account of social process for the community for whom it was first articulated? The events of each phase of the drama are set in motion by the action or reaction of the king. Conchubar spares the infant Deirdre, whose untimely cry in the womb had led the druid to prophesy ill-fortune on her account. Yet this magnanimity is marred by the king's decision to rear the girl for his own purposes. His angry response to her elopement forces the exile of members of his warrior band. Moreover, it is his perfidious attitude to reconciliation which brings the exiles back to their death, and causes a further breach in the relationship between ruler and warriors.

The tale, therefore, may be viewed as an *exemplum* regarding the conduct of kingship. Comparative studies have shown that the early Irish ideology of kingship reflected a common Indo-European heritage. The king incarnated and represented the total social unit, and his wise and judicious rule ensured the prosperity and fruitfulness of the land. Failure in the observance of precepts governing royal behaviour, on the other hand, brought misfortune, social disruption and dysfunction (Lincoln 156–69; Binchy 2–10). In the narrative, Conchubar's actions as king are marked by jealousy, vindictiveness and treachery. Yet these attitudes derive ultimately from his primary transgression of the principle of *fír*, the wisdom and justice which ensured cosmic harmony (Binchy 10). By arrogating to himself control of Deirdre's life, the king exceeds the limits of just authority. His sin is, fundamentally, one of pride, an assertion of self, rather than the transcedence demanded by his status as "the very embodiment of the social totality" (Lincoln 163). As we see, Conchubar's behaviour profoundly affects the body politic. Societal bonds are sundered, the kingdom is weakened by the defection of warriors. As the text graphically declares, "for sixteen years thereafter neither weeping not trembling ceased among the Ulster people" (Gantz 263).

It is evident that power and its exercise are fundamental concerns of the tale. Is Deirdre simply an object in the transaction of power, a possession, perhaps interchangeable with any other? Or is she a representation of power itself, an adaptation in human terms of the goddess of sovereignty? In the universe of early Irish mythology, this female deity was the embodiment both of the physical land and of its dominion. Societal rule was conceived of as a sacred marriage between goddess and king-spouse, and the intimate association between sovereignty and sovereign was epitomized in physical manifestations. Thus, in early Irish narrative, on both conceptual levels, we see the goddess, as aged or demented hag, restored to youth and beauty by coition with a fitting spouse, while the land is restored to fruitfulness by the rule of a just king.[2] The choice of spouse seems to have been the prerogative of the goddess, who is often depicted as taking the initiative in the mating game. In our tale, therefore, is Deirdre's initiative in instigating her union with Naoise a reflex of the action of the goddess who selected her own partner? Is the conflict between Conchubar and Naoise at base a conflict over possession of sovereignty? Is the young warrior a potential claimant of kingship who seizes power prematurely? (Tymoczko 154–8).

Such a reading, it seems to me, involves selection from the story of certain elements which fit the sovereignty pattern while neglecting others. It is evident that Conchobar's possession of the kingship of Ulster pre-existed his possession of Deirdre, and was not dependent on it. Nor does Deirdre's choice of Naoise effect any transfer of power to the young warrior. Deirdre does not have the capacity to influence either the outcome of the conflict over her destiny, nor the future of the kingdom of Ulster. The female embodiment of the realm should of necessity be coeval with it (Mac Cana, "Women" 7). Yet Deirdre is depicted as a mortal female whose entire life-span is encompassed within the limits of the story. She is not, therefore, the incarnation of royal power. Yet a social drama about kingship begins with her traumatic entry into the world, and ends with her equally traumatic exit. What, then, is the nature of her role?

Deirdre enters as disruption of the convivial male environment of the feast, as she cries out from the womb of the host's wife. While the assembled warriors wish to have this child of ill-omen killed, the king judges justly that she be spared. He goes on, however, to declare that the infant will be taken by him on the morrow, to be reared by him as future companion. This takeover of the whole of the girl's future existence has already been interpreted as a prideful transgression of the limits of power. But what was its rationale? The cry of the unborn child intruded an unpredictable natural force into the ordered world of society. The warriors, according to their function, sought to redress the situation by physical action. While the king exercised judgement, in accordance with his societal function,[3] he too wished to neutralize the external element rather than accepting it on its own terms. He chose, therefore, to devise a means of its subjection to his control. Thus, Deirdre, the female epitome of unsocialized nature, is taken over by the king to be brought utterly under social domination.

Such a reading inevitably invokes the classic question "Is female to male as nature is to culture?"[4] Our present purpose is not to discuss the general appropriateness of the equation, but to examine the relationship between the domains in the world of early Irish mythology. The feminization of the land is amply in evidence in the sovereignty myth. Moreover, natural features of the land such as rivers and springs were also incarnated as female deities. Single or triplicate goddesses represented forces of fertility and of destruction (Mac Cana, *Celtic Mythology* 85–91). A notable feature of the system was the dual aspect of the goddesses. The figure of sovereignty could appear repulsive or beautiful. Death and slaughter were the reverse sides of the personifications of growth and fertility. It has been stated that "such a series of associations seems to reflect a conception of the world in its totality: the theatre of unending conflict in which oppositions can be neither disentangled nor ignored" (Carey 275). However, the realm of the goddesses is not an undifferentiated "world", but rather the natural world, which appears to man as having two faces, at one time benign, at another malign.

It has, indeed, been noted by Sjoestedt that in the Celtic mythological tradition there were "social forces of male character opposed by natural forces of female character" (112–13). However, the relationship between the two was not one of hostile opposition. We may interpret the sovereignty myth as depicting nature amenable to socialization. The king-god is chosen to mate with the goddess, whose earthly realm reacted either positively or negatively to the manner in which kingship was exercised. According to early Irish ideology, therefore, the relationship of female/ male, nature/culture was not one of simple evaluation on the level of inferiority/superiority, but rather a system of complementarity in which the fortunes of the sociocultural domain were linked with its respect for the power vested in the natural world.

Conchobar's act of possession of Deirdre thus may be read as an attempt to subvert this equilibrium, to achieve a position of dominance of the male principle over the female. The infant Deirdre is not viewed in her full human dimension, but rather as an unsocialized and disruptive force. Her name, derived from the verb *derdrithir* ("to resound"), brands her in terms of her cry from the womb (Dooley 155–9). Her depersonalization is reinforced by her being reared apart, separated from family and society.

Yet in seeking thereby to control ominous nature, Conchobar caused the development of a child of nature, who grew to womanhood unschooled in societal norms. Thus Deirdre's direct approach to the young warrior Naoise is completely outside of learnt cultural conventions. She "leapt at him and grasped him by the ears" saying "let these be two ears of shame and mockery unless you take me with you" (Gantz 261). Naoise, for his part, has no learnt response to her behaviour, and his capitulation is swift and unmediated. He and his brothers forsake loyalty to king and warrior band for Deirdre's familiar habitat, in the wilderness, on the margins of settled society.

Conchobar's pursuit is not so much motivated by jealous lust as by the need to regain control of his creature, to reassert his power, to bring unpredictable existence back within confinement. Though finally, in response to the wishes of his warriors, he feigns forgiveness, his design, nevertheless, does not allow acceptance of Deirdre's alienation to Naoise. Moreover, having declared this design in a public assembly, acceptance of its reversal meant, for the king, public diminishment of his power. Having taken the first injudicious decision with regard to Deirdre, all the king's subsequent breaches of the principles of justice and truth seem to follow inevitably.

Though he repossesses Deirdre after luring the returning exiles to their deaths, Conchubar finds his victory hollow. Deirdre is not now taken as a helpless infant, but as a woman who, having experienced an existence involving choice and freedom, cannot assent to one of control and confinement. A brief narrative sequence which follows the elopement episode (Gantz 261–2) describes how, in the course of subsequent exile, the king of Scotland discovered the presence of Deirdre and sought her. She, however, relayed to Naoise all the messages sent to her by the king's steward, and provided the warning that flight was necessary once more. While the episode serves the well-attested narrative purpose of reprise of the main theme, it also depicts Deirdre's growth in awareness. She now acts on information rather than on instinct. Thus, as the drama begins with the unborn girl, an invisible agent of disturbance, it progresses to a view of her as a fully realized human.

We are all the more conscious, therefore, of the fact that her final act is a considered one. Physical appropriation by the king did not mean that Deirdre accepted the role of his creature. Her defiance is initially passive. "She never smiled, nor did she ever take sufficient food or sleep, nor raise her head from her knee" (Gantz 263). Frustrated design then led Conchubar to exert power over her by petty cruelty, by sending her to his partner in crime, Eogan mac Durthacht. As she is being borne in a chariot, Conchobar taunts her: "It is the eye of a ewe between two rams that you make between myself and Eogan". As she is being thus publicly reduced to helpless sexual object, Deirdre breaks free by the only direct route open to her, by taking her own life. "There was a large boulder in front of her. She dashed her head against it, so that it broke her head in fragments, and she died" (Gantz 267).

The final image, the shattered skull of Deirdre, is a graphic realization of disintegration. At the societal level, what Dumézil terms "the sin of the sovereign" (*Destiny of a King* 111–12), upset the balance between male and female forces in the universe. Conchobar sought to demonstrate the mastery of the natural sphere by social rule. The tale, however, reinforces by negative *exemplum* the early Irish view that the welfare of the community rested on a system of interdependence rather than of domination. As the whole environment responded to the nature of the relationship between its constituent elements, the social harmony of the kingdom was sundered by the king's ill-judgement.

The mythic model of the relationship between male and female principles in the governing of the universe seems to have served also as a paradigm for male–female relations in social life (Sanday 55–75). Thus, as Deirdre's human dimension is realized, the story's import refers to the sphere of ordinary human behaviour as well as the sphere of power and government. On the human level, the concept of domination is once more depicted as destructive. Conchobar views Deirdre as object rather than as subject, and denies her the freedom as a social being which is her due. Though she has achieved her human potential in her life with Naoise, she remains for the king an object subordinate to his power. Her suicide, therefore, is a refutation of this power. Oppression of female by male thus is shown to achieve nothing but negative results. Instead of fruitful joint participation in the world, there is tragic waste, as the female who should produce life is driven to rend this life apart.

The narrative representations, therefore, provide what Clifford Geertz calls "symbolic templates" (Sanday 3) to set the limits of behaviour both at the social and personal level. Sanday has argued that male–female power structures and "sex-role scripts" are unique to each particular culture (1–12). Certainly, the evidence of early Irish story contradicts the generalizing model which posits universal male dominance through woman's association with nature. The script presented here is one of complementarity at both the social and individual levels. Refracted through the deeds of the *dramatis personae* of the Deirdre story is a view of the folly of seeking to distort the balance of the universe. Communal and individual welfare rested, not on the triumph of authority, but on mutual respect and cooperation.

Does this world-view persist into the Christian period? A textual distinction has been drawn between the foregoing main narrative and the speech passages composed in a Christian milieu. The first of these passages occurs in the opening sequence, after the unborn infant's dramatic cry. The mother is questioned by her husband about the source of the "violent noise". She however, turns to the seer, Cathbad, since "no woman knows what exists within her womb". The seer then utters the prophecy of the birth of a beautiful woman "over whom there will be great slaughter among the warriors of Ulster". In a separate poem this theme is reiterated at length. Deirdre will be an agent of destruction. Ulster heroes will die, others will be exiled, because of her "ugly harsh deed", committed "out of anger" against the king (Gantz 258–9).

The second speech section occurs close to the end of the story, when Deirdre laments her lot with Conchobar after Naoise's murder. Images from her past life in the company of Naoise and his brothers are contrasted with those of the present. The food of the wild forest was sweeter than the "honeyed food" of Conchobar's court. The singing of the brothers was more melodious than the king's pipers and trumpeters. Deirdre, however, does not merely bewail her changed world. She blames herself for having brought it into being. She takes responsibility for Naoise's death, claiming that "For him I poured out . . . the deadly draught that killed him." In further stanzas addressed to Conchobar, she is depicted as refusing his comfort. Yet there is only passing reproach of him for his part in Naoise's killing. Ironically, her main reproach is directed against Fergus, who "sold his honour for beer" (Gantz 264–6).

It is evident, therefore, that in these passages an alternative reading of the events of the story is being shaped. The public and private tragedies are traced back to a single, simple cause. That cause is Deirdre, the "woman of fate". She was responsible for the death and exile of great men. She offended against a king who apparently professed love for her. She led to his doom a fine warrior whose praise is extolled at length. The viewpoint is consistently patriarchal. Deirdre's mother is made to defer to the druid since "no woman" is knowledgeable about what she bears in her womb. The druid's prophecy describes Deirdre as a beauteous object of male desire, "whom champions will contest, whom great kings will seek" (Gantz 258). The emphasis is on the extent to which Ulster will suffer on her account. Deirdre's own suffering is depicted entirely in the conventional terms of mourning for the loss of a lover.

It would appear, therefore, that the Christian redaction of the tale found the earlier encoded representation of male–female relationships unacceptable. From a patriarchal perspective, Deirdre had broken free from the legitimate authority of Conchobar, and had entered into unlawful union with Naoise. When returned to the just custody of the king, she had committed a sin abhorrent to Christianity, by taking her own life. Therefore, her depiction had to be made to reflect her culpability. Yet tradition, and the traditional power of story, had to be respected. Thus, the original narrative framework was left intact. However, insertions were made which manipulated the rhetoric of the characters so that woman as subversive, as denier of rightful male authority, could be brought into focus.

Is this a representation of fundamental change in the structures of male–female relationships in Irish society consequent on the adoption of Christianity? Available evidence suggests otherwise. Laws on marriage, written close to the time of the Christian redaction of our story, accord pride of place to "marriage of common contribution", in which both parties contribute equally to the common pool of marital property (Ó Corráin 6–9). What we must bear in mind are the different levels of discourse in the Deirdre story. The mythic narrative articulated the communal ideology of a pre-Christian society. However, the written text represents the privatized word, produced by literate Christian scholars. It reshapes the narrative to suit the outlook of a male monastic society, which had interiorized the patriarchal views espoused by its religion.

Apart from the image of a single, all-powerful male deity, one of the most potent Christian images involving male–female relations derived from the interpretations of the Genesis account of Adam and Eve. In these, the female was viewed as the temptress, the cause of man's downfall (Pagels, *Adam* 53–71, 168–9; Daly 44–50). This projection of guilt on Eve is attested in the writings of early Irish Christianity.[5] One particular poem represents Eve as accepting blame, not only for transgression, but also for visiting her sins on her children. Her weakness transfers to the whole female sex. Because of Eve's folly in yielding to her desire for the apple, "women will not cease from folly as long as they live" (Murphy, "Early Irish Lyrics" 50–3). The misogyny present here may be seen as an indication of the source of the representation of Deirdre by Irish monastic *literati*. Like Eve, Deirdre transgressed against the male authority, the king. She, too, lured a man to transgression along with her. Society could be seen to suffer turmoil and tribulation as a result. It would appear, therefore, that, within the mind-set formed by Christian representations of male–female relationships, Deirdre's role underwent revision.

Yet this was accomplished with subtlety and style. The monastic writer involved in the literary marriage of pagan and Christian outlook within our version of the story consciously harmonized tradition and innovation, and fused all the elements of the narrative into a compelling whole. The power and poignancy of the story of Deirdre remained intact, though its designs on its audience may have been manipulated to suit a new societal ethos. Far from revealing "a concise yet utterly convincing image of the feminine psyche" (Mac Cana, "Women" 9), the early Irish representation reveals the richness and complexity of the societal and literary milieux which produced it. Moreover, though the story speaks from past times, it deals with fundamental and perennial preoccupations. In its exploration of concepts central to the life of early Irish society, it focuses on the relationship between the social group and its environment, and on the relationship within the social group of the roles of male and female. We may now take closer cognizance of the manner in which subsequent cultural eras have produced their own definitions of these relationships. We may also, perhaps, consider it more timely than ever to consider the extent of their own departure from the mythic view that cosmic well-being rests, not on a dominating power, but on a system of equality, balance and interdependence.

Notes

1 For complete text, translation, and commentary, see Vernam Hull. The translation alone can be found in Gantz 256–67. As the latter is the more accessible, in all instances of textual citation, reference is made to its relevant passages. The translations, however, are my own.

2 For discussion of the sovereignty goddess in Irish literature, see, in particular, Mac Cana, *Celtic Mythology* 94–5, 120–1; and "Aspects".

3 The term "function" derives from Dumézil's *L'idéologie tripartite des Indo-Européens*, and his other works. See Littleton 7–19, 130–2.

4 On this debate, see, in particular, Ortner; Mathieu; MacCormack and Strathern; Ruether 72–102; Sanday 4–6, 163–83.

5 For Irish adaptations of biblical apocryphal texts on this theme, see Greene and Kelly; Murdoch.

2

Elise and the Great Queens of Ireland: "Femininity" as constructed by Sinn Féin and the Abbey Theatre, 1901–1907

Elin Ap Hywel

Synge's "great queens of Ireland, with white necks on them the like of Sarah Casey, and fine arms would hit you a slap the way Sarah Casey would hit you" (Saddlemyer IV:25) have attracted their fair share of academic notice. Until recently, it has been obvious that it is the heroines of the Abbey stage – the Deirdres, Pegeens and Emers – who have been the focus of most of the attention which has been brought to bear on constructs of "femininity" in Ango-Irish literature. That this should be so is no doubt largely due in the first instance to the furore caused by the first staging of *The Playboy of the Western World* in 1907. It was recognized at the time, and has been debated since, that the portrayal of female sexual behaviour in that play was a specific focus of nationalist anger. Yet although Cairns and Richards, for example, have expanded our understanding of the nationalist construct of "Woman" by placing her within a familist economy, little attention has been paid to the specific question of the construct of "femininity" (both hereafter used without quotation marks, though retaining the distance they imply) espoused by mainstream cultural nationalism in Ireland at this period. That there was a gulf between Pegeen Mike, for example, and the kind of woman who inhabited the pages of *Sinn Féin* (for whom I am here substituting the metonymic Elise), has long been recognized, but little, if any work has been done to delineate the exact nature and extent of that gulf.[1]

The fact of the gulf's existence is the more ironic when one considers what the writers and dramatists associated with the early Abbey had in common with mainstream cultural nationalists. By 1907, it is true, the heady days of agreement over *Cathleen Ní Houlihan* were over, as also was the cooperation between the Gaelic League and the Irish Literary Theatre of the early days. Still, the same materials, to a large extent, enthused both parties, and both constructed their views of the Irish past from a similar fund of the mythological and folkloric materials which were increasingly being "discovered", collected, translated and popularized from the beginning of the twentieth century onwards.[2] It might also be said that both parties had broadly similar aims – to create and portray a community which could be presented as a coherent and viable alternative to the denationalized Ireland of the first decade of the twentieth century. Both imaginary communities were intensely patriarchal in structure, but Woman inhabited a different locus in respect to the seat of power in the imaginary community of the cultural nationalists to that of playwrights such as Synge, Gregory and Yeats. Adherents of both these imaginary communities drew on the same kind of materials but inflected the constructs of femininity which they found there in differing ways. Both were intensely concerned with topics such as sexuality, power, nature and language, but again these bore different alignments with respect to the figure of Woman. In certain cases, mainstream nationalism's view of female sexuality prevented it from adequately mining the ore of what it claimed to be its cultural heritage. Within a discourse of nationalism which was still formulated in terms of Arnoldian "Celtism", these differing emphases had varying implications for the construct of femininity within that discourse.

In an attempt, then, to situate what I will call the "Abbey woman"[3] against the background of the nationalist construct of femininity at this period, I will be looking at the way femininity is constructed in the pages of *Sinn Féin* in the period directly before the riots in 1906–1907. I will then move on to consider different treatments of the Deirdre tale in order to highlight some of the ways in which similar material shows different attitudes to the position of the woman and the articulation of her sexuality within a patriarchal society. Finally, I will deal with attitudes to Nature and Spirituality.

At the turn of the century, the Gaelic League had published *Irishwomen and the Home Language* by Mary E. Butler in its series of "useful" pamphlets, presumably as a kind of blueprint for behaviour for women wishing to take up their places in a struggle which was more often than not described in terms of a war. Butler's pamphlet made it quite clear from the outset that the place for nationalist woman was not with the men in the public arena. "Shrieking viragoes" and "aggressive amazons" were specifically discouraged, and it was emphasized that Irish women were not "required to plunge into the vortex of public life". Instead, the woman was to exchange any claim to autonomy outside the home for a kind of divine rule within:

Woman reigns as an autocrat in the kingdom of her home. Her sway is absolute. She rules and serves simultaneously in the home circle. Not

only does she attend to the organisation of the practical details, and the
supplying of material wants, but the spiritual side of home life is starved
or satisfied according as her nature is noble or ignoble. . . . The spark
struck on the hearthstone will fire the soul of the nation. (3)

It was taken for granted that this figure would be a mother, and it was
portrayed as a privilege for her to guide the first faltering steps of her
children's spiritual odyssey. Butler speaks with almost breathless approba-
tion of "gentle low-voiced women who teach little children their first
prayers, and, seated at the hearth-side, make those around them realize the
difference between a home and a dwelling" (2). This static creature sitting
by the fire, unwilling to venture out into the great world, fixed in her
domestic sphere, is iconized by her connection with spirituality into a
secular Irish Madonna. Her world revolves around the twin poles of Altar
and Hearth. She barely exists in her own right; she is simply a channel for
the life-giving milk of an Irish Ireland, and as such strongly contrasted to
the denationalized mother who appears in an article in *The Leader* for 15
September 1900, whose nipples are a "poisoned fount" to her children.
Although she possesses, by implication, the attributes of fecundity, these are
stressed at the expense and to the exclusion of any expression of individual
sexuality.

It is perhaps understandable that the Gaelic League placed such an emphasis on the figure of the nurturing mother. Hyde well recognized the
literal importance of the mother tongue to the mother land, making it clear
at the time of the Intermediate Education controversy in 1899 that mothers
were both front-line and bastion against the loss of the Irish language. This
was all the more true if the mother figure were placed in the setting of
Western peasant (and therefore at this date, still largely Irish-speaking)
society. There had been a consensus as to the connection between fluency
in Irish and a genuine moral superiority for quite some time (Hyde, *The
Irish Language* 15–16), and when Woman was added to the mixture as
prescribed, the brew at times became almost transcendental. As Pearse
rhapsodized in 1902:

What wonderful faces one sees in Irish-speaking crowds! Truly the
lives of those whose faces are so reverent and reposeful must be beautiful beyond your and my ken. A painter might find here many types for
a St. John, a St. Peter, or a Mater Dolorosa. I often fancy that if some
of the Old Masters had known rural Ireland, we should not have so
many gross and merely earthly conceptions of the Madonna as we
have. (Edwards 39)

This same network of concerns – spirituality, the Irish language, an apparent negation of sexuality, the West, the peasantry – is still to be found
clustered around the figure of Woman on the pages of the *Sinn Féin* of the

1906–1907 period. "Beartin Fraoch"[4] unleashed the following flow in an article called "Coláiste Connacht" on a college for the teaching of Irish to adults:

> I somehow thought a beautiful maiden of peerless grace, virtue and modesty, called us, and led us on. Her language was so sweet, so musical and poetic, so full of love and truth and innocence, that no mortal could resist. On and on we followed, leaving the press and throng, the whirr and noise, the din of crowded cities, and the whish and thud of trains and tramcars, this peerless maiden still leading us on, until the noise of the busy world died away on the evening breeze, and we reached a land where people were happy, where men whistled as they strolled leisurely homewards from the fields; where simple maidens sang songs of occupation and old women crooned sweet snatches of old world songs which blended with the whirring of their spinning wheels. And in this land of majestic hills, of shining lakes, of dark green woods, quiet glens, and rushing mountain brooks, the maiden stood, and gracefully lifting her right hand, in which she held a sword of light, pointed to a large mansion, situated on a beautiful hill overlooking a sparkling lake, shaded from the west winds by cloud-capped "eternal hills", she said, "Foghluim agus bighidh saor" ("Learn that ye may be free"). (3)

It is interesting that we have here a maiden rather than a mother: her affinity with the *spéirbhean* or sky-woman of eighteenth-century classical vision-poetry in the Irish language is remarkable. Although attention is drawn to her sexuality by the repetition of her claims to purity, it should be noted that, as with the figure of the mother, individual sexuality is hinted at only to be denied. She is emblematic, general; yet there are far more mothers than maidens on the pages of the contemporary nationalist press.

In general, then, it is the figure of the mother which is privileged in cultural nationalism's discourse of Woman as shown by the pages of *Sinn Féin* in 1906–1907. Once again, individuality disappears and Irish women are reduced to self-effacing ciphers, literally living through their children. "Eibhlin" wrote on 5 May 1906:

> Thank God for those mothers of ours – who have faced life and its sorrows and terrors and its labours without even seeming to realise the possibility of shirking them. We Irish women have never deserved the reproach of cowardice – and shall we of this generation not strive to pass on the previous heritage of that tradition as untarnished as we get it? Yes, surely, – or we are degenerates – and not worthy the life our generous mothers gave us. (4)

There is, once again, an emphasis on spirituality, this time linked to the idea of visible physical attributes:

We are rapidly becoming the worst-shaped people on the face of the earth. . . . Irish beauty – with its exquisite purity of colouring, and its wonderful spiritual appeal – is the legacy of many generations of white-souled, clean-living men and women – and as such we should cherish it, and hold it among our most precious possessions . . . if the men of our race don't give up drinking, and smoking in excess, and if the physical culture of our sex is not attended to – we might as well give up the attempt to assert our nationhood again, and quietly allow ourselves to be branded as the most cowardly people in the world. ("Eibhlin", 16 June 1906: 3)

A poem entitled "Herself" is interesting in this context. It is written from the point of view of a dreaming peasant lad who has conjured up an imaginary creature to live with him, and it is impossible to make out whether she is mother, sweetheart, Ireland or some combination of the three. What is unambiguous, however, is the emphasis on spirituality ("E.B." 3). That this is a specific form of spirituality may best be illustrated by the advice given elsewhere as to what to do with a broad ledge which is too high to be turned into a window-seat: install a statue of the Virgin and you will miraculously have created "a gracious shrine to our lady" ("Eibhlin", 19 May 1906: 4).

There is, throughout, an emphasis on placing Woman in her context within a patriarchal society. Having forgotten that Irish men drink and smoke to excess, "Eibhlin" goes on to say:

It is the men of Ireland – strong of will, strong of heart and purpose, strong of principle, and with bodies strengthened by manly exercises and pure and sober living who shall win the Great Victory. It is the women of Ireland – fit helpmates and mothers of a nation of men – who shall help them to it.

All this rhetoric was punctuated by the small, still voice of Riobard Ua Fhloinn, who warned that men:

. . . are as terrified at the thought of the independence of women as Englishmen are at the thought of the independence of Ireland. . . . If you train a woman to look up to men and not to her own sex, you are fitting her with the servile spirit of the seoinin, and the seoinin mother will, by a fatal consequence, bring up a family of seoinin children . . . If we consider how much boasting we have lavished on Irish women, and how little real respect we have paid them – how little real liberty we have allowed them – we need not be surprised at the degraded and denationalised condition in which we find Ireland today. (3)[5]

The pages of the journals of the day certainly contain a number of attempts to puncture the myth of Irish male chivalry towards women –

however, it seemed to have little effect on the general tenor of rhetoric. A few weeks later, Maire De Buidleir (presumably the Mary E. Butler of the Gaelic League pamphlet) was writing on the subject of "Our Irish Homes":

> The women of present-day Ireland have come into a goodly inheritance; secure homesteads in a magnificent country which shall certainly be free before their infants now in their cradles are grown to manhood and womanhood. It is their pleasant, their charming duty, to make their homes worthy of Irish-Ireland. (De Buidleir 1)

It is perhaps unsurprising, given the author, to find her remarking further, "The Altar and the Hearth – these are the two most sacred spots on earth, and to none so sacred as to Irish hearts." Butler's earlier pamphlet had been reticent to the point of silence on the role to be played by unmarried or childless women in the higher endeavour; not even envelope-licking is mentioned. Although the single woman makes more of an appearance on the pages of *Sinn Féin* for 1906–1907 than she does in Butler's writing, it is not exactly in her capacity as a political organizer that she is mentioned, but as a homemaker. In 1906, *Sinn Féin* ran a series under the title "Letters to Nora", purporting to be letters from an older woman friend to a young girl who had newly completed her convent education and was looking around for ways of employing herself in the nationalist cause. As the series goes on, the domestic arrangements seem to become a metaphor for setting Ireland's house in order for what is perceived as the coming battle, and yet it is painfully obvious that once again "Woman" had become frozen along with the pretty little fripperies in the domestic sphere: "No Irishwoman can afford to claim a part in the public duties of patriotism until she has fully satisfied the claims her 'home' makes on her" ("Eibhlin", 19 May 1906: 4). To this end, having talked at length about the problems of choosing menus and wallpapers, the mentor continues:

> . . . if I boldly claimed a column of a paper whose every line is devoted to a splendid and heroic cause – if I claimed, I say, a whole column of it for the discussion of subjects as homely and workaday as these, it is because I felt that through them, above all, shall "Sinn Féin" as a working policy for more than half our race – that is to say for the women – best be tested. ("Eibhlin", 2 June 1906: 3)[6]

As far as leaving the domestic sphere went, women were allowed as far down the road as it took them to buy a bolt of Irish-made cloth, and that was it. (The fact that so much attention was paid to women's clothes has more to do with the growing recognition of cultural nationalism as a consumer market which would eagerly purchase such items as an eau de toilette called "Erin's Tears" than with any particular broadening of woman's role.) This was a period when Irishwomen's sorties into nationalist endeavour could be reduced to an article entitled "Elise in search of a blouse", which chronicled the frustrations of attempting to find "black material of 'gossamer texture' " manufactured in Ireland. "Elise" characteristically and humorously describes this long and frustrating process in terms of dramatic struggle:

> The situation is becoming strained. My need for a new blouse has grown more imperative with the lapse of time. Christmas is approaching. My heroic soul abhors compromise. Must I have a blouse made of tweed or serge – both unsuitable materials? Or must I go blouseless for the sake of my country? (Anon.)

Comic – and suggestive – as this vision is, responses to it in the correspondence columns of the paper underline the elevated terms in which this one active expression of nationality was allowed to exist by *Sinn Féin*. As "Banba" said:

> I will say that any woman can be dressed – elegantly and tastefully dressed – in Irish manufacture from head to foot for three pounds, and oh! the delightful, the triumphant feeling of walking out, knowing that it is so, and that every article on one's person has been made by a pair of Irish hands in some corner of Ireland, and that every shilling we have spent on our clothes has helped to keep some Irish boy or girl at home in the dear land. It is glorious, inspiring, let mere man say what he will. (1)

Women outside the North had to wait until the appearance of the suffrage paper *The Irish Citizen* for any rational public discussion of the relationship between nationalism and feminism, or mention of any role models of militant nationalist females. I have quoted at length here because, although the content of passages such as this last are to a large extent what might be expected, their style perhaps is not. Is it a kind of mock-heroic compensation for inability or unwillingness to write about nationality in a more abstract sense, or is it, perhaps, an attempted deflation – conscious or unconscious – of the nationalist rhetoric which placed maidens, not on pedestals but on Irish hilltops clutching swords of light? Again, it does much to reinforce the sense of a gulf between these women and the figures portrayed on the stage of the Abbey; it is extremely difficult to imagine Deirdre of the Sorrows choosing wallpaper. Despite Elise's blouselessness, sexuality is subsumed completely in the passages by an exclusive concentration on the small externals of life, the swagged curtains and the kid gloves, and it is made quite clear that even childless, unmarried women should concentrate on "homemaking".

It should have become obvious from these passages that the possible variations on the construct of femininity available to mainstream nationalism at this date – 1906–1907 – were few, and how firmly the alternatives were fixed around a kind of static negation of sexuality. On the whole, the

Good Irishwoman was the Good Mother, spiritual, fixed at home, trans-
mitting Irishness to her children. The emphasis was on conservation and
conservatism. Nor is this surprising. Those who articulated cultural
nationalism knew what they wanted by this stage and what kind of community they wished to recognize as their own, and the only change sought
was to have that recognized in terms of consensus. They wanted to con-
serve the Irish language, to stop the flow of emigration and thus stabilize
the rural population. They also wanted to project this view onto the past.
The community projected by Synge and Gregory, however, was different,
and its women were different. Not only did many of the plots of their plays
revolve around the exploration of barriers to the heroine's free expression
of her sexual choice, but those heroines, far from being transfixed in their
context by the hatpin of conventional roles, were free to roam the stage of
the heroic past in as capricious a fashion as they would.

The extent to which writers such as Hyde and Gregory had collaborated
on projects and the use they made of each others' materials have slightly
obscured the jealousy that the adherents of mainstream cultural nationalism
felt at what they saw as the Abbey's monopolization and de-bowdlerization
of the stock of Gaelic material. Reviewers such as "Scrutator" could be
intensely scathing about portrayals of these legends, as in this comment on a
production of Scawen Blunt's "Fand":

> Miss Maire O'Neill (the most unsuitable member in the company to
> play the part) came on as Fand. She was restrained at first, so long as
> she posed as the ancient crone who was going to cure Cuchulain. But
> when she flung aside her outer garment, and revealed herself, arrayed
> in delicate blue, as the goddess herself – then was the very spirit of
> melodrama rampant. She could not keep quiet for a moment. She
> ranted and raved and waved her hands, the very incarnation of the
> wronged and injured heroine of the amateur theatrical society. Why,
> Mr. Stage-Manager, did you not tone this down a little? Is your
> conception of a Celtic goddess, the English parlour-maid in a fit of
> hysterics? (3)

As the gibes at "melodrama" and "English parlour-maid" show, "Scrutator" was attempting to identify the Abbey's portrayal of the Irish heroic
past with present English music-hall offerings, in nationalist terms not only
hopelessly "anti-national" but also "immodest" and "immoral". If Hyde's
re-assemblage of the Deirdre tale is anything to go by, however, Celtic
goddesses, if not related to English parlour-maids, had certain affinities with
well-brought-up convent girls who had rather gone off the rails at the first
sight of male beauty.

The version of the Deirdre tale (the earliest written version of which can
be found in the twelfth-century *Book of Leinster*) which Hyde popularized
in his *A Literary History of Ireland* is curiously patchwork. Beginning with

the opening of a translation of the late eighteenth- or early nineteenth-century Belfast manuscript which he had previously published in *Zeitschrift für celtische Philologie*, the tale progresses through Hyde's retelling of the 1801 O'Flanagan version to two alternative endings, the first from O'Flanagan and the second from the *Book of Leinster* itself. The Deirdre who appears in the Belfast manuscript version is as far removed from the Deirdre of the Book of Leinster as she is from the eponymous heroine of Yeats's play; as Eleanor Hull puts it, "it is curious to find the wild woman of the 12th century *Book of Leinster* version transformed into the Lydia Languish of a later age"; (235). The absence of the *geasa* motif of the original (whereby Deirdre compels Naoise to elope with her to Scotland by laying bonds on him) endows Deirdre with a measure of free will in that decision which she does not possess in the medieval version, losing the sense that she and Naoise are fated to run away together and are merely acting out an event which has long since been decided by agencies outside their control. As with the rest of Hyde's translation, the episode is couched in language which does more to evoke the polite drawing-room of Victorian fiction than the brutal great outdoors of the twelfth century:

> When Naoise beheld the splendour of the girl's countenance he is filled with a flood of love, and Deirdre beseeches him to take her and escape to Alba. But Naoise thought that too hazardous, for fear of Conor. But in the course (?) of the night Deirdre won him over, so that he consented to her, and they determined to depart on the night of the morrow. (*Literary History of Ireland* 309–10)

The effect of this degree of autonomy, coming as it does in the middle of a linear narrative progression which begins by setting the newly born child firmly in the context of her predestined relationship to Conor and thus to the community into which she is born (like the nationalist woman of 1907), is to highlight Deirdre's moral fall in her refusal to accept the framework within which her life has been placed. Of the two endings, O'Flanagan's has Deirdre simply fall into the grave of Naoise and his brothers, and die there: "After her lay of lamentation she falls into the grave where the three are being buried, and dies above them" (*Literary History* 316). Hyde, however, also goes on to quote the stark ending of the *Book of Leinster*, privileging it over O'Flanagan by the copiousness of his quotation:

> "What is it that you see that you hate most?" said Conor. "Thou thyself and Eoghan (Owen) son of Duthrecht", said she. "Thou shalt be a year in Owen's couch then", said Conor. Conor then gave her over to Owen. They drove the next day to the assembly at Muirtheimhne. She was behind Owen in a chariot. She looked towards the earth that she might not see her two gallants. "Well, Deirdre," said Conor, "it is the glance of a ewe between two rams you

cast between me and Owen." There was a large rock near. She hurled her head at the stone, so that she broke her skull and was dead. (*Literary History* 317)

The net effect of this peculiar hotchpotch is to erect a narrative structure which casts the normative conventions of a community whose prescriptions and proscriptions are mediated exclusively by males such as Cathfaidh the druid as the touchstone for the consequent development of both Deirdre and the story. Coupled with her choice to elope with Naoise and the means by which she persuades him to do so, the effect is to rob the story of its sense of fatality and human powerlessness in the face of the force of destiny. This blushing, vacillating Deirdre is, almost paradoxically, seen to be her own moral agent, and in conjunction with her horrifying death as described by Hyde – a combination of sexual humiliation and gore – her whole career can only be taken in this version as a moral exemplum, a forewarning of what happens to silly, pretty little girls who stray from the paths prescribed by a paternalistic family unit.

In Yeats's *Deirdre* (1906), however, the location which sexuality occupies in relation to the conventions of family and (patriarchal) community is quite different. The play does not begin with Deirdre's birth and her being fated to marry the old king (in this version, named Conchubar rather than Conor), but with the return of Deirdre and Naoise to the court. The conversation between the musicians and Fergus at the play's very beginning, before the entrance of the protagonists, concentrates on Conchubar's jealousy and thus draws very explicit attention to the element of gratified sexuality in the relationship between the two lovers (*Collected Plays* 172–4). This, coupled with the king's seeming acceptance of the situation, leads to a growing impression, before Deirdre and Naoise even appear, that it is the free expression of sexuality rather than the confining bonds of family which constitutes this play's status quo. The order of events in itself suggests that it is not Deirdre's wilful sexuality which has transgressed against the stability of a patriarchal order (as represented by Conchubar), but rather the rigid structures of Conchubar's understanding of the relationship between sexuality and community which have transgressed against Deirdre and Naoise's love. The fact that Conchubar's acceptance of the relationship between these two is only skin deep simply serves to stress his deviation from the romantic norms erected by Yeats. The musicians' insistence upon the jealousy of old men at the play's beginning, coupled with Deirdre's recurring references to Conchubar's absence from the guest-house (*Collected Plays* 180), restore to this version of the tale its sense of fatality – thus encouraging the audience to align its sympathies with the now truly tragic Deirdre. (These sympathies can only be deepened by her attempts – made in order to save Naoise's life – to convince Conchubar that she will return to him.)

Deirdre's death is silent, spectacular only in its proof of her adherence to Naoise and her sense of the integrity of their relationship. We get no sense that here is the harrowing and unusual end of one who has broken the rules of community and convention; Yeats's *Deirdre* is a cautionary tale only in so far as it warns against the death of the heart. Rather than placing his heroine's demise within a moral framework of free will abused and potentially redemptive action ignored, the quiet and dignified death of Yeats's Deirdre draws our attention back to Deirdre superb and living, and it is her glorious esprit which is stressed at the play's end, even by Conchubar:

Howl, if you will; but I, being King, did right
In choosing her most fitting to be Queen,
And letting no boy lover take the sway. (*Collected Plays* 203)

Here, it is not Conchubar rather than Naoise who has "taken the sway", but Deirdre rather than either of them. Throughout the play our attention has been focused on her and her conception of love, and the whole of conventional, male-dominated courtly society is largely merely a foil and a contrast to this. As with Pegeen in *The Playboy* and Nora in *In the Shadow of the Glen*, the male characters seem to exist in order to provide a setting for the main focus of the female debate.

Gregory's *Kincora* provides a particularly good example of the way in which Woman can be seen to exist at an intersection of different kinds of power in a patriarchal community, for it is Gormleith's relationships with the male characters of the play which lead directly to its outcome. As Malachi's ex-wife, Brian's present wife, Maelmora's sister and Sitric's mother, she exists in a direct causal relationship to power which is constantly being discussed by the male protagonists (Fitzgerald 45, 49–50, 61–2). Gormleith is situated at the intersection of different strands in the power struggle in Ireland in the twelfth century, but the play's end brings home to us the realization that her power, far from being solely a reflection of her relationship with these men, is meant to be seen as immanent in her femaleness. For Gormleith, by giving her assurances to the Danes in order to save her son Sitric, withdraws power from her husband Brian, leading not only to his loss of sovereignty but also to his death at Clontarf. Here, Woman is specifically portrayed as possessing the power either to sanction or destroy hopes for Irish autonomy in the face of foreign invasion; she is also, more generally, cast in the role of bestower or withholder of sovereignty. Hence, at least in this formulation, there is some congruence between the position of the woman as visualized by Gregory, and that outlined by Ashis Nandy in his descriptions of Indian colonial and pre-colonial formations of "womanliness".[7] To this extent, the writers of the Abbey were far more able than the rhetoricians of cultural nationalism at the time to resurrect and redefine the medieval Irish-language trope of *flaitheas* or sovereignty, whereby the king, copulating with the earth-goddess, fertilized the kingdom and in return had sovereignty temporarily vested in him (Gallagher 229–37; Nulty 520–4). Cultural nationalism, though sometimes embarrassed by the earthiness of Irish texts – the Intermediate Education controversy was a case in point – could hardly acknowledge the kind of vocabulary to deal with these particular aspects of ancient Irish royal history. As Woman in nationalist terms was not located at the meeting place of power and sexuality, this option was not available to its writers. Instead, cultural nationalism provides an example of the sanitization of the female figures from its own Irish-language tradition.

Another aspect of differing slants on the same subject from the nationalist and the Abbey viewpoints is to be found in the relationship between women and Nature. Where nationalism linked women and Nature with images of fecundity but could not quite bring itself to use the whole *flaitheas* trope, the women in the Abbey plays are seen to exist in a close and dynamic relationship to natural forces which fills the lacuna left by conventional spirituality. In his discussion of Synge's *Deirdre of the Sorrows* in *Seven Types of Ambiguity*, Empson draws attention to the part played by pathetic fallacy in mirroring the motions of the achievement of sexual desire in the play. Speaking of the episode of the flooding of the stepping-stones, he says "what in the story is done heroically by her (Deirdre's) own choice is, in dumb show, either as an encouragement or as an ironical statement of the impotence of heroic action, done by the weather" (39). There are other examples in Synge's plays of an equation between female action and the forces of nature, often linked, for instance in the repetition of moon images in *The Tinker's Wedding*, by metaphors of mutual mutability.

Perhaps the most specific and extended connection between Woman and the changeable, treacherous forces of Nature, however, is that contained in Synge's *Riders to the Sea* (1904). Here Maurya is shown to have grown into an alliance with the sea which, in its bitter compulsion, has uprooted conventional religion from her heart; as she says of the priest, "It's little the like of him knows of the sea" (Saddlemyer III: 21). The priest's exact prescriptions are scrupulously repeated by Nora at the play's beginning:

"I won't stop him [Bartley]", says he; "but let you not be afraid. Herself does be saying prayers half through the night, and the Almighty God won't leave her destitute," says he, "with no son living." (5)

But their hollowness is cruelly exposed by the play's end. For it is not only Catholicism which fails, but also the language in which it is expressed, which is shown to possess only the mimeticism of ritual utterance without its magic power. The failure of religious blessing is shown when Maurya goes down to the well in an attempt to break the "dark word" spoken to Bartley:

I tried to say "God speed you", but something choked the words in my throat. He went by quickly; and "The blessing of God on you," says he, and I could say nothing. (19)

Language, however, *is* perceived as having power and authority in, for example, the "dark word" itself, which has all the self-fulfilling prophetic quality of the curse it in fact is. Here it is the woman who, rather than re-enacting language prescribed from above by patriarchal religious authority, generates language which itself pre-enacts reality. When Cathleen says to Maurya:

Why wouldn't you give him [Bartley] your blessing and he looking round in the door? Isn't it sorrow enough is on every one in this house without your sending him out with an unlucky word behind him, and a hard word in his ear? (11)

woman is once again seen in her classic role as giver or withholder of language as well as life, an impression which is reinforced later on in the same speech when Cathleen reiterates: "It's destroyed he'll be surely. There's no sense left on any person in a house where an old woman will be talking forever" (13). This attribute is shared by the nationalist construct of "Woman", who is also portrayed as the giver of language and life, albeit in a more positive way.

Riders to the Sea shows an almost exclusively female community. Not only are the men all taken, one by one, by the forces of nature, but at the play's end, when the inevitable tale of Bartley's death by drowning is brought to Maurya, it is the women of the community who, in chorus, describe what really happened, as opposed to the priest's sanguine forecast. Despite her vision of Michael riding on the grey pony, then, it is not the supernatural which comes to directly occupy the space left by a specifically Catholic spirituality, but Woman, Nature and Community, lending a barbed irony to Maurya's words:

It isn't that I haven't prayed for you, Bartley, to the Almighty God. It isn't that I haven't said prayers in the dark night till you wouldn't know what I'd be saying; but it's a great rest I'll have now, and it's time surely. (25)

This was the single play of the whole of Synge's *oeuvre* which was most approved of by the nationalist critical press, possibly because rather than presenting the Western peasantry as materialistic, despite the failure of Catholicism, it showed them as concerned with the larger issues of life and death. Cultural nationalists had a horror of seeing the Western peasant portrayed as grasping or money-loving, and this again blinded them to tropes in their own heritage such as the extreme importance of material goods as a prerequisite for marriage in the folksongs of the West. (One has

only to think of a song such as "Meidbh Ni Mhulloidh" in Hyde's own
Love Songs of Connacht (O'Conaire 54–60).)

Hyde's dramatic work presents a contrasting view of the relationship
between language and community to that of Synge. In Hyde's *Casadh an
tSugáin* (1901), translated and published by Lady Gregory in her collection
Poets and Dreamers as *The Twisting of the Rope*, Hanrahan the poet is seen to
have the same power as Synge's women to make things happen with
words. Maurya says of him: "He's a great poet, and maybe he'd make a
rann on you that would stick to you for ever, if you were to anger him"
(Gregory, *Poets and Dreamers* 141). Again, when it is suggested that she
should throw him out, she claims:

> he is a great poet, and has a curse that would split the trees, and that
> would burst the stones. They say the seed will rot in the ground and
> the milk go from the cows when a poet like him makes a curse, if a
> person routed him out of the house. (142)

Hanrahan's greatest sin, in the context of the community which is described in the play, is that, given his power to make language realize fact, he
succeeds in investing another man's future wife with a regal and poetic
sexuality:

> The swan on the brink of the waves, the royal phoenix, the pearl of the
> white breast, the Venus among the women, Oona ní Regaun, is
> standing up with me, and any place she rises up, the sun and the moon
> bow to her, and so shall ye yet. She is too handsome, too sky-like, for
> any other woman to be near her. (143)

It is noteworthy that it is the sensual exchange of love-poetry between
Oona and Hanrahan ("I call on yourself and I praise your mouth . . .")
which eventually goads Sheamus into action in order to reclaim Oona
before she is lost to him in more than one sense of the word. One of the
phrases which Hanrahan uses to "woo" Oona refers to Deirdre as an ideal:
"By my word, since Deirdre died, for whom Naoise, son of Usnech, was
put to death, her heir is not in Ireland today but yourself" (146). Hanrahan
is eventually ejected from the house by a ruse, and the potential marriage
between Oona and Sheamus remains intact, the largely passive Oona presented as having been saved, virtue intact, from the ravishing blandishments
of the poet. Hyde seems to be saying, here, that poetic language can indeed
bring into being an alternative reality, but that this very language poses a
threat to the Irish-language community by introducing destabilizing forces
such as sexuality, normally proscribed. Both cultural nationalists and the
Abbey writers believed that language could somehow make reality happen,
and that given her relationship to words, Woman was central to this site of
the tussle for the artistic licence to portray a validated community.

There is a passage in Yeats's "J.M. Synge and the Ireland of his time" in which his discussion of the relationship between the creative artist, his language and his community explicitly evokes the femininity of poetic language:

> . . . so it is that enlargement of experience does not come from those oratorical thinkers, or from those decisive rhythms that move large numbers of men, but from writers that seem by contrast as feminine as the soul when it explores in Blake's picture the recesses of the grave, carrying its faint lamp trembling and astonished or as the Muses who are never pictured as one-breasted Amazons, but as women needing protection.
>
> Indeed, all art which appeals to individual man and awaits the confirmation of his senses and his reveries seems, when arrayed against the moral zeal, the confident logic, the ordered proof of journalism, a trifling, impertinent, vexatious thing, a tumbler who has unrolled his carpet in the way of a marching army. (*Essays and Introductions* 317–18)

Although it seems at first as if Yeats is here categorizing the feminine in terms very different from those suggested by the female characters of both his own plays and those of Synge himself, the image of the tumbler needs careful scrutiny. It makes clear that those qualities in art which Yeats perceives as needing protection and defence arise rather from that same art's maverick compulsion to create an unpopulist alternative reality, than from its innate weakness. The feminine is therefore aligned not with physical feebleness, as at first seems to be the case, but with change and magical self-transformation, in much the same way as his own Cathleen Ní Houlihan is transformed from an impotent old woman into a vibrant and youthful sovereign (*Collected Plays* 88). The difference in emphasis between the play and the passage from the essay lies in the fact that while it is the nationalist principle (in its masculine form) which transforms Ireland-as-Woman in the former piece, in the latter Woman bears the seeds of her own creative instability.

Another graphic indication of Woman's mutability may be found in Gregory's playlet *The Gaol Gate* (1906). Within a very short space its two female characters, interacting on each other, move from the conviction that the man who is son to one and husband to the other is an informer, to the conclusion that he has been hanged for the (unspecified, nationalistic) crime he has committed, to the true realization that he has died protecting the other men implicated in the affair. During the course of the short one-act play, the disposition of the women themselves has changed.

The movement in Yeats's *Deirdre* between sexuality and convention is mirrored over and over by parallel movements in the work of Synge and Gregory, creating an area where the issue of female sexuality finds its points of debate crystallized around the twin poles of alliance and misalliance. In the two plays singled out for condemnation on the specific issue of their portrayal of Irishwomen's sexual behaviour, *The Playboy of the Western*

World (1907) and *In the Shadow of the Glen* (1903), Pegeen Mike's and Nora Burke's expressions of their own sexuality are directly contingent upon their sense of the inappropriate nature of the alliances which convention has decreed for them; Nora's with an old, "cold" man and Pegeen's with a man who may be her contemporary but is her match neither in intelligence nor passion (Saddlemyer III: 35; IV: 77). Their respective refusals of the conventional and community-sanctioned match are an explicit function of desire fulfilled; in this sense, their unions (however brief and illusory Synge suggests they may be) with the Tramp and Christy, the consorts of their choice, may be termed alliances of desire.

The extent to which the possibility of "true" union is held forth in *The Tinker's Wedding* and *The Playboy*, only to be exposed as a chimera, or, as with *In the Shadow of the Glen* and *Kincora*, predicated only to be shown to be false, suggests that in these plays it is once again achieved female desire which is the norm, with the free expression of sexuality being equated with female self-knowledge (Saddlemyer III: 57; IV: 49; 169; FitzGerald 86–8). It is deeply ironic that, given the outspokenly passionate character of the female figures who inhabited the mythic materials which cultural nationalists utilized – figures such as Medbh and Grainne – their potential to transform the discourse of Arnoldian Celtism should be denied by Irish Catholicism's received pieties. Given the nature of the male/female union which Arnold erects as a model for the relationship between Teuton and Celt, where not only is the Celt accorded a position of "feminine" submission comparable to that of the wife in Victorian marriage (FitzGerald 81–3), but has his/her "feminine" qualities of mutability, creativity and undependability allowed and domesticated within certain carefully husbanded boundaries, then there is a very real sense in which figures such as Yeats's Deirdre and Synge's Nora Burke are committing adultery by proxy against a Union which does not answer to Irish desires and needs, but constitutes itself in terms of a misalliance of legislative as well as human bodies.

Notes

1 "Sinn Féin", meaning "Ourselves", was the phrase attached by Arthur Griffith to his proposals for the achievement of Ireland's independence from Britain in *The Sinn Féin Policy* (1905). A vigorous and gifted journalist and polemicist, Griffith founded a series of newspapers: *The United Irishman* in 1899 with his friend William Rooney, and *Sinn Féin* (1907), founded to replace its predecessor which was bankrupted by poor management and a law suit. Both these journals were weeklies. *Sinn Féin* ran as a daily (evening) paper from August 1909 to January 1910 and, thereafter, for financial reasons, reverted to a weekly format. See Younger 15–52 *passim*. See also Davis; Cairns and Richards, *Writing Ireland* 89–94.

2 The extent to which this is true was perhaps not recognized until Declan Kiberd's pioneering work on the relationship between Synge's themes and those of the Gaelic League: see *Synge and the Irish Language* esp. Chapter IX, 216–60.

3 By "Abbey woman" I mean the main female characters of the mythological and "historical" plays of Yeats and Gregory and their imitators, and all of Synge's, belonging to an earlier period in the theatre's artistic history than, for example, Robinson's and Colum's work. For writing on Abbey women, see, in particular, Parkin; and Saddlemyer, "Synge and the Nature of Woman" 38–57 and 58–73.

4 Literally "a little bunch of heather" or, with play on words, "a little act of fury".

5 The word "seoinin" here refers to an aper of foreign ways, and is meant to convey a flavour of "servility" and "flunkeydom".

6 *The Sinn Féin Policy*, Griffith's political manifesto, had been published in 1905 (see note 1).

7 See "Woman Versus Womanliness in India": "The concept of *adya shakti*, primal or original power, is entirely feminine in India . . . It is by protesting against or defying the traditional concepts of woman and womanhood that all Indian modernizers have made their point. On the other hand, all forms of conservatism and protests against modern Western encroachments on Indian society have taken shelter in and exploited the symbol of motherhood" (Nandy, "At the Edge of Psychology" 34–7).

3

Mina's disclosure:
Bram Stoker's *Dracula*
Mary FitzGerald

Gothic fiction is about power; specifically about the negotiation of power structures which are in some way inaccessible and inscrutable. It is no surprise, therefore, that Gothic should have been such a hospitable form for Irish writers writing in Ireland after the Act of Union. Maturin, Le Fanu and Bram Stoker all constructed works which may interestingly be read as analogues of Irish politics. However, it is not only National politics which the strategies of their texts suggest. It is the sexual politics of *Dracula* which are undoubtedly the source of the text's neomythical status.

In *Dracula*, Bram Stoker created one of the most popular dramatic archetypes of twentiety-century culture. Although the text has been redrawn in many different ways in many different plays and films, it still provides some of the most suggestive and disturbing representations of fear, power and violence in gender relationships. Stoker's original handling of these emblematic hierarchies overturns the binary logic of patriarchy and presents female sexuality as radically and terrifyingly promiscuous, predatory and subversive of male identity. Male sexuality, on the other hand, becomes not a means of satisfying this insatiability, nor even a project for self-satisfaction, but a means of sterilizing the "pollution" which the insatiability of women represents. Male sexuality is simply the negation of the female sexuality which threatens men. It is experienced as a need to breach the privacy and mystery of the individual, and thereby to assert power. The breaching of individual consciousness, a denial of the privacy and autonomy of the self, is presented as the crux of sexual power. The text becomes a dramatic focus in itself, for it is a repository of consciousness; it stores a point of vulnerability which is also the ultimate weapon.

The means of storing consciousness are marked by modern and scientific techniques and equipment – the business shorthand script and the phonograph – and there is a sort of quasi-scientific fetishizing of the paraphernalia required to combat the vampire. The garlic, the consecrated host, the wild rose and the crucifix merge with the scientific instruments of the Doctor's bag and create a disturbing continuum between the daylight, controlled, closed, male world of science, and the irrational, open and predatory world of the vampire (Stoker 207–10).

Dracula – the source of "pollution", the power which threatens the virtuous, daylight world – is male. He is associated with intellect, nobility, heroism, the law, authority. He reads the ultimate male text – Bradshaw's railway timetable – a text which threatens no personal intrusion, but promises control of space and time (22). He displays none of the disgusting voluptuousness of the female predators, but he is the ultimate predator, and it is from the earth and the night – traditionally female terms in the binary logic – that he draws power; without these bonds he is powerless. He is also, for all his power, to be found making Jonathan Harker's bed, and laying the table for dinner (27).

Mina, we are told, has a "man's brain" (234). It is her analysis of the diaries and letters which establishes the vulnerable patterns of Dracula's habits. Renfield, the lunatic, is not a "madwoman in the attic", but a man. He represents another transgression of the binary code, his erratic rationality contrasting strongly with Mina's relentless "knitting together in chronological order every scrap of evidence" (225). The occasion on which the men decide to exclude Mina from their activities is also, inevitably, the occasion of Dracula's greatest triumph, his assault upon Mina's independence (280–3).

The men are reluctant to be open with each other, and are naturally discreet and closed. For a very long time, Van Helsing cannot bring himself to explain his surmises and fears explicitly to Dr Seward. The men do not confide their relations with Lucy to each other. The women, on the other hand, have no such sense of vulnerability to each other, no such sense of discretion, and tell each other everything.

> There it is all out. Mina, we have told all our secrets to each other since we were *children*; we have slept together and eaten together, and laughed and cried together; and now, though I have spoken, I would like to speak more. Oh, Mina couldn't you guess? I love him. I am blushing as I write, for although I *think* he loves me, he has not told me so in words. But, oh, Mina, I love him; I love him! There, that does me good. I wish I were with you, dear, sitting by the fire undressing, as we used to sit; and I would try to tell you what I feel. I do not know

how I am writing this even to you. I am afraid to stop, or I should tear
up the letter, and I don't want to stop, for I do so want to tell you all.
(55)

Mutual confession is obviously an intense and quasi-sexual pleasure here,
something to be enjoyed most in circumstances of physical intimacy, when
they are by the fire undressing together. It is obviously an almost irresistible
impulse, a necessary personal indulgence. However, it is not a pleasure
which the women will acknowledge to the men. Some months later, Lucy
primly says to Dr Seward: "I cannot tell you how much I loathe talking
about myself" (111). The men's code is very different: Van Helsing advises
Dr Seward:

> "And my good friend John, let me caution you. You deal with mad-
> men. All men are mad in some way or other; and inasmuch as you deal
> discreetly with your madmen, so deal with God's madmen, too – the
> rest of the world. You tell not your madmen what you do nor why
> you do it; you tell them not what you think. So you shall keep
> knowledge in its place, where it may rest – where it may gather its
> kind around it and breed. You and I shall keep as yet what we know
> here, and here." He touched me on the heart and on the forehead, and
> then touched himself the same way. "I have for myself thoughts at the
> present. Later I shall unfold to you." (118)

The intimacy symbolized by the touch here enforces a separateness, and a
privacy of thought which is not to be breached. It is a sign of their unusual
mutual confidence that they can be so intimate as to acknowledge that they
dare not be intimate. Van Helsing indicates that thought may only "breed"
when enclosed in privacy. The privacy of thought is understood and valued
in very different ways by the men and the women. Harker uses a shorthand
which excludes Dracula from his diary, and marks not only the privacy of
his sexual relation to Mina, but also, simultaneously, and paradoxically, her
independence, which is to be so crucial. The shorthand represents for her
the ability to earn her own living, her competence in a male world, her
ability to move beyond the domestic world into a more public arena. He
gives her his diary, but asks her to keep it unread as "an outward and visible
sign for us all our lives that we trusted each other" (105). It signifies that
trust for him exactly by being silent, but Mina soon finds that she must fulfil
her trust by breaching that silence and scrutinizing his text (173).

Lucy confides "heresy" to Mina (50). Her confessions have all the aura
of forbidden pleasures. She does feel that perhaps she should "tear up the
letter", but she does not want to (55). The women are aware of transgress-
ing the male codes of silence to which they yet feel obliged to do lip
service. Similarly, when Mina finds Lucy in the graveyard at night, she is
concerned for her reputation, concerned that she might be seen out *without*

shoes. She makes Lucy wear her shoes, and daubs her own feet with mud to disguise her transgression (91). She does feel obliged, not necessarily to conform to the enclosures which the male world requires of her, but at least to appear to do so. It is interesting symbolically that she must walk in mud to conform. The act of conformity is itself a pollution for her.

Dracula tries to establish access to the plans of his opponents by turning Mina into the aggressor. He makes her suck his blood, and it is at the moment of being aggressor that she seems most totally the victim (282). He gains access to her consciousness and can use it to exert his power and to evade the daylight powers of the men. However, he cannot accomplish this without making himself vulnerable to her, and even when he tries to distance himself from her, and foregoes his access to her mind in an attempt to exclude her from his, he cannot fully deny her knowledge of his consciousness, and this knowledge is power. To combat Dracula the men must relinquish their privacy, discover the subversion of it in the letters between the women, and stand embarrassingly exposed. Mina confronts the necessity to of leaving off the "mud" to abolish the silences and deny the privacies to which the men are accustomed. She thinks sympathetically of the plight of the "Poor fellows . . . However, I thought the matter over, and came to the conclusion that the best thing I could do would be to post them in affairs right up to date" (229). Mina consoles Lord Godalming by offering him a reassuringly familial and unthreatening version of the sexuality suggested by such a breach of his privacy. She takes his hand and asks:

> "Will you not let me be like a sister to you" . . . I felt this big, sorrowing man's head resting on me, as though it were that of the baby that some day may lie on my bosom, and I stroked his hair as though he were my own child. (230)

When she sees her manuscript in Mr Morris's hands, however, and "knew that when he read it he would realise how much I knew", she offers him similar comfort, and their conversation ends with him calling her "little girl". She thus offers every familial possibility in her attempts to reassure them; she is sister, mother, child.

Mina tempers the disquieting revelation of the openness of female discourse by suggesting domesticated versions of its presence within the deliberations of the men. Lucy, on the other hand, regrets in her letter to Mina that she cannot marry them all: "Why can't they let a girl marry three men, or as many as want her, and save all this trouble? But this is heresy, and I must not say it" (59). Arthur regards his giving of blood as a form of marriage to her, and "as something like life seemed to come back to Lucy's cheeks . . . through Arthur's growing pallor the joy of his face seemed absolutely to shine" (122). But his blood is not enough, she takes blood from them all and leaves them all exhausted, although the others discreetly keep this from Arthur. When she is vampire she is depraved and lascivious.

Her "purity" turns to "voluptuous wantonness", she takes on a "languorous, voluptuous grace" (211), "the whole carnal and unspiritual appearance seeming like a devilish mocker of Lucy's sweet purity" (214). It is seen as appropriate that her would-be husband should be the one to "sterilize" this depravity by penetrating her with the stake, thereby returning her to her asexual, virtuous and unthreatening image:

> Arthur placed the point over the heart, and as I looked I could see its dint in the white flesh. Then he struck with all his might. . . . He looked like a figure of Thor as his untrembling arm rose and fell, driving deeper and deeper the mercy-bearing stake, whilst the blood from the pierced heart welled and spurted up around it. His face was set, and high duty seemed to shine through it. (216)

This memory will give him great solace thereafter. He saved her soul by penetrating her heart, the very core of her being, with the stake. The only moments of male sexual desire recorded explicitly are the moments when Harker almost falls prey to the female vampires who would suck his blood:

> I felt in my heart a wicked, burning desire that they would kiss me with those red lips. . . . I lay quiet, looking out under my eyelashes in an agony of delightful anticipation. . . . Then the skin of my throat began to tingle as one's flesh does when the hand that is to tickle it approaches nearer – nearer. I could feel the soft, shivering touch of the lips on the super-sensitive skin of my throat. . . . I closed my eyes in a languorous ecstasy and waited – waited with beating heart. (38)

There is no active force and no "high duty" here. It is an entirely passive, very pleasurable, and absolutely lethal version of male sexuality. It is a sexual pleasure which is to be feared as a death-wish. But it is only when male sexuality thus confounds its own codes that it becomes pleasure.

The promiscuity and lasciviousness of Lucy-as-vampire appear to the men to be totally unrelated to her normal virtuous self, but her letters to Mina reveal a promiscuity with knowledge in her recounting of their approaches to her, and a promiscuity of desire in her responses to these approaches; "heresies" which suggest to the reader a continuity which the men cannot contemplate between her different personae.

Dracula seeks to know and to control the consciousness of the women. The men in their false security assume a comforting and supportive closure in the women. The supposed privacy and mystery of the woman is crucial to her attractiveness. Lucy notes of Dr Seward, who is in love with her, that "He has a curious habit of looking one straight in the face, as if trying to read one's thoughts. He tries this on very much with me, but I flatter myself he has got a tough nut to crack" (55). The conventional desire to penetrate this mystery and enter the private sphere of the woman's consciousness parallels the satisfaction of penetrating the woman's heart with the stake and turning the openness of her voluptuous desire to the closed purity of death. Dracula seeks to use a breach of privacy but this intrusion ultimately defeats him. Renfield perceives himself as competing with other beings for life and turns predator. This is perhaps a "mad" version of the terror of a female openness which threatens to breach the closure and impersonality of the men's world. To breach, indeed, even the crucial barrier Dr Seward perceives between "conscious" and "unconscious cerebration" (69). It threatens their control of experience, the privacy of their minds, and the privacies they prefer to preserve even within their minds. They must penetrate this openness to close it in death. The world of *Dracula* is marked not by penis envy, but by terror of the vagina.

In this deadly version of the battle of the sexes, where the penetration of consciousness, its openness or closedness, is such a crucial issue, the text which records it becomes intensely contentious. For it is not just the sexuality of the women which is threatening in its refusal of closure, and its insatiability: their discourse is also subversive, open, insatiable. We are never allowed to forget that the text of *Dracula* is a text, that it is *produced* and may be read and used in different ways. It is a journal, a letter, a newspaper cutting, a memorandum, a phonographic recording. We are told of it being written and recorded, and told of it being re-transcribed. Its physical presence is acknowledged throughout. The use to which Mina puts these letters and journals is not one that was foreseen at the moment of their production, and it is a usage which confers power: the power to counter another power. These texts not only communicate, but also store consciousness. They may hide it in shorthand, inscribe it as a private letter, or publish it for the world to purchase and read. Whatever the intention behind their production, and whatever the first reading of them, they may be re-examined and analysed. The knowledge lost within it may be retrieved and exploited. *Dracula* is a text which presents itself as exactly that problematic and contentious repository which all texts must become for feminist criticism – a privileged sphere where heresies may be hidden or revealed, where strategic elisions may naturalize any construction. It is a field, above all, which may be analysed by women and made to reveal patterns and power structures to which we need access. Mina is the figure of the feminist critic, scrutinizing her own texts, and those of men, for traces of a knowledge and a power forgotten therein.

4

Yeats: The anxiety of masculinity[1]
Elizabeth Butler Cullingford

Like our colleagues the feminist critics of Shakespeare or Milton, feminist readers of Anglo-Irish literature want both to interrogate and to recuperate our Master Texts and Master Genres.[2] Despite his frequently problematic statements about women, Yeats is a poet whose verse retains the power to fascinate and disturb feminist readers. This chapter concentrates on his early career in order to demonstrate his tenuous and intermittent identification with traditional models of masculinity, and his consequently oblique relationship to the canonical genre of the love lyric. To paraphrase Simone de Beauvoir, one is not born a man, one becomes one; and Yeats had considerable trouble becoming a man. Instead of playing the "strong poet" of Harold Bloom's extravagantly masculinist poetics, Yeats was a "weak poet" whose gender identification was inherently unstable. Although I rely to some extent on strategies borrowed from deconstruction and Lacanian psychoanalysis, I reject the ahistorical implications of these methods, in order to stress the importance of the material, social and literary contexts of Yeats's poetic development.[3]

Yeats's relationship to the discourse of phallocracy was always uneasy. As a white, male, middle-class citizen of the British Empire, who acknowledged his enormous debt to canonical English writers (*Letters* 872), he belonged to the dominant patriarchal tradition. As a colonized Irishman, however, he was acutely conscious of repression and exclusion. His commitment to occult studies marginalized him further, for the occult tradition represents centuries of opposition to the ruling discourses both of patriarchal religion and of male science. The so-called irrationality of occult investigation conventionally identifies its practitioners as "feminine", and many of Yeats's fellow theosophical students were women, who were seeking new sources of power in a religious organization that did not bar them from office because of their sex.

Yeats inherited the male-dominated literary tradition of poetic love at a moment of historical crisis and change in gender relations. In the late nineteenth century, men's ancient and unconscious fear of women's sexuality received a new impetus from the growing demand for female emancipation. The proliferation of literary and pictorial images of women as vampires, monsters, Medusas and Salomés can be partly explained as the product of male apprehension that women, subordinated for so long, would in the course of their liberation exact a terrible revenge upon their oppressors.[4] The male modernists' obsession with masculine impotence and female power may spring from a similar source (see Gilbert and Gubar, *No Man's Land* 1: 35–6). At the same time, and possibly in reaction to the same phenomenon, the medievalism fostered by the Romantic poets and obsessively pursued by the Pre-Raphaelites had led to a literary reinvention of the idea of courtly love: women had to be persuaded that it was preferable to be adored than to be emancipated. As a young man Yeats, who had "gathered from the Romantic poets an ideal of perfect love", was determined that although he might never marry in church he would "love one woman all my life" (*Memoirs* 32). Paradoxically, however, the woman with whom he fell in love was an Irish nationalist organizer who had little time for romance. The political circles within which he moved were also notably sympathetic to emancipation. His father was a disciple of John Stuart Mill, an early male champion of women's rights. The drama of Shaw and Ibsen, with which Yeats was thoroughly familiar, offered powerful feminist analyses of the "Woman Question". Through his early involvement with the socialist group that gathered around William Morris[5] and his friendship with actresses like Florence Farr, Yeats met many "New Women".[6] His occult studies brought him into contact with social reformers like Annie Besant, and Madame Blavatsky was interested in the advancement of women. Although Maud Gonne was primarily a nationalist, she acted on feminist principles, founding her women's association, Inginnidhe na hEireann, on behalf of "all the girls who, like myself, resented being excluded, as women, from national organizations" (MacBride, *Servant* 278). The contradiction between the politics of his historical situation and the generic conventions of nineteenth-century verse informs his early love poetry, which, although it obsessively rehearses the formal gestures of the courtly speaker, is also ironically aware of their futility.

As a nationalist poet, Yeats was expected to produce "manly" verse in order to counteract the colonial stereotype of the Irish as effeminate and childish.[7] Yet he conceived of his poetic vocation as demanding a "feminine" receptivity and passivity, and as inheritor of an organic romantic poetic he saw the production of verse as analogous to the female "labour" of producing a child.[8] "Man is a woman to his work and it begets his thought", he wrote in 1909 (*Memoirs* 232).[9] His concept of creative bisexuality never changed: 26 years later he told Ethel Mannin, "You are doubly a woman, first because of yourself and secondly because of the muses, whereas I am but once a woman" (*Letters* 831). Yeats's feminine identifications engage two disputed areas of feminist theory: childbirth and androgyny.

In her survey of the differences between male and female use of childbirth as a metaphor for creativity, Susan Friedman argues that men who adopt the model of pregnancy are indulging in "a form of literary *couvade*, male appropriation of procreative labor to which women have been confined" (56). The comparison between poetic and physical creativity "obscures women's real lack of authority to create art as well as babies" and "subtly helps to perpetuate the confinement of women to procreation" (64). In the abstract, Friedman's argument is persuasive; but in the context of Yeats's constant encouragement, support and promotion of women artists like Katharine Tynan, Althea Gyles, Lady Gregory, Dorothy Wellesley, Elinor Wylie and Edith Sitwell, his use of the childbirth metaphor resembles a gesture of solidarity rather than an appropriative strategy. He exhorted Dorothy Wellesley: "Write verse, my dear, go on writing, that is the only thing that matters" (*Letters* 860).

Yeats's insistence on the androgyny of the male artist, an idea which gained enormous currency during the 1890s (see Praz 366; Marcus 3–4), is also problematic. Freudian and Jungian critics of Yeats concur in describing him as female identified, but while the Freudians regard this identification as a neurosis caused by his unsatisfactory relationship with his mother,[10] the Jungians celebrate it as evidence that Yeats was able to accept and express his anima.[11] Although the Jungian reading is more positive, both psychological methodologies essentialize the feminine, and thus perpetuate traditional gender stereotypes. Our valuation of the idea of androgyny depends upon whether, like Carolyn Heilbrun, we see it as the deconstruction of stereotypes, a "movement away from the prison of gender" (ix), or whether, like Toril Moi (pers. comm.), we regard it as the superimposition of one stereotype upon another. Reading androgyny historically, as a characteristic of the decadents, Jane Marcus concludes that it "often extends the range of male sexuality into the feminine, but continues to regard the extension of female sexuality into the historical masculine as perverse" (251). Reading Yeats historically, one may observe that while he temporarily affected the dandyism of the decadents he outlasted the Tragic Generation, and as a modernist he investigated more deeply than they did the problematics of androgyny. Noting that "the Greek androgynous statue is always the woman in man, never the man in woman. . . . It was made for men who loved men first" (*Letters* 875), he showed himself sensitive to the possible colonization of the feminine represented by the androgynous ideal which he had embraced. His relationship with the lesbian Dorothy Wellesley, moreover, demonstrates clearly that he did not regard the extension of female sexuality into the historical masculine as "perverse": "Your lines have the magnificent swing of your boyish body. I wish I could be a girl of nineteen for certain hours that I might feel it even more acutely" (*Letters* 875). Although he subscribed to the theory of a feminine essence (especially in his courtly worship of the Rose as goddess), he also celebrated deviations from that essence; in addition, historical, social and psychological factors combined to render his conceptions of masculinity unstable and indeterminate. I see this indeterminacy as one of the sources of his interest as a love poet. The autonomous, unified phallic self of patriarchal tradition constitutes itself as sole author of both history and the literary text. Yeats, whose most aggressively phallic symbol, the tower, is "Half dead at the top" (*Poems* 239), subverts the potency of his male self, which for him is always an ironic mask. He described himself as "one that ruffled in a manly pose/For all his timid heart" (*Poems* 243). His theory of the gyres, in which opposites alternately increase and decrease in strength but always contain and never obliterate each other, demonstrates his inability to speak from the position of the unitary, phallic self.

Indeed, Yeats's feminized gender position helped him to deconstruct several of the constituent terms of the patriarchal binary opposition Male/Female. Hélène Cixous outlines the series of pairs in which woman always occupies the subordinate place in "Sorties":

Activity/Passivity
Sun/Moon
Culture/Nature
Day/Night
Father/Mother
Head/Heart
Intelligible/Palpable
Logos/Pathos
Form, convex, step, advance, semen, progress.
Matter, concave, ground – where steps are taken,
holding- and dumping-ground. (63)

Yeats was unable to identify consistently with the dominant masculine side of this perennial opposition. Although he was a male poet involved in the production of Culture, he exalted emotion (Pathos) over reason (Logos). His loathing of the Victorian myth of science and progress, and his early desire to cast out of his verse "those energetic rhythms, as of a man running" and replace them by "wavering, meditative, organic rhythms" (*Essays* 163), express his rejection of masculine form. His horoscope showed him to be a man dominated by the moon (Moore 216), and in his later years he developed a philosophy based upon a lunar myth, which privileged moon over sun, night over day. Although his father praised active men, Yeats knew himself to be timid and passive, a poet dependent upon reverie and dreams for his inspiration.

At the beginning of his career he was metaphorically ravished by a Muse who displayed the traditionally masculine qualities of aggression and initiation. His first love, Laura Armstrong, whom he described as a "wild creature" (*Autobiographies* 76), "woke me from the metallic sleep of science and set me writing my first play" (*Letters* 117). Although Laura played a feminine role in rescuing Yeats from the "metallic" sterility of rational and scientific thought and turning him toward the intuitive world of poetry, Yeats's portrait of himself as a Sleeping Prince awakened by an energetic Princess reverses traditional gender stereotypes. His account of his first meeting with Laura emphasizes his passivity:

> I was climbing up a hill at Howth when I heard wheels behind me and a pony-carriage drew up beside me. A pretty girl was driving alone and without a hat. She told me her name and said we had friends in common and asked me to ride beside her. After that I saw a great deal of her and was soon in love. I did not tell her I was in love, however, because she was engaged. She had chosen me for her confidant and I learned all about her quarrels with her lover. (*Autobiographies* 76)

Laura, unconventionally hatless and driving alone, literally carried off the poet, who adopted in relation to her the sexually indeterminate role of vicarious listener to tales of love. He admired her style, and when he first met Maud Gonne he was reminded of Laura.

An early playlet written for Laura, *The Island of Statues*, explicitly explores ambiguities of gender. Laura was to play the part of an Enchantress who lives on an island, guarding the flower of immortality within a "brazen-gated glade" (*Variorum Plays* 667). Penetration of this symbolically feminine enclosure is archetypally dangerous: male questers in search of the flower must be certain to choose correctly. If they fail, the Medusan Enchantress will turn them to stone: the statues of the title are innumerable men who have made the wrong choice. The plucking of a flower is an ancient metaphor for the taking of virginity, and we hardly need Freud's interpretation of the Medusa as the castrating female genitals surrounded by snaky hair to see in *The Island of Statues* a thinly veiled expression of Yeats's doubts about his own ability to conform to the expected standards of "masculine" behaviour. Indeed, the impotence of all the male characters in the play is striking. The lovers of the shepherdess Naschina, Thernot and Colin, are the first in a long line of passive Yeatsian poets mesmerized by inaccessible and courageous females: Aillil in early versions of *The Shadowy Waters*, Septimus in the drafts of *The Player Queen* and Aleel in *The Countess Cathleen* (an obvious self-portrait that was written to be played by a woman, Florence Farr). Naschina gives her love to Almintor, an ostensibly more heroic types who promises to pluck the coveted flower and defeat the Enchantress. Yeats, however, could not at this stage of his development create or perhaps even imagine a successful, competent, "masculine" male. Conforming inadvertently to the ideal of male chastity, a facet of the courtly love tradition reworked for nineteenth-century Europe most powerfully in Wagner's *Parsifal*, Almintor chooses the wrong flower and is duly turned to stone.[12] The resourceful Naschina then assumes a male disguise and confronts the Enchantress herself. In a plot development reminiscent of Shakespearian comedy, the Enchantress falls in love with the disguised shepherdess, but her infatuation destroys her, and the victorious Naschina restores the statues to life. Like Rosalind, Portia and Viola, the androgynous female in male clothing apparently unites the best qualities of both sexes. Yet while Shakespeare's transvestite heroines are reincorporated into conventional patriarchal society at the close of the action, Naschina's success transforms her into a figure for the triumphant, immortal and excluded Eternal Feminine: at the end of the play we see that, unlike her male lover, she casts no shadow. To add to the complexity and indeterminacy of effect, the defeated Enchantress attracts our sympathy, and her passion for the shepherdess is tinged with pathos. Perhaps she is fatal to men because she has been waiting for centuries for a woman to love.

The Island of Statues was written before Yeats's meeting with John O'Leary and his decision to become a national writer. Once he had read Thomas Davis he realized that an audience accustomed to the patriotic verse of *The Spirit of the Nation* would not appreciate his own delicate ambiguities. In "To Ireland in the Coming Times" (1892), therefore, he attempted to establish himself as a male writer in a primarily political context:

> Know, that I would accounted be
> True brother of a company
> That sang, to sweeten Ireland's wrong,
> Ballad and story, rann and song.

One who needs to insist that he is the "true brother" of Davis, Mangan and Ferguson, however, obviously expects the audience of his poem (explicitly constructed as male, as "him who ponders well") to have had doubts about the writer's gender identification, and to have been alienated by the femininity of his subject matter:

> Nor be I any less of them, [the true brothers]
> Because the red-rose bordered hem
> Of her, whose history began
> Before God made the angelic clan,
> Trails all about the written page. (*Poems* 50)

Yeats identifies the occult with the feminine: "the red-rose bordered hem" of the Gnostic Sophia leaves its traces all over his writing. He knows that his pursuit of "elemental creatures" or of "faeries dancing under the moon" situates him on the margins of acceptable discourse. He suspects that the intensely subjective and arcane poetry that he has chosen to write may not be viewed as sufficiently manly by the propagandists of the nationalist movement.

"The Madness of King Goll", for example, first published in 1887, depicts the renunciation of male political authority and prowess in war for the metaphorically female domain of nature, poetry and madness.[13] The king abandons his defence of Ireland against the Viking invaders and becomes a crazed wanderer in the woods, a celebrant of the nature goddess Orchil. Only the "kind wires" of his poetic instrument afford him relief from the "whirling and the wandering fire" that drives him on: poetry alone justifies his madness and alienation from masculine pursuits. The poem ends ambiguously, however, with the poet unable to sing, and yet still an exile from the world of political action:

> But lift a mournful ulalu,
> For the kind wires are torn and still,
> And I must wander wood and hill
> Through summer's heat and winter's cold. (*Poems* 18)

Yeats's intense personal identification with this sexual impasse is suggested by his father's portrait of him as the mad king holding the broken harp.

Goll's pattern is repeated by Fergus, who in "Fergus and the Druid" seeks to cast away the responsibilities of authority in order to gain the "dreaming wisdom" of the Druid. The Druid warns him of the loss of power, of the capacity for masculine action, and of male sexuality itself, that are inherent in the choice of wisdom, dreams, and poetry:

> Look on my thin grey hair and hollow cheeks
> And on these hands that may not lift the sword,
> This body trembling like a wind-blown reed.
> No woman's loved me, no man sought my help. (*Poems* 32)

As Allen Grossman suggests, in Yeats's early poetry the wind is a symbol for the libido (55–6). The image of the Druid's body "trembling like a wind-blown reed" suggests that, in choosing dreams, the Druid and Fergus open themselves to the sorrow of infinite and unsatisfied desire.

Desire, in "The Man who Dreamed of Faeryland", destroys what society has defined as masculinity. The dreamer is on the threshold of manhood – as lover, as money-maker, as perpetrator of violence – but he is distracted by the image of a perfect, "dreamless" world where

> There dwelt a gay, exulting, gentle race
> Under the golden or the silver skies;
> That if a dancer stayed his hungry foot
> It seemed the sun and moon were in the fruit.

Faeryland is a place where desire is unknown because it is always already satisfied. The alchemical opposites, Sol and Luna, gold and silver, male and female, are united in the perfect fruit, which refreshes the lovers and the dancers. In the first and third stanzas of the poem, Yeats juxtaposes gold and silver with the amniotic waters of the sea: the fish

> . . . raised their little silver heads,
> And sang what gold morning or evening sheds
> Upon a woven world-forgotten isle
> Where people love beside the ravelled seas.

This world suggests the Lacanian Imaginary, which Kristeva identifies with the pre-Oedipal state of symbiotic and undifferentiated union with the mother. Although the Imaginary depends upon the presence of the mother's body, for the infant gender differences do not yet exist. The Imaginary is therefore at once a female state and a state that obliterates the distinction between masculine and feminine. While the mortal man is identified in the first word of every stanza as "He", the sex of the faery lovers and dancers is indeterminate:

> . . . glittering summer runs
> Upon the dancer by the dreamless wave.
> Why should those lovers that no lovers miss
> Dream, until God burn Nature with a kiss? (*Poems*, 43–5)

Although the man's active life is destroyed by dreaming, the object of his fantasies, is, ironically, "dreamless". No-one dreams in faeryland, because no-one lacks anything, for desire is a function of absence: "Why should those lovers that no lovers miss/Dream . . .?" Desire, Lacan has argued, is produced by the repression of the Imaginary, a repression that creates the unconscious. In the Imaginary itself there is no unconscious, and therefore no dreaming, since there is no lack. The pre-Oedipal child, however, must leave faeryland, give up his identification with his mother and, in acquiring a language structured by *différance*, accept the Law of the Father and enter what Lacan calls the Symbolic Order. The man who dreamed of Faeryland is ruined by his inability to accept his patriarchal order, and by his obsession with the maternal paradise: he cannot function in the world.

Yeats seldom wrote about his mother. When he did, he often associated her with Ireland, and emphasized her fondness for exchanging stories with the fishermen's wives at Howth (*Autobiographies* 61). As his essay "Village Ghosts" makes clear, these stories all concerned fairies and the supernatural

(*Mythologies* 15–21). When he later became a collector of Irish fairy stories he was associating himself with the only happiness he had ever observed his mother enjoying. In 1887, after suffering a stroke, the already silent and withdrawn Susan Yeats became mentally impaired. In *The Celtic Twilight*, Yeats recounts numerous tales of people who have withdrawn from the world into total or partial insanity; he explains that, having been "touched" by the fairies, they are "away" or absent: their spirits are in fairyland. Yeats's description of his mother's stroke as a liberation into "perfect happiness" (*Autobiographies* 62) suggests that he saw her too, in her 12-year "absence", as an inhabitant of fairyland. Lacan and Kristeva agree that, although the realm of the Imaginary offers the only wholeness we shall ever know, it is uninhabitable by adults except at the price of a psychosis. Yeats's vision of fairyland as the place of the mother, a psychic retreat from the problems and challenges of the world, was deeply ambivalent: the cost of female wisdom might be insanity. Writing about the fairies, he argued that:

> It is natural, too, that there should be a queen to every household of them, and that one should hear little of their kings, for women come more easily than men to that wisdom which ancient peoples, and all wild peoples even now, think the only wisdom. The self, which is the foundation of our knowledge, is broken in pieces by foolishness, and is forgotten in the sudden emotions of women, and therefore fools may get, and women do get of a certainty, glimpses of much that sanctity finds at the end of its painful journey. (*Mythologies* 115)

Women, fairies, primitives, lunatics and saints deconstruct the phallic, unified Cartesian self, foundation of the Law of the Father. As a poet, Yeats felt his male selfhood dispersed and threatened but his poetry powerfully enabled by his identification with these marginal figures.

The question of male selfhood and its constitution in language is central in "The Song of the Happy Shepherd" and "The Sad Shepherd". The Happy Shepherd rejects the traditionally masculine pursuits of war, philosophy and science. Yet, believing that "Words alone are certain good", he clings to the masculine Logos, to the constitutive importance of language: "The wandering earth herself may be / Only a sudden flaming word". The speaker defiantly affirms the unified self and its speech against meaningless flux, "the many changing things / In dreary dancing past us whirled". Yet the myth of the phallogocentric self can be maintained only by a female Other who will hear and repeat it:

> Go gather by the humming sea
> Some twisted, echo-harbouring shell,
> And to its lips thy story tell,
> And they thy comforters will be,
> Rewording in melodious guile

> Thy fretful words a little while,
> Till they shall singing fade in ruth
> And die a pearly brotherhood. (*Poems* 7–8)

The "twisted, echo-harbouring shell" to whose lips the fretful speaker will entrust his sad story appears to be, like the mythical nymph Echo, no more than a melodious hollow chamber, a sounding-board for male complaint. The Ovidian reference, however, provides an ironic comment on the speaker himself: Echo's beloved was the ultimate solipsist, Narcissus. Yeats depicts the happy shepherd as a verbal narcissist, who suggests that the male should find a sympathetic female who will not only listen to him, but repeat his words in her own way. She will add nothing original, nor will she speak of herself, but her female melody will embody male Logos. Man provides the spirit, woman the flesh.[14] Cixous' Intelligible/Palpable opposition appears to inform this idea, but it is complicated by the fact that in rewording Logos the "echo-harbouring shell" also transforms it into poetry: for Yeats the supremely important act. The masculine "brotherhood" of words will take a "pearly" colour from the vessel through which it has passed: the poet's voice as it returns to "comfort" him is inevitably a feminized one.

"The Song of the Happy Shepherd" is in any case subverted by its companion poem, "The Sad Shepherd", in which the sea-shell seizes the initiative. When the protagonist attempts to communicate with the stars, the sea and the dewdrops, these archetypally female presences are busy talking to themselves, and ignore him. He therefore:

> Sought once again the shore, and found a shell,
> And thought, I will my heavy story tell
> Till my own words, re-echoing, shall send
> Their sadness through a hollow, pearly heart;
> And my own tale again for me shall sing,
> And my own whispering words be comforting,
> And lo! my ancient burden may depart.

The words "I", "my" and "me" dominate this passage, but the egotistical shepherd discovers that the "wildering whirls" of the sea-shell distort and dissipate the imperial male self:

> Then he sang softly nigh the pearly rim;
> But the sad dweller by the sea-ways lone
> Changed all he sang to inarticulate moan
> Among her wildering whirls, forgetting him.

The world is not a single male word, Logos, comprehensible to all, but many female voices singing, "inarticulate" melodies among themselves. In Kristevan terms, one who speaks the language of the father, the language of lack and desire, confronts but cannot understand the semiotic language of the mother, the song of self-presence and self-containment:

> The sea swept on and cried her old cry still,
> Rolling along in dreams from hill to hill.
> He fled the persecution of her glory
> And, in a far-off, gentle valley stopping,
> Cried all his story to the dewdrops glistening.
> But naught they heard, for they are always listening,
> The dewdrops, for the sound of their own dropping. (*Poems* 9)

The relationship between these two poems demonstrates the constant process of self-undermining, and questioning of the relation of gender to poetry at work in Yeats's verse. As Cixous argues, the hierarchical ideology in which the male element of the binary opposition always defeats and destroys the female has not been monolithic; gaps and inconsistencies always occur:

> Sometimes I find where to put the many-lifed being that I am. Into elsewheres opened by men who are capable of becoming woman. For the huge machine that ticks and repeats its "truth" for all these centuries has had failures, or I wouldn't be writing. There have been poets who let something different from tradition get through at any price – men able to love love; therefore, to love others, to want them: men able to think the woman who would resist destruction and constitute herself as a superb, equal, "impossible" subject, hence intolerable in the real social context. Only by breaking the codes denying her could the poet have desired that woman. Her appearance causing, if not a revolution, harrowing explosions. . . . (Only for poets, not for novelists who stick with representation. Poets because poetry exists only by taking strength from the unconscious, and the unconscious, the other country without boundaries, is where the repressed survive – women or, as Hoffman would say, fairies.) (98)

Yeats is one of those poets who frequently, though not always, "let[s] something different from tradition get through". His adherence to the English poetic tradition, for example, was disrupted by his identification with Ireland. When he started to read versions of early Irish saga material, he found models of femininity that differed radically from those current in Victorian poetry: the great queens and warriors Maeve, Aoife and Emer, who own property, dispose of their own bodies, control and even defeat men.[15] In desiring Maud Gonne he desired a woman like these, one who fully intended to constitute herself as a "superb, equal, 'impossible' subject".

Maud Gonne's autobiography reveals that she wanted to live in the male world of political action, and was trying to remove herself from the sphere of conventional romance. She was, she later told Ethel Mannin, too busy working for Ireland's freedom to fall in love.[16] This reversal of traditional feminine priorities partly motivated her disastrous marriage to John Mac-Bride, whom she saw not as romantic lover nor as head of the family, but as equal companion in the struggle for Irish freedom. Her attempt to redefine the matrimonial paradigm ended in divorce proceedings that destroyed her political effectiveness in Puritan Ireland, and led to a 10-year exile in France. It was during this exile that Yeats wrote "No Second Troy", which celebrates her as "superb" and "equal", but also suggests her "impossibility" in the social context:

> Why should I blame her that she filled my days
> With misery, or that she would of late
> Have taught to ignorant men most violent ways,
> Or hurled the little streets upon the great,
> Had they but courage equal to desire?
> What could have made her peaceful with a mind
> That nobleness made simple as a fire,
> With beauty like a tightened bow, a kind
> That is not natural in an age like this,
> Being high and solitary and most stern?
> Why, what could she have done, being what she is?
> Was there another Troy for her to burn? (*Poems* 91)

"No Second Troy" is a difficult poem for the feminist reader, whose positive response to the celebration of female agency and power is qualified by the poet's restrictions on the exercise of that power. Maud Gonne transgresses all the conventions of femininity: she is violent, courageous, noble, fiery, solitary and stern; her beauty is a weapon – a tightened bow – rather than a lure. In figuring her as Helen, Yeats radically modifies the archetype: Homer's passive queen, the sex object over whom men fight their battles, becomes herself a warrior, identified by the simile of the bow as an Amazon. In his choice of active syntax, Yeats attributes to her the agency of a subject: instead of causing its destruction by men, she burns Troy herself. Nevertheless, Maud Gonne lives in an age that, according to Yeats, affords no fitting outlet for the energy of the superb woman. He refuses to consider that revolutionary nationalism and militant socialism (hurling "the little streets upon the great") might in fact provide a perfectly appropriate outlet for her power. Thus the poem takes back with one hand what it gives with the other: the superb woman is acknowledged, but her freedom to constitute herself as a subject through political action is denied.

The freedom to constitute herself as a subject has been routinely denied to the beloved woman in the canon of Western male love poetry. The politics of this influential genre are crucially important because love poetry participates in the cultural production of the discourse of "love", which is neither natural nor essential. Courtly love, for example, with all its accoutrements of passionate longing, religious worship and self-abasement on the part of the male, is a particular variant of the discourse, one which according to C.S. Lewis began "quite suddenly at the end of the eleventh century in Languedoc" (2).[17] La Rochefoucauld said that people would never fall "in love" at all if they had not heard love talked about: which does not mean that men and women would cease to form partnerships, but rather that the conventions regulating this activity are socially defined. The question to ask, according to Michel Foucault, would be "What strategies of power are furthered by these conventions?" Obviously, they have been produced to serve the interests of men, who until recently were the sole arbiters of discourse. Much love poetry naturalizes and universalizes what are in fact common male assumptions about women: that they are passive, vain and coquettish. Telling women that they are beautiful, mysterious and romantic, but also silent and incapable of agency or of logical thought, the "courtly" love poetry of the troubadours, Dante and Petrarch reinforces patriarchal ideology and contributes to the oppression of women even as it pretends to worship at the shrine of "Woman".[18] Poems in the contrasting *carpe diem* tradition, which is neither courtly nor romantic, insist that a woman's only value resides in her transient beauty and its power to satisfy male lust. Neither as Madonna nor as sexual toy can a woman voice her own desire, figure as a speaking subject. In its deployment of conventional tropes (woman as rose, love as war or hunting, the blazon) and formalized discourse positions (the abject but loquacious lover, the elevated, absent or dead, and always silent Beloved) the genre has been extremely conservative, while masking and universalizing its own ideological premises.

Yeats himself understood the enormous importance of love poetry in the production of gender identity:

> It seems to me that true love is a discipline, and it needs so much wisdom that the love of Solomon and Sheba must have lasted, for all the silence of the Scriptures. Each divines the secret self of the other, and refusing to believe in the mere daily self, creates a mirror where the lover or the beloved sees an image to copy in daily life; for love also creates the Mask. (*Autobiographies* 464)

In giving women an "image to copy in daily life", love poets have insisted that they have divined – and divined correctly – the "secret self" that is the "essence" of femininity. Adrienne Rich has described her experience as a female reader of such male writings:

> And there were all those poems about women, written by men: it seemed to be a given that men wrote poems and women frequently inhabited them. These women were almost always beautiful, but threatened with the loss of beauty, the loss of youth – the fate worse

than death. Or, they were beautiful and died young, like Lucy and Lenore. Or, the woman was like Maud Gonne, cruel and disastrously mistaken, and the poem reproached her because she had refused to become a luxury for the poet. ("When We Dead Awaken" 39)

Rich is, I think, correct to isolate the concatenation of beauty, transience and death as central to male love poetry. I would, however, qualify her analysis of what Yeats did to Maud Gonne. Certainly "No Second Troy" reproaches his beloved even as it rejects doing so: "Why should I blame her that she filled my days / With misery?" This double-edged rhetorical strategy, however, also informs "The Fish", a poem that Rich would read as unmitigatedly reproachful:

> Although you hide in the ebb and flow
> Of the pale tide when the moon has set,
> The people of coming days will know
> About the casting out of my net,
> And how you have leaped times out of mind
> Over the little silver cords,
> And think that you were hard and unkind,
> And blame you with many bitter words. (*Poems* 58)

Here the speaker's overt appeal for sympathy is undermined by his choice of metaphor. We have only to read the poem on a literal level to see the ridiculousness of blaming a fish for avoiding capture. Fish that get caught usually get eaten. When the fisherman in the romantic love lyric "The Song of Wandering Aengus" catches "a little silver trout", he undoubtedly intends to fry it for breakfast:

> When I had laid it on the floor
> I went to blow the fire aflame. (*Poems* 59)

Although the trout is saved from the pan by its metamorphosis into a "glimmering girl", Yeats's touch of realism demonstrates his awareness of the implications of the "hunting" metaphor so dear to male love poets. A much later poem, "The Death of the Hare", deliberately deconstructs this trope:

> I have pointed out the yelling pack,
> The hare leap to the wood,
> And when I pass a compliment
> Rejoice as lover should
> At the drooping of an eye,
> At the mantling of the blood.
>
> Then suddenly my heart is wrung
> By her distracted air
> And I remember wildness lost

> And after, swept from there,
> Am set down standing in the wood
> At the death of the hare. (*Poems* 222–3)

If the male is a hunter, then the only possible end for the prey is death. The game of compliment has a cruel aim: the curtailment of the woman's freedom, the loss of her "wildness". Yeats, who valued wildness, understood that for women patriarchal marriage is no better than captivity. In his youth, he had worshipped heroines like Shelley's proto-feminist Cythna, "lawless women without homes and without children" (*Autobiographies* 64). Although he certainly wanted to marry Maud Gonne, he knew what a sacrifice he was demanding of her. On one of the rare occasions when his courtship was going well, he wrote: "She had come [to] have need of me . . . and I had no doubt that need would become love . . . I had even as I watched her a sense of cruelty, as though I were a hunter taking captive some beautiful wild creature' (*Memoirs* 49). Of "The Death of the Hare" he said, "the poem means that the lover may, while loving, feel sympathy with his beloved's dread of captivity" (*Letters* 840–1). Yeats's sympathetic identification with the female gender position kept him alert to the political implications of apparently dead metaphors.

The revisionary nature of Yeats's deployment of the genre of love poetry is nowhere clearer than in his handling of the *carpe diem* formula. Poems in the *carpe diem* tradition, modelled on the works of Horace, Catullus and Ovid, urge immediate sexual enjoyment in terms that devalue the object of their desire. In *Twelfth Night*, Shakespeare's Orsino voices the master metaphor of the genre: "For women are as roses whose fair flow'r / Being once display'd doth fall that very hour" (Act 2, Scene 4). Innumerable manipulators of the formula use the rosebud cliché to insist that the woman who refuses to yield her chastity will wither on the branch, her essential biological purpose unfulfilled. Edmund Waller's "Go, Lovely Rose" is a classic of the genre, one in which the perennial conflation of woman with nature emphasizes the passivity of the female,[19] whose function is to display herself for male "commendation" and consumption:

> Bid her come forth,
> Suffer herself to be desired,
> And not blush so to be admired.

Even the syntax is passive. The comparison becomes overtly coercive in the final stanza, where the rose is instructed to:

> . . . die! that she
> The common fate of all things rare
> May read in thee;
> How small a part of time they share
> That are so wondrous sweet and fair! (128)

Instead of concluding that the cruel mistress was afraid of getting pregnant, had objections to his character or his looks, or preferred someone else, the *carpe diem* poet frequently expressed his disappointment through an arrogant insistence that the woman's virginity was like uninvested capital: unless "used" by him it was "wasted". Waller implies that he is the young woman's only chance: if she refuses him she will never find another. In "To the Virgins, to Make Much of Time", Herrick also deploys withering rosebuds to underscore the ideal that a woman sexually unused is a woman dead:

> Then be not coy, but use your time;
> And while you may, goe marry:
> For having lost but once your prime,
> You may for ever tarry. (84)

Herrick is specific about the social implications of his economic and horticultural metaphors: if a woman "spends" time without "using" it to acquire a man, she will become a superfluous old maid. The message is repeated in poem after poem: woman's time is short. Since her only function is to please physically and to procreate, she needs to make the most of her brief bloom: once it has gone she is worthless. Poets admit that men die too, but their useful life and their natural life more nearly coincide. Loss of manly beauty does not mean loss of manly function.

Although he must have been turned down as often as any love poet in history, Yeats did not present Maud Gonne with Marvell's grotesque choice: yield your virginity to me or to the worms. His rejection of this destructive convention may be demonstrated by comparing "When You Are Old and Grey and Full of Sleep" with Ronsard's "Quand Vous Serez Bien Vielle", from which it derives:[20]

> Quand vous serez bien vielle, au soir, à la chandelle,
> Assise aupres du feu, devidant & filant,
> Direz chantant mes vers, en vous esmerveillant,
> Ronsard me celebroit du temps que j'estois belle.

Ronsard uses the conventional theme of mutability as an "erotic threat" (Broadbent 153). If his mistress fails to satisfy him, "Vous serez au fouyer une vielle acroupie, / Regrettant mon amour et vostre fier desdain". She will be lonely and regretful because she has missed her chance with him, and he seems pleased to imagine her unhappiness. Yeats does not resort to such sexual bullying. His beloved is not admonished, like Ronsard's, "Vivez, si m'en croyez, n'attendez a demain: / Cueillez des aujourd'huy les roses de la vie". Yeats makes no mention of those perennially transient roses, nor is his poem an attempt at seduction. The woman will age whether or not she requites his love: he offers her the poem as a source of melancholy pleasure during the sleepy twilight of old age, a reminder that

> . . . many loved your moments of glad grace,
> And loved your beauty with love false or true,
> But one man loved the pilgrim soul in you,
> And loved the sorrows of your changing face. (*Poems* 41)

Although his verses will recall her lost youth they do not accuse her of cruelty towards her celebrant: Love has "fled", she has not repelled him by her "fier desdain". The deterioration caused by ageing is not used as a weapon against her; instead the poet lovingly details her present charm: the "soft look" and the shadows in her eyes, her moments of glad grace. Ronsard's object of desire has no particular characteristics; she is, simply and unoriginally, "belle". Yeats values particular beauties of her body, but is even more attracted by beauty of soul: unlike other suitors he loved "the pilgrim soul in you / And loved the sorrows of your changing face". In the Introduction to his *Penguin Anthology of Love Poetry*, Stallworthy notes with pained surprise that throughout the entire amatory tradition, "We look in vain for the features, lineaments of a living woman" (25). It is Stallworthy's surprise that is remarkable: women in this tradition are objects, not individuals. Yeats's "pilgrim soul", however, a phrase we associate with Maud Gonne's courage and determination, provides an exception to this rule. It associates her, moreover, with the journeying quester of male mythology rather than with the passive maiden of the courtly tradition. Nor can a pilgrim soul wither like a youthful body: Yeats subverts the *carpe diem* genre even as he employs it. His refusal to imitate Ronsard's sonnet form (his poem has 12 lines instead of 14) may even suggest a stylistic disengagement from that most traditional vehicle of the amatory tradition.

Instead of using mutability as a coercive strategy, Yeats promises to love his mistress even when she has lost the bloom of youth, and whether or not she actually yields to him. While others may desert her, he will remain faithful:

> Time's bitter flood will rise,
> Your beauty perish and be lost
> For all eyes but these eyes. (*Poems* 71)

In assuring her that what he values is a beauty that he will always see, no matter what her outward appearance, Yeats abandons the crude assumption that a woman is good only for a few years, and that all she is good for is having sex with him. "The Folly of Being Comforted" enacts dramatically his rejection of that assumption:

> One that is ever kind said yesterday:
> "Your well-belovèd's hair has threads of grey,
> And little shadows come about her eyes;
> Time can but make it easier to be wise
> Though now it seems impossible, and so

> All that you need is patience."
> Heart cries, "No,
> I have not a crumb of comfort, not a grain.
> Time can but make her beauty over again.

The beauty of Yeats's beloved, which consists in energy rather than passivity, in "nobility" rather than in freshness of the flesh, can only increase with the passage of time. Here Yeats employs a modified form of the Shakespearian sonnet, but his claim that "Time can but make her beauty over again" deliberately challenges Shakespeare's basic premise, which is that nothing but art or procreation can withstand the depredations of "Devouring Time" (Sonnet 19). Despite his use of the concluding Shakespearian couplet, Yeats refuses to claim that "in black ink my love may still shine bright" (Sonnet 65): an assertion that witnesses to the poet's desire for immortality as much as to the qualities of the beloved. In "The Folly of Being Comforted" the 35-year-old woman inspires a devotion unlinked to the flawless skin and auburn hair of the 23-year-old:

> Because of that great nobleness of hers
> The fire that stirs about her, when she stirs
> Burns but more clearly. O she had not these ways
> When all the wild summer was in her gaze. (*Poems* 78)

Clearly, Yeats's unstable conception of his own masculinity prevented him from employing the macho poetics of the *carpe diem* mode. Although he made considerable use of the woman-as-rose metaphor he completely reversed its implications. Early in his career, he wrote that "the only two powers that trouble the deeps are religion and love" (*Uncollected Prose* 2: 133), and he combined them into a religion of woman in which the rose became a Dantesque sacred symbol. In "The Rose of the World", female beauty, figured in the conventionally "fatal" archetypes of Helen and Deirdre, is eternal and indestructible:

> We and the labouring world are passing by:
> Amid men's souls that waver and give place
> Like the pale waters in their wintry race,
> Under the passing stars, foam of the sky,
> Lives on this lonely face.
>
> Bow down archangels, in your dim abode:
> Before you were, or any hearts to beat,
> Weary and kind one lingered by His seat;
> He made the world to be a grassy road
> Before her wandering feet. (*Poems* 36)

Here the male poet represents transience, and the woman partakes of immortality. The last stanza makes it clear that Yeats's female principle is at least coeval with, if not equal to, the male Deity: she exists alone with God before the creation of the world.

Yeats's religion of woman can be explained not only by his adoption of the Victorian version of courtly love adumbrated by Rossetti, but also by his occult studies. Elaine Pagels has documented the suppression of the female elements of divinity by the orthodox fathers of the early church. Yeats, however, rejected Christian orthodoxy. The occult mystical tradition made available to him by Blavatsky and Mathers was strongly influenced by Gnosticism, which was much more sympathetic to women than is patriarchal Christianity. God's female counterpart, the Shekinah, is centrally important in the Jewish Cabbala, which played a major role in the rituals and studies of the Golden Dawn. Introducing the *Kabbalah Unveiled*, Mathers wrote:

> I wish particularly . . . to direct the readers' attention to the stress laid by the Qabalah on the Feminine aspects of the deity and to the shameful way in which any allusions to these in the ordinary translations of the Bible have been suppressed. (Grossman 87)

Theodor Reik says of the Torah, "She is considered older than the world and is assigned a cosmic role. . . . Even in this diluted form we recognize the primal female goddess" (Rich, "Antifeminist Woman" 75). Clearly, Yeats's Rose is also an avatar of the primal female goddess. His discovery of her in his occult studies symbolizes his rejection of Victorian rationalist science and his search for an alternative culture that would subvert patriarchal history and theology.

Radical advocates of female difference like Mary Daly celebrate goddesses as offering powerfully enabling images for women deprived of female divinity by the masculine Christian Trinity. Yeats shares their rejection of traditional theology: his heretical holy man Ribh denounces the father of Irish Catholicism, St Patrick:

> An abstract Greek absurdity has crazed the man,
> A Trinity that is wholly masculine. Man, woman, child
> (daughter or son),
> That's how all natural or supernatural stories run. (*Poems* 284)

Feminists opposed to the principle of female difference, however, argue that goddess-worship simply valorizes the previously inferior partner in the masculine/feminine hierarchy instead of deconstructing it, while perpetuating concepts of the Eternal Feminine.[21] Like Beatrice and Laura, Yeats's Rose is beautiful, remote, and self-preoccupied; like Helen and Deirdre, she is the passive cause of the destruction of many men: he therefore invites the charge of essentialism. I would argue, however, that the current condemnation of essentialism should be modified to take into account the historical circumstances of earlier writers. The search for the goddess was part of a Victorian revolution against patriarchy that theorized matriarchy as the origin of civilization. The discipline of anthropology was founded upon the speculations of such men as Bachofen, McLennan and Morgan about the primacy of mother-right.[22] For the purposes of my argument, whether they were feminists is as irrelevant as whether they were correct: what is important is their questioning of the patriarchal family as the essential and immutable model for social relations. Drawing on Morgan's *Ancient Society*, Marx and Engels posited the matriarchal gens as the originary, pre-capitalist form of social organization, and argued that this primitive communist grouping was destroyed by the twin institutions of slavery and private property, that were embodied in the authoritarian paternal household. In *The Origin of Family, Private Property, and the State* (1884), Engels described this transition as the "world-historic defeat of the female sex" (736). He also argued that although the patriarchal family was well established among the classical Greeks, "the position of the goddesses in mythology represents an earlier period, when women still occupied a freer and more respected place" (737). Feminist classical scholars question the historical accuracy of this judgement (Pomeroy 15), but I wish to establish only that Yeats, who from 1887 to 1890 frequented William Morris's Sunday evening socialist gatherings, would have seen the recovery of the goddess as a project compatible with advanced socialist and feminist thought. His occultism, which is often attacked as symptomatic of reactionary and even neo-fascist views, can be more accurately characterized as an alignment with the progressive late Victorian movement towards alternative models of social organization.

The politics of Yeats's historical situation, his love for a "New Woman", the indeterminacy of his gender identity, and the obliquity of his relationship to the canonical tradition, make it impossible to categorize his love poetry in any simple way. In approaching his early work, therefore, I find myself compelled to alternate between a recuperative and a suspicious hermeneutic. I am convinced that this dual response is demanded by Yeats's complexity and historical position in culture; and that a criticism that would do full justice to the insights of feminism and still engage with his poetry must accept such heterogeneity as a concomitant of its enterprise.

Notes

1 I would like to thank Alan Friedman, Jane Marcus and Toril Moi for their helpful comments on earlier drafts of this essay. My excellent graduate students from "Love Poetry: Gender and Genre" influenced my thinking in many ways. A summer grant from the University of Texas Research Institute provided me with the time to write the essay, which was first delivered as a lecture at the Yeats International Summer School, Sligo.

2 The practice of "gynocritics" (the study of women by women) advocated by
   Elaine Showalter in "Toward a Feminist Poetics" has been widely adopted by
   the Anglo-American feminist community, but at a 1987 conference at the
   University of Texas, Showalter herself suggested that the next direction for
   "gender studies" should be the examination of masculinity as a social construct
   rather than as an unmarked universal. Nina Auerbach has always maintained
   that "I do not want to give up writers I love because my allegiance to women
   tells me to do so: we have been told for too long that being a woman means
   giving things up" ("Engorging the Patriarchy" 157).

3 In adopting certain features of the work of male theorists, without concerning
   myself particularly about whether the uses to which I put my borrowings are
   consistent with the overall logic of their theoretical systems, I am following a
   course already advocated by the French feminists Cixous and Irigaray: I steal in
   order to fly (voler). Feminists are divided about the question of theory: some
   view it as the last gasp of a sterile male-dominated academic orthodoxy; others
   feel that the work of Derrida and Lacan, patriarchs though they undoubtedly
   are, has many useful strategies to offer the resourceful female critic. Derridian
   deconstruction, which occupies itself with exposing and undoing the hierarchical binary oppositions that are the basis of Western phallogocentric
   thought, can, when we employ the practice upon the opposition male/female,
   be a powerful tool for women readers.

4 See Auerbach, *Woman and the Demon, passim*; Marcus 3–4; Gilbert and Gubar,
   No Man's Land 2: Chapter One. For a full discussion of these "fictions of
   feminine evil" see Dijkstra, *passim*.

5 For an account of his early socialism, see Butler Cullingford, *Yeats, Ireland and
   Fascism*, Chapter Two.

6 For a discussion of the effect of the "New Woman" actress on Yeats, see Laity.

7 In the nineteenth century, the new racist pseudo-science of ethnography characterized the Irish as a feminine people. According to Ernest Renan: "If it be
   permitted us to assign sex to nations as to individuals, we should have to say
   without hesitance that the Celtic race . . . is an essentially feminine race" (81).
   Matthew Arnold interpreted the passivity, excitability, and inefficiency evinced
   by this conquered people as evidence of their need for a firm "masculine"
   ruler: a circular argument which perfectly served the ends of imperialism. The
   nationalist response to this caricature was to invert it, and insist on Irish masculinity: to attempt to become, in Ashis Nandy's formulation,"hyper-
   masculine" (*Intimate Enemy* 7–10). See Cairns and Richards, "Woman in the
   Discourse of Celticism".

8 For an extended discussion of this metaphor as used in "Adam's Curse", see
   Butler Cullingford, "Labour and Memory".

9 While Gilbert and Gubar spend the first chapter of *The Madwoman in the Attic*
   arguing that in the nineteenth century literary creativity was metaphorically
   defined as a male generative activity, with the pen as penis, the author as father,
   Ellmann points out that there is an equally strong habit of association between
   "childbirth and the male mind" (15). Friedman shows that both the phallic and
   the feminine analogies are common in male writers (49). Castle traces the
   rejection of the organic childbirth metaphor in neo-classical poetics (197–202),
   and its revivification by the Romantics (203–5).

10 Freudian critics David Lynch and Brenda Webster agree that Yeats was female identified (Webster 7), and attribute what they see, revealingly, as a "problem" to Yeats's unsatisfactory relationship with his mother (Lynch 47–51), a relationship documented in some detail by William Martin Murphy in his biography of J.B. Yeats.

11 Declan Kiberd uses the Jungian model first proposed by James Olney to argue that Yeats became unusually aware of the feminine aspect of his personality. Although in his youth he was "an unconscious slave to his anima" (Olney 128), in his later work he accepted and expressed the woman within. He wrote to Dorothy Wellesley, who must have told him of her sexual preference for women: "My dear, my dear – when you crossed the room with that boyish movement, it was no man who looked at you, it was the woman in me. It seems that I can make a woman express herself as never before. I have looked out of her eyes. I have shared her desire" (*Letters* 868).

12 I am indebted to Jane Marcus for his observation.

13 He constantly revised his depiction of Goll, who in 1887 is "A gentle yet a kingly child"; in 1888 "A gracious, gentle, kingly boy"; in 1889 "Peace-making, mild, a kingly boy", but who by 1895 is capable of striking terror into "The hearts of the world-troubling seamen" (*Variorum Poems* 81–2).

14 Yeats repeats this opposition in a later poem, "On Woman", when he praises the female sex for providing male "thought" with "her flesh and bone" (*Poems* 146).

15 See Mac Cana's "Women in Irish Mythology" for the classic discussion.

16 See unpublished letters in the National Library of Ireland.

17 Lewis's thesis has been the focus of numerous attacks (see, for example, Dronke; Robertson; Benton), and is now considered old-fashioned by medievalists. Yet the politics of the debate about courtly love have not been clearly discerned by the participants. Dronke's insistence that courtly love is an eternal and unchanging expression of the human psyche (2–3) is fundamentally conservative in its implications: it is the old-fashioned Lewis who turns out to be allied with current theorists of sexuality like Michel Foucault and Stephen Heath. His recognition that the forms in which sexual feeling find expression are culturally produced, and therefore subject to change, is perhaps more radical than he himself understood.

18 For the classic feminist denunciation of courtly love see Millett 37.

19 See Sherry Ortner for a feminist discussion of the Woman/Nature, Man/Culture opposition first analysed by Lévi-Strauss.

20 The similarities between these poems have been more frequently noted (see, for example, Mackey) than their differences.

21 I am grateful to Toril Moi for clarifying my thinking on this point, although the conclusions I have reached are different from hers.

22 See Coward, Chapter One, esp. 28–9, for an account of the nineteenth-century debate.

5

Narcissus re-vised: Constituting the female subject in three Beckett plays

Toni O'Brien Johnson

All That Fall, *Happy Days* and *Not I* were all first written in English, and women play an "active" part in all three, but otherwise, on the surface, they have little in common. They are generically different, for *All That Fall* is a radio play, commissioned by the BBC and first performed in 1957.[1] *Happy Days* is a stage play written in 1960–1 and first performed in New York in 1961, and through the intensity of its lighting and the spareness of its set and movement, it exploits to the maximum the visual dimension present in any stage play.[2] Although *Not I* is also a stage play, first performed in New York in 1972, it entirely abandons the traditional notion of "dramatic dialogue", while its set and movement are minimal, with the stage in darkness except for a mouth and the figure of an auditor who never speaks.

From their different generic angles, these three plays explore some gender-related difficulties in the constitution of the speaking subject. It is as though their author were attempting to see in the first two how male and female try to satisfy their need for reflection in each other in the process of self-definition, whereas in *Not I* he attempts to go beyond gender and on stage eliminates apparent intersubjective communication whether through the ear or the eye. This last play might be described as an attempt to represent a space, outside the patriarchal order, where the excluded woman as speaking self continues to deny or hide her own subjectivity by insisting on telling her life-story in the third person rather than the first. The particular dilemma of the women of the first two plays in constituting themselves arises from their being trapped in a limiting, male-authorized version of "femininity". This entrapment is presented only to the audience's ear in the radio play, while it is also evident to the eye in *Happy Days*. It is avoided in *Not I* through the complete elimination of social context and the confinement of signs of gender to voice and language. As a consequence of their generic variety, these three plays offer different modes of representing presence and absence as well as reflection, which can be visual or vocal.

The work of Luce Irigaray and Julia Kristeva, which attends to specular and psycholinguistic issues, provides a substantial part of the theoretical underpinning of this study. Irigaray, in *Speculum of the Other Woman*, has shown how woman has come to be outside representation in patriarchal culture. She points out that the basic assumption underlying all male-dominated Western philosophical discourse is of a postulating subject that is capable of reflecting on its own being. In this discourse, the woman has become the negative required by the male subject's speculation/ specularization, from Plato to Freud, whose definition of sexual difference continues to depend on the eye, using man as norm, and seeing the female in terms of absence or lack. Although Kristeva's theories differ from Irigaray's in important respects, she shares her view of woman as being outside presentation. In particular, she sees patriarchy as frustrating in women the narcissism which in its positive form could enable them to become the subjects of representation.

The gaze, which is crucial to narcissism, ultimately derives from touch, which it extends and displaces (Heath, "Difference" 86), while for Irigaray the gaze objectifies and masters. Voice and gaze are separated in the story of Narcissus and Echo, with Narcissus's attachment to the gaze causing his death. Echo's fate, however, is audible immortality (Segal 12–15). It may be said that when the child begins to learn language, the mother enters into a game of linguistic mirroring with it, repeating the sounds and words that it utters. In this originary dyad, there is no silent mirroring, for the mother does not offer the infant a voiceless gaze. The mutuality of this speech is displaced in the process of creating written texts, which imply a substitution of the gaze for the voice (221–2).

The Lacanian theory of the construction of the subject and entry into the symbolic order provides an important basis for the positions of Irigaray and Kristeva. According to Lacan, as Nelly Furman succinctly tells us in "The Politics of Language":

one's entry into language is due to a fundamental alienation resulting from a splitting within the subject. . . . The primitive union with the mother is ruptured at the mirror-stage, which is the moment when the child recognizes its reflected image, identifies with it, and becomes aware of being a separate entity from the mother. The moment at which the infant perceives itself as an image, as "other", is also the

moment when the "I" which does the perceiving is split off from the
"I" which is perceived. Seeing oneself as other determines an everlast-
ing frustration and vain attempts at making one's "I" and one's imago
coincide, as well as a desire for oneself (sameness) under the guise of
otherness. The splitting of the subject and the separation from the
mother allow for the eruption of desire, determine the need for intersubjective communication, and force the child into the oedipal
triangle. (70)[3]

Irigaray, however, insists that at the Oedipal stage, there is a necessarily
different disposition on the part of the little girl towards her mother com-
pared with that of the little boy, and at the same time points out the
operation of the (false) "logic of the same" in Freud's conclusion that if the
boy desires his mother, the girl must learn to hate her.[4]

The libidinal investment or desire set up at the mirror stage when the
primitive union with the mother is ruptured is called *primary* narcissism
(Lacan, *Écrits* 98). This narcissism, Kristeva suggests, is a defence against the
emptiness of separation. Separation, she claims, "is our opportunity to
become narcissists or narcissistic, at any rate subjects of representation"
(*Reader* 257). But, of course, women are the *objects* of patriarchal representation, not its subjects. Women are the site of the specular, are meant to
exist for others, and to attract the gaze of these others through studying
themselves in the mirror (Lenk 56–7). Costume and mirrors are essential to
the *secondary* narcissism that patriarchy thus confers on women who, as a
result of their gazing in mirrors, create elaborate surfaces for the male gaze
to penetrate (Irigaray 113; Segal 213). The psychological dilemma that
women face as a result is how to escape from this limiting male-authorized
secondary narcissism which is inevitably unsatisfying for themselves: by
engaging them as objects, it disables them from constructing themselves as
subjects.

The mythological account of Narcissus might be regarded as an early
male-produced myth rendering the psychological process of becoming
locked in the image of the self-same. In Ovid's version of the tale, Tiresias'
knowledge of the difference between the sexual pleasure of men and that of
women (owing to his having spent 7 years as a woman) is the pretext for
the story of Narcissus. Tiresias, when asked by Jupiter to judge which of
them has the greater pleasure, decides that women have, thus siding with
the male god's view. Juno, since she holds the opposite view, is angered by
this, therefore she strikes Tiresias blind. Jupiter, to compensate, grants him
the gift of prophesy, insight for sight. Thus it is that when Tiresias is asked
whether Narcissus will live to ripe maturity, he can answer "if he doesn't
ever know himself". When in time Narcissus reaches puberty, many youths
and maidens seek his love. He, however, remains cold and aloof, including
when he is pursued by Echo. Echo has no parents, is from nowhere, and has

had her voice curtailed by Juno so that she can neither remain silent when others speak, nor begin to speak until they address her. Accordingly, when Narcissus says "May I die before I give you power over me" as she tries to embrace him, her reply is "I give you power over me". Spurned, she fades away bodily from grief, but her haunting voice remains. Narcissus stoops to drink from a clear pool, and falls in love with his own reflection. Caught in this self-love, he drowns in the pool (Segal 1–9). This myth incorporates the process of reflection in both specular and linguistic terms, while separating voice and gaze.

The relationship between voice and gaze, presence and absence, and the possibilities of reflection will concern me in the course of this chapter. The levels on which these factors operate in the plays are multiple and various. For all three plays, the audience is a necessary presence to justify performance, though it is also largely absent on stage (or on radio). Its gaze is necessary to a high degree for *Happy Days*, to a lesser degree for *Not I*, and not at all for *All That Fall*. If as Irigaray and Kristeva suggest, the woman is outside representation, then she should be invisible. Beckett indeed attempts to make her so by burying her or disembodying her voice, which is at times the only evidence of her presence. The voices of all the characters are audible against the necessary silence of the audience. However, there is frequent doubt as to whether the characters on stage actually hear each other's voices: silence is no proof of absence. Voice, even when disembodied, seems to prove the presence of the speaker, though not necessarily of her/his auditor on stage, for there are failures of sought verbal reflection. Also, there is a progressive integration of the voice of the Other (as predominantly male) in that of the female speaker from the earliest play to the latest.

Beckett's plays repeatedly raise the question of why the characters keep on talking when they seem to have so little to say and what they do say so little advances intersubjective communication. Since it is what the women say that is the dominant focus of attention in the three plays chosen for discussion, I shall concentrate on that. The chattiness of Mrs Rooney in *All That Fall* and the loquaciousness of Winnie in *Happy Days* suggest both frustration of their need for intersubjective communication, and an inordinate struggle to construct themselves as speaking subjects. The form of *Not I* is suggestive of "a tale told by an idiot"; the voice is female and the tale of "her" life might be seen as a talking cure taking place outside of the analytical situation, or as an aborted autobiography.

Agency, which is necessary to autobiography, and its curtailment, is a recurrent concern in Beckett's work and is strikingly presented to our eyes through Winnie's physical confinement in *Happy Days*. Her apparent passivity enables her endless talk, and could thus be responsible for her becoming buried in linguistic debris, rather than using language for constructing an autobiography. In the radio play *All That Fall*, the central female character is presented as physically less passive than Winnie. Despite the burden of Mrs Rooney's two hundred pounds of unhealthy flesh (30), she retains some power to move in a social context – a power almost lost to Winnie who is confined to her male partner as her only (present) interlocutor, whereas Mrs Rooney can engage in verbal exchange with a range of people. While the sound of her dragging feet establishes her presence for the audience, she becomes identifiable as a woman only through her voice. This begins with her reflection on the suffering of another woman listening to "Death and the Maiden": "Poor woman. All alone in that ruinous old house" (7). Overall, Mrs Rooney's reflections appear somewhat freer from prescription than Winnie's but another kind of entrapment emerges.

This entrapment takes the form of identification on Mrs Rooney's part with the female and suffering, frequently in combination, and it characterizes Mrs Rooney's position throughout the play. It arises from her own personal experience of "death and the maiden", which is embodied in the figure of her still-born daughter, who would now be reaching the menopause had she lived (12). It becomes evident that the primary source of Mrs Rooney's suffering is frustrated motherhood when she identifies herself as follows: "Oh I am just a hysterical old hag I know, destroyed with sorrow and pining and gentility and churchgoing and fat and rheumatism and childlessness. (*Pause. Brokenly.*) Minnie! Little Minnie!" (9)

The indications are that this identification of herself as frustrated mother informs most of her reflections, and also arrests her self-definition. For example, as the character Christy is introduced by her, she admits that it was not himself that she recognized, but his hinny (7). This hybrid, who has an ass for a mother and a horse for a father, is sterile, and thus engages Mrs Rooney's identification with frustrated motherhood. (She also goes on to identify with the suffering of Christy's mother and daughter.) On the other hand, she finds it especially painful to have her own childlessness reflected when the hinny refuses to take its eyes off Mrs Rooney: "How she gazes at me to be sure, with her great moist cleg-tormented eyes! . . . Take her by the snaffle and pull her eyes away from me. Oh this is awful. . . . What have I done to deserve all this, what, what?" (9) The hinny's gaze (moist with "tears" and suffering from horse-flies) objectifies Mrs Rooney, who identifies with the childlessness of the hinny-as-subject. This sparks a memory which makes it impossibly painful for Mrs Rooney to continue defining herself, so that she wishes to "just flop down flat on the road like a big fat jelly out of a bowl and never move again". Her grief at this point, as well as on another occasion when she remembers Minnie (12), leads her to long not only for stasis, but for absolute formlessness, so that there would be no question of identification, hence no further need for self-definition, so that she could disappear into a state of unconsciousness. It is this state she also longs for when she wishes to release herself into physical formlessness and declares: "oh to be in atoms, in atoms" (13). In the unconscious state, she

could in theory return to the pre-oedipal phase where there would be no
problem of identity because no individual identity separate from the
mother, no language, before the gaze into the mirror had forced entry into
the symbolic order where Mrs Rooney is not represented and she has such
difficulty defining herself.

This difficulty is apparent from the outset in the domain of language.
Mrs Rooney conveys her alienation from her own language as follows: "I
sometimes find my way of speaking very . . . bizarre" (8), an alienation in
no way relieved by Christy, who does not reply to her. Later she reflects
her husband's negative view of her as "struggling with a dead language",[5]
while he discounts any opinion she might have, and is content with hearing
and judging his own voice. She in contrast takes consolation in the future
demise of the language she is speaking ("it will be dead in time, just like our
own poor dear Gaelic"), for that would be another means of returning to
before the mirror phase, before the intervention of language. This return is
also emblematically present in the "baa" of the "pretty little woolly lamb"
seeking union with the mother's body. In a reference to "Arcady" (35),
Mrs Rooney shows her consciousness of the ideal nature of the unchanging
language of pastoral, and thus lives with the contradiction of longing for
what is impossible – a return to symbiotic union with the mother.

It is not only Mr Rooney and Christy who refuse to reflect Mrs Rooney.
She encounters this with other characters too. At the station, when
Tommy ignores her she ironizes: "Don't mind me. Don't take any notice
of me. I do not exist. The fact is well known" (16). She also chides Miss Fitt
who fails to acknowledge her: ". . . Am I then invisible, Miss Fitt? Is this
cretonne so becoming to me that I merge with the masonry?" (19). And
when the group of people at the station all greet each other but leave her
out, she reproaches them: "Do not imagine, because I am silent, that I am
not present, and alive, to all that is going on" (23). Thus through her talk,
this woman asserts her presence at the periphery of a patriarchal order
which will not acknowledge her. Her intrusion into discourse is enabled by
her manipulating the rhetorical structure of what she says. Like Echo repeating the words of Narcissus, she can mime male discourse, but she alters
the figure so as to demand a reading between the lines. By actually saying "I
do not exist", she negates the meaning-value of the assertion; and by asking
the question "Am I then invisible?", her words impose responsibility for
reflecting her on her interlocutor. When she is silent, she is still "alive to all
that is going on" – going on without her, that is, for although clearly
present to the audience, she is excluded from re-presentation by the failure
of other characters to acknowledge her, and is present only in her voice.

Voice has become associated for Mrs Rooney with a series of questions
concerning species, gender and fertility, for instance when she hears
Christy's hinny cry, she comments: "So hinnies whinny. Well, it is not
surprising" (8). Her lack of surprise that the hinny whinnies rather than

brays arises from her expecting the power of the voice to originate with the father, not the mother. Also, when an ass brays later in the play she says: "That was a true donkey. Its father and mother were donkeys" (29). Later again, when her empathizing with the "lovely laburnum" is evoked by the loss of its potential fertility – "Poor thing, it is losing all its tassels" (37) – this leads her to muse:

> *Mrs Rooney*: Can hinnies procreate, I wonder?
> *They halt.*
> *Mr Rooney*: Say that again.
> *Mrs Rooney*: Come on, dear, don't mind me, we are getting drenched.
> *Mr Rooney*: (*forcibly*) Can what what?
> *Mrs Rooney*: Hinnies procreate. (*Silence.*) You know, hinnies or jinnies, aren't they barren, or sterile, or whatever it is? (*Pause.*) It wasn't an ass's colt at all, you know, I asked the Regius Professor. (*Pause*)
> *Mr Rooney*: He should know.
> *Mrs Rooney*: Yes, it was a hinny, he rode into Jerusalem or wherever it was on a hinny. (38)

The nexus of interests species/gender/fertility is interwoven in Mrs Rooney's mind to the point where confusion overtakes her and she addresses herself to the blind male for authoritative knowledge on fertility.

Several features of this speech merit attention. First, her reticence in questioning Mr Rooney directly concerning engendering, brought about by his response, "Say that again", conveying either incomprehension or disbelief that she should wish to know. Second, her concern with their physical well-being functions as a distraction from the knowledge she is pursuing, aided by Mr Rooney's total failure to understand her question as he repeats "Can what what?", which effectively causes her to shift from the question of engendering to that of classification, which presumably she thinks he will understand. Third, her deference to the authority of the Regius Professor on the patriarchal text is endorsed by Mr Rooney. Finally, there is a distinct shift from the clarity of her original question "Can hinnies procreate?" to the vagueness and inaccuracy of her identifications of hinnies or jinnies, barren or sterile, and Jerusalem or wherever. This suggests that she has been made to feel that naming itself is not her business, as though she has been placed outside the practice of identifying.

All this suggests that the woman's curiosity is curtailed, through her own reticence as well as through the man's discouragement and failure to reflect her; through her submission to the patriarchal text, the discrepancies of which have been kept hidden;[6] through her weak engagement with definition; and through her misplaced deference to male authority overall for knowledge. For there is no evidence that this blind male is significantly knowledgeable; and given the arbitrariness with which areas of knowledge are carved up, the Regius Professor here as professor of theology is an expert on the text *per se*, not an authority on the genetics of solid-hoofed quadrupeds. Given all these impediments, Mrs Rooney's attempts at using language for constructing her own position in relation to voice, gender and fertility can scarcely be effective, for she allows herself to get involved in a wild and profitless chase of the non-arbitrary in reference, or in an endless process of deferral.

The blindness of Mr Rooney (with its psychological and mythological associations with castration) calls attention to the gaze in a particular way in a radio play. Because of his blindness, he has to be led by the young male to the men's lavatory: "Jerry led me to the men's, or Fir as they call it now, from Vir Viris I suppose, the V becoming F, in accordance with Grimm's Law" (36). Mr Rooney is repressing some anxiety about gender here, for the important distinction to be made where culturally men and women are segregated in public for excretary purposes is between male and female, linguistically between masculine and feminine, that is Fir and Mná in Irish, not between the voiced and voiceless fricatives. A knowledge of Grimm's Law is of little help in reading these signs. Although the blind Mr Rooney may have learned the laws of philology, and something of his Latin nouns, he ignores the feminine gender and depends on the support of another male to be led to the correctly gendered lavatory.

Mr Rooney's ignoring of the feminine gender is also apparent when he introduces a reference to Dante, after his infanticidal urge is activated by the jeering of the Lynch twins (31). He suggests that he and Mrs Rooney "go on backwards", which she questions, but he insists: "Yes. Or you forwards and I backwards. The perfect pair. Like Dante's damned, with their faces arsy-versy. Our tears will water our bottoms." The allusion here is to Canto XX of Dante's *Inferno*, where the poet meets the prophets, fortune-tellers, and augurers whose punishment for having access to forbidden knowledge is to have their heads twisted backwards, so that they can only see the direction in which they are moving by walking backwards (Dante 195–200). These figures are weeping, so that indeed their tears *are* watering their bottoms. However, even allowing for the multiple irony in Mr Rooney's idea of "the perfect pair", his proposal ignores the implication of his suggestion that if Maddy were to continue leading him (blind as he is), facing forwards without having her head twisted backwards, then her tears could not water her bottom. On the other hand, if he is implicating her in the same damnation as himself, so that her head would be twisted backwards, then they would both have to move either forwards or backwards if they were to remain moving as a pair. A ruthless logic of the same is operating, eliding both subjective positional and gender difference.

There is a virtual embodiment of the elision of gender difference in one of the figures in the Dante passage alluded to (Canto XX), the blind Tiresias who would be the logical focus for Mr Rooney's identification.

The important forms of "forbidden knowledge" here to which Tiresias has access are his prophesy relating to Narcissus, and his experience of both female and male sexual pleasure. His birthplace, Thebes, is also mentioned, which is where the story of Oedipus takes place, as well as being the birthplace of another pertinent character, Athamas, whose madness had driven him to infanticide. He would be another focus for identification for Mr Rooney, given both the remarks about killing a child that precede his reference to the *Inferno* and the evidence that builds up that he has killed a child by pushing it out of a train. That Mr Rooney should identify himself with these damned may be fair enough, but his implicating Mrs Rooney in this state is less fair since she is still grieving for the *loss* of her child. Instead of protesting at his elision of *her* difference, she expresses concern about *him*, having perhaps assumed a compensatory mothering role *vis-à-vis* her husband, so that she reflects him vocally saying "What is the matter, Dan? Are you not well?" This mirroring strategy enables him to talk about himself, while he marginalizes her and implicates her in a negative light.

Two effects of Mrs Rooney's strategy of mirroring the male emerge. First, her immense difficulty in maintaining herself as a clear, separate, complete entity. In addition to longing to dissolve into a slop of jelly or atoms as we saw earlier, she also envisages herself as a "bale" to Mr Slocum, suggesting that he push her up into the car as if she were one (*All That Fall* 14), playing between the sense of "bale" as "bundle" (of hay) and the archaic sense of "bale" as "misery"; and she wearily longs to waste away (18). Moreover, she asks Miss Fitt to prop her up against the wall as if she were a "roll of tarpaulin" (23), and she replies to Miss Fitt's admission that she had seen Mrs Rooney as "just another big pale blur": "Maddy Rooney, née Dunne, the big pale blur. (*Pause.*) You have piercing sight, Miss Fitt, if only you knew it, literally piercing" (21). It is one thing to have one's premarital identity elided by that of one's husband, but more painful when the Other can perceive the uncertainty, indefiniteness and opacity of what might be an individual "identity". The other effect of Mrs Rooney's mirroring strategy is the secondary narcissism that causes her to worry about her appearance in a similar way to Winnie, despite the fact that her husband is blind. For instance, when her dress is caught in Mr Slocum's car door she screams: "Look what you've done to my nice frock! . . . What will Dan say when he sees me?", to which Mr Slocum replies, "Has he then recovered his sight?" (15). Also, it is clear that she has gone to the trouble of putting on a hat, for Tommy says "Mind your feather, Ma'am" (16). Given the fundamental health problems from which this woman suffers, such attention to surface matters can only be other-oriented, and is further evidence of her failure to direct energy towards the construction of herself as subject.

If we accept Mrs Rooney's talkativeness as symptomatic of a woman's struggle to construct herself as subject, then it is not surprising that patriarchal literature has repeatedly endorsed the ideal of the silent woman.[7] In the Middle Ages, logorrhoea was diagnosed as a disease, and Renaissance books on conduct (devised to maintain patriarchal order by ensuring the silence of women as the necessary negative for the male logos) advised women against "babbling out all at large" (Gilbert and Gubar, *No Man's Land* 1 (, 231). In *Happy Days* Winnie clearly did not heed women's conduct books, for she utters an almost constant flow of trivia, clichés, traditional pieties and "familiar quotations" (Knowlson and Pilling 94). She is trapped in habit, buried as she is in inherited linguistic debris (a reflection of her physical/visual position on stage) in which she as a woman is not inscribed. Besides, she has submitted her will to Will/ie:

> Bid me put this thing down, Willie, I would obey you instantly, as I have always done, honoured and obeyed . . . No? (*Happy Days* 28)

Locked into the patriarchal text of which the marriage service here alluded to is emblematic, she is forced to adopt for the purposes of self-assertion and agency the voice for which Willie's silence becomes the background.

It is not the female alone who is locked into the text: Willie keeps reading the same old, yellowing newspaper where he could scarcely find his present self reflected. His first utterance is prompted by male identification when he quotes a headline announcing the death of a self-evidently patriarchal figure: "His Grace and Most Reverend Father in God Dr. Carolus Hunter dead in tub" (14). Willie's speech, however, betrays none of the need for verbal reflection inherent in Winnie's constant efforts to get him to reply, but then her presence is guaranteed for him by her voice. Also, her constant solicitousness for his welfare, even advising him on how to negotiate his entrances to and exits from his hole (14) affirm him. Her consulting him on linguistic matters extends this affirmation, and give him the opportunity to reply authoritatively concerning for instance "hair" being singular or plural (19), and the meaning of "hog" which he faithfully defines according to the *Oxford English Dictionary* (*Happy Days* 35–6).

The suggestion is that Winnie does not have direct access to the language of definition and delimitation while Willie does. She shows a remarkably refined lexical knowledge in certain instances, with a preference for less popular or more "correct" terms, suggesting that she has in the past consulted the dictionary (which is, of course, traditionally seen as a male-authored text) for the inherited meanings of rare words like "emmet", "bast", "anthrax" and "setae". Yet this linguistic knowledge serves no useful purpose for her and can be interpreted as only an extension of her finical concern with the correct pronunciation for the name of the gentleman who gave her her first kiss, which leads her inappropriately towards stressing the fixity of "stone" in "John*stone*" (15). Such concern with "prestige" linguistic practice follows one of the common stereotypes of women's speech identified by sociolinguists on both sides of the Atlantic

(Cameron 48). It is symptomatic of a disabling perfectionism, which rather than making the woman linguistically more free and competent, actually hampers her in the use of language for her own expression. Thus she continues passively to reflect the male-authorized text, rather than authoring her own.

This disabling perfectionism also underlies Winnie's hesitation over word-order on a number of occasions when the alternative is not particularly significant.[8] Moreover, she feels compelled to expend inordinate effort on establishing what the text inscribed on her toothbrush is, despite its surface irrelevance to her situation. She is repeatedly "taken over" by the prescribed verbal forms of prayer, song and quotation, and tries (somewhat obsessively) to get Willie to repeat one of her Shakespeare quotations – "Fear no more the heat of the sun" – but he obstinately refuses to go further than "Fear no more" (*Happy Days* 21). Here we have an inversion of Echo's curtailment of speech: whereas Echo can only repeat the *last* words of her interlocutor, Willie wilfully curtails his "response" to Winnie to the *first* words, taking for granted that she has learned the whole quotation. The original text is male-authored, yet the verbal energy invested in it by the female surpasses that of the male. The man can depend on the woman's learning the patriarchal script, although her position allows her no purchase on this language, to the point where it does not help her to construct herself, because definition, delimitation and control reside with the male.

Willie's silence constitutes his refusal to reflect her presence, yet the absence which it suggests is denied both by what we see, and by the authority Winnie goes on to find in her own voice for the necessary presence of the Other:

> . . . I used to think that I would learn to talk alone (*Pause.*) By that I mean to myself, the wilderness. (*Smile*) But no. (*Smile broader.*) No no. (*Smile off.*) Ergo you are there. (*Pause.*) Oh no doubt you are dead, like the others, no doubt you have died, or gone away and left me, like the others, it doesn't matter, you are there. (37–8)

Here, Winnie goes beyond the egotistical, primary-narcissistic Cartesian *cogito ergo sum* to a recognition of the inherently dialogical nature of language, "I speak, therefore you are there", so that speech becomes the proof of presence. Thus her talk, though learnt according to the law of the father, acquires the power to compensate for the failure of her male interlocutor both to confirm his presence to her and to reflect hers. It is as though, paradoxically, through this talk, she acquires a power of agency which allows her to substitute, not constitute both Willie and herself.

Earlier, before reaching this recognition of the substitutory power of language, Winnie is still dependent on Willie's reflection, convinced that "something of this is being heard, I am not merely talking to myself", while she also imagines that if Willie were not there at all, she would have nothing to do but seek reflection in her looking glass (18). This reference to her looking glass (a prominent prop in the first act) serves as a reminder that she has developed a patriarchially acceptable secondary narcissism (mention of her looking glass immediately evokes anxiety about her hair). It also anticipates her shattering her mirror later on.[9] Having disposed of the mirror that encourages her to see herself as if through the eyes of the desiring Other, Winnie can assert her own desire to see Willie, to become herself the subject, not the object of the gaze:

> Do you know what I dream sometimes? (*Pause.*) What I dream some-times, Willie. (*Pause.*) That you'll come round and live this side where I could see you. . . . I'd be a different woman. (*Pause.*) Unrecogniz-able. (*Turning slightly towards him.*) Or just now and then, come round this side every now and then and let me feast on you. (35)

By distancing herself from seeking the reflection of the gaze, she can imagine herself as subject, and would thus be unrecognizable to Willie.[10] By rejecting secondary narcissism, she is enabled to tap certain powers of language.

When finally Willie does present himself to Winnie's gaze, she adopts a series of different (vocal) positions. Having first "castrated" him with the words "What a get up, you do look a sight" (45), she reverts to habit and invites *his* gaze: "That's right, Willie, look at me. (*Pause.*) Feast your old eyes, Willie." This immediately makes her think of her "beauty", or the surface for the male gaze to penetrate (46). After repeating her invitation to Willie to gaze, she moves from associating the gaze with touch, to affec-tion, and ultimately violence (47). Here, her distress must arise from con-necting the gaze with a desire for control, aggravated by the presence of the gun on the mound, all compounded by hints of displaced sexual desire. What the audience sees as a last tableau is Winnie and Willie gazing at each other, silently. Thus *it* is excluded from seeing what is reflected in the characters' respective eyes, and is reminded that its look is not where it would see, nor can it ever be so. The inadequacy of the gaze is neatly established in theatrical terms.

A number of theatrically self-conscious passages other than Winnie's shattering her mirror show her awareness of the eye of the beholder (God or audience): "Strange feeling that someone is looking at me. I am clear, then dim, then gone, then dim again, then clear again, and so on, back and forth, in and out of someone's eye" (31). It is remarkable here how the movement of the gaze as she experiences it resembles that of the speculum, as though the woman were actually seeing herself in reverse, as Other, through the frame of the specular instrument. She also experiences herself as the object of the audience's gaze at the beginning of act two, when her own eyes are all she can move and she says "Someone is looking at me still. (*Pause.*) Caring for me still. (*Pause.*) That is what I find so wonderful.

(*Pause.*) Eyes on my eyes" (37). Thus the idea of the audience as mere voyeur is undermined, since the voyeur is usually redundant to the object of his gaze. Instead, Winnie/the actress experiences the audience as providing the reflection denied by Willie.[11]

Willie's refusal to reflect Winnie either visually or vocally could be expected to drive her to other strategies for self-definition. Autobiography offers such a strategy, but Winnie's autobiography has been arrested in her childhood, at the age of four or five. She recounts it at one remove from the self, giving the protagonist in it the name Mildred,[12] and she retains it as the ultimate activity for her increased immobility during the second act, when her speech becomes self-reflexive (she repeatedly prefaces her statements with "I say" or "I always say"):

> There is my story, of course, when all else fails. (*Pause*) A life. (*Smile.*) A long life. (*Smile off.*) Beginning in the womb, where life used to begin, Mildred has memories, she will have memories, of the womb, before she dies, the mother's womb. (*Pause.*) She is now four or five already and has recently been given a waxen dolly. (*Pause.*) Fully clothed, complete outfit. (*Pause.*) Shoes, socks, undies, complete set, frilly frock, gloves. (*Pause.*) White mesh. (*Pause.*) A little white straw hat with a chin elastic. (*Pause.*) Pearly necklace. (*Pause.*) A little picture-book with legends in real print to go under her arm when she takes her walk. (*Pause.*) China blue eyes that open and shut. (*Pause. Narrative.*) The sun was not well up when Milly rose . . . (41)

The elision of time-division here is a reflex of the blurring of identity, both between Winnie and Mildred, and between Winnie and the dolly: the little girl Mildred has a doll-image of the woman given to her (with costume motifs that mirror Winnie's), and this prescribed image carries a prescribed text with "legends in real print". Having no language of her own, the dolly has to carry a book of legends to be reiterated to her as stories. Besides, although her china-blue eyes can open and shut, she cannot become the seeing subject. Similarly, Winnie can only tell her own story between the lines, in the third person, and the development of this story is arrested at the "little girl" stage. Winnie's capacity for using autobiography for self-definition is restricted to emblematic form. Likewise, Mrs Rooney is only able to recount her story at one remove through that of the little girl who had never been properly born, in the words of the "mind-doctor".

Prompted by a reference of Mr Rooney to "the feeling of being confined" (evoking childbirth for her), Mrs Rooney reports a talk she once heard by a psychiatrist, about a girl whom he had treated unsuccessfully, with whom he could find nothing wrong, and who died when he gave up the case. Mrs Rooney quotes: "The trouble with her was she had never been really born!" (37). To have not been properly born is the ultimate failure in self-definition, and Mrs Rooney identifies with it to the point of weeping. This reference to the "mind-doctor", as Mrs Rooney calls the psychiatrist, encapsulates an autobiographical story: Beckett attended a lecture by Jung at the Tavistock Clinic in London in October 1935, in which he talked about the personal unconscious consisting of an unknown number of fragmentary personalities. He spoke in particular about the writer who "When he creates a character on the stage, or in his poem or drama or novel, he thinks it is merely a product of his imagination; but that character in a certain way has made itself" (Bair 208). This, Beckett found, coincided with his own experience of writing. He also found that the story of the little girl who had never been born entirely shed light on his own psychological difficulties in gaining appropriate distance from his mother (another form of failure to have been properly born) resulting in problems in defining himself. Thus we can see that something of the author's own "life" lies behind Mrs Rooney's "life". He objectifies his experience by translating his personal difficulty into the struggle for self-definition of Mrs Rooney, who in turn translates hers into that of the little girl with whose position she/he could identify.

Although Mrs Rooney's difficulties in defining herself could in theory be mitigated by her becoming the subject of her own autobiography, she cannot take this step either, for her life in the form we are shown it is almost entirely subjected to or inscribed in that of her husband. Despite her own ill-health and his egotism, she drags herself to the station to meet him on his birthday. Furthermore, her continual empathizing with the misery of others prevents her from living out the personal suffering at the centre of her own existence. And the language that is available to her for autobiography has gendered structures at its roots, in addition to having misogyny inscribed in it.[13] Moreover, as a frustrated mother, she can never construct the "identity" that patriarchy favours for her. The theme of frustrated motherhood permeates the play, not only in the case of the woman listening to "Death and the Maiden" whose daughter had presumably died, but also in the killing of the hen: in Tommy's and Jerry's orphaned state; in Miss Fitt's search for her mother; in the reduction of the daughter on the station platform to "Dolly"; and above all in Mr Rooney's killing of the child. Living as a failed mother in a world dominated by men, Mrs Rooney finds no reason to conceive of herself as fit subject for autobiography.

The cause of Winnie's autobiography being arrested in *Happy Days* is less evidently the result of frustrated motherhood. Nevertheless, the stasis, sterility and "birthing difficulties" that receive so much attention in the play induce notions of the displacement of the mother. Winnie might be considered as either having herself been never quite born because she is buried in the ground, or as slowly retreating into "mother earth". Likewise, Willie seems to be caught in a reiterative pattern of "going back into the womb". Winnie instructs him in this process in the first act (20) in a manner that re-infantilizes him, as well as anticipating the difficulties of a

breech delivery. This concern recurs in the second act: "God grant he did
not go in head foremost! (*Eyes right, loud.*) You're not stuck, Willie? . . .
You're not jammed, Willie? (*Eyes front, distressed.*) Perhaps he's crying out
for help all this time and I do not hear him!" (42). This might be interpreted as both the wishful thinking of the frustrated mother and the trace of
a still birth after breech delivery: Winnie's own physical state is such that
she can do nothing to promote birth or motherhood.

Yet considerable attention is drawn to Winnie's bosom in the play, and
the bosom can be taken as metonymic for the mother: not only is it
designated as "big" in the stage directions and revealed by a low bodice
but, in the course of the first act, Winnie anticipates: "And should one day
the earth cover my breasts, then I shall never have seen my breasts, no-one
seen my breasts" (30). One should remember that seeing the breasts is not
essential to their primary function: again Winnie is caught in the secondary
narcissism that makes her conceive of herself as an object for the male gaze.
This is evident when, towards the end of the first act, she recalls the
comments of Mr Shower (or Cooker) as the last person (with his wife as
interlocutor) to pass by; the words she remembers are: "What's she doing?
he says – What's the idea? he says – stuck up to her diddies in the bleeding
ground – coarse fellow" (32). However, when she recalls that same scene in
the second act, her memory has edited it, for what she recalls is: "Can't
have been a bad bosom, he says, in its day. (*Pause.*)" (43). Winnie, like Mrs
Rooney, is childless, is not reflected by her male partner, but has nevertheless internalized the words of prescribed patriarchal texts. Thus she finally
submits to a popular song for self-definition, rather than constitute herself
through autobiography.

In the case of *Not I*, a compulsion to tell the story of the life underlies the
speaker's utterance. The silent Auditor functions as a presence on stage with
which the audience can identify, but there is little evidence that the speaker
is conscious of this presence. However, the speaker has internalized a voice
which repeatedly interrupts the "flow" of the story to add details for its
"objective" accuracy.[14] The Auditor's most repeated intervention is to
remind the speaker of the buzzing she heard in her head; and its most
dramatically marked intervention is four attempts to get the speaker to
assume the first-person position in relation to her narrative. Although these
"interventions" are registered only within the discourse of the speaker,
these last four are animated for the audience through the Auditor's
response: four times "he" makes diminishing gestures of compassion after
the speaker has vehemently insisted on maintaining the third-person singular feminine for the narration. It is as though there were an inherent
incapacity on the part of the female speaker for saying "I", for asserting the
self as subject. Moreover, this insistence not only highlights the thirdness or
otherness of the subject of the autobiography, but also her gender, for the
speaker is driven to repeat "what? . . . who? . . . no! . . . she! . . ." four

times, repeating the "SHE", more vigorously, on the last occasion (*Not I* 222). It is as though the speaker believes that her gender distinction would be lost were she to say "I".

The question of gender is first raised in *Not I* by the fact that the voice is feminine, whereas the disembodied mouth could in principle be either male or female. Besides, the script of the "autobiography" begins with the premature birth which allows the first pronominal reference to be neuter, when the speaker refers to the infant as a "tiny little thing", which then with the prompting of the internalized voice becomes a "tiny little girl" (216). Significantly, the auditor is of "sex undeterminable" (216), which is underwritten through "his" being enveloped in a "loose black djellaba" and having nothing to say, therefore no voice that would identify gender.

The positions of the Mouth and the Auditor in relation to each other are such as to suggest those of the Freudian analyst and patient. The Auditor/ analyst is behind the Mouth, in a less prominent position, and is "shown by attitude alone to be facing diagonally across stage intent on MOUTH", in other words is not seen by the Mouth/patient who is facing the audience and whose eyes, in any case, are not visible. (It is worth noting that the Auditor is a tall figure, which would encourage the audience to conceive of it as male, as was the prototype of the analyst.) Moreover, the buzzing in the head is the kind of symptom that psychiatrists are reputedly so interested in. One can take the title of the play as indicating a schizophrenic separation from the self, borne out in the refusal of the subjective position, or in the avoidance or denial of the boundaries between the self and the Other in the discourse of the speaker.

This discourse is already in process when the curtain goes up and continues after the curtain falls, as unintelligible ad-libbing from the text. The suggestion here is that the point of entry into the "story" is arbitrary, but in effect it "begins at the beginning" with the birth of the little girl. Although the discourse is characterized by repetitions which evoke a circular structure, it also provides material for the creation of a sequence, and while what is audibly uttered does not consist of discrete sentences, it becomes intelligible when reflected on as a "talking cure", a stream of consciousness. Moreover, it is recounted within the story that when speech first came to her, she herself had "no idea what she was saying" (219).[15] What the Mouth in *Not I* actually does say remains outside traditionally structured logical discourse, so that the levels of alienation are multiple, and the presence of the Other (male?) is purported as necessary for analysis/ interpretation.

The origin of the psychosis which marginalizes the speaker in *Not I* and interferes with her autobiographical capacity is identified within her story: she was abandoned as a "speechless infant", so that all she experienced was the voiceless gaze both in infancy and later in life:

. . . speechless all her days . . . practically speechless . . . even to herself . . . never out loud . . . but not completely . . . sometimes sudden
urge . . . once or twice a year . . . always winter some strange reason
. . . the long evenings . . . hours of darkness . . . sudden urge to . . .
tell . . . then rush out stop the first she saw . . . nearest lavatory . . .
start pouring it out . . . steady stream . . . *mad* stuff . . . half the vowels
wrong . . . no one could follow . . . till she saw the stare she was
getting . . . then die of shame . . . crawl back in . . . (222, emphasis
added)

Without the stimulus to enter the symbolic order through speech, her
development was arrested before the mirror phase. Hence her failure to
speak throughout her life until she was 60 or 70, and the current "stream"
she pours out.

The stream of this woman's speech differs from that of Mrs Rooney and
Winnie principally in the degree of its alienation from itself. Whereas Mrs
Rooney is struggling with a dead language, and Winnie, despite being
virtually buried in linguistic debris makes continual efforts at accuracy, the
Mouth in *Not I*, besides not using complete, logical structures, uses language only for the compulsive purpose of "something she had to . . . had to
. . . tell . . . something that would tell how it had been . . . how she had
lived' (221). At the same time, there is "nothing she could tell . . . nothing
she could think" (222), so we have the classic Beckettian situation of
someone talking with nothing to say. None of the three women can remain
silent (as tradition would like them to be), yet none of them has the chance
to develop a fully self-conscious ego, for none of them is adequately reflected either in language itself, or by their partners. The roles of Mrs
Rooney and Winnie are clearly prescribed in relation to their male partners, while the Mouth is entirely deprived of social role through isolation
and disembodiment.

Beckett's speech in the female voice, then, is less than promising for the
prospect of women constituting themselves as subjects – not that the linguistic prowess of his men is reassuring either, but their superior judgemen-
tal position, including their relation to the woman's language, assures them
some capacity for authority. These plays are not indifferent to difference.
Progressively, they increase the woman's dependence on an interiorized
interlocutor, forcing her back into the inherently dialogical nature of language, while at the same time depriving her of the social reflection that is
necessary for the healthy development of the ego. They show her to herself
increasingly in the "negative" so that her ego is diminished ("auto"), her
life is restricted ("bio") and her capacity for linguistic expression hampered
("graphy"), thus autobiography is precluded for her.

Perhaps salvation from the apparent inevitability of such a progression
lies in reducing the importance attributed to the gaze as metaphor for

understanding, and in the refusal of the silent gaze – a refusal of the silent, passive reading of the text, including Beckett's texts, which invite anything but a passive reading. These texts suggest that it could also lie in women consciously assuming autobiographical responsibility, and in discontinuing that practice of depriving the Other, whether male or female, of reflection as subject. Women, who as mothers have a primal experience of the splitting of the subject (Kristeva, *Reader* 206) and can "normally" accompany their gazing at the infant with voice effortlessly, can re-vise the Narcissus myth and liberate themselves from this male sentence, whether Beckett's, Ovid's or the mythical Tiresias': a more enabling myth may be produced by women themselves, in time. For we should not forget the displacement of the mother in the three plays we have been considering: a displacement which is also present in the case of Echo, and in the story based on Jung's lecture.

This is particularly troublesome when we trace the origins in Beckett's imagination of the apparently sexless djellaba and of the female voice of *Not I*. During a visit to Morocco in February 1972, he was struck by the figure of an Arab woman shrouded in a djellaba, waiting intensely for her child, and periodically flapping her arms against her sides (Bair 622). Clearly, this was a powerful image of attachment for him, yet he shows a progressive diminution of human attachment in these plays, pushing the isolation of the individual to its limits in *Not I*. Of the voice in this play he has said:

> I knew that woman in Ireland, I knew who she was – not "she" specifically, one single woman, but there were so many of those old crones, stumbling down the lanes, in the ditches, beside the hedgerows. Ireland is full of them. And I heard "her" saying what I wrote in *Not I*. I actually heard it. (Bair 622)

Since up to now there has been no material social space outside of patriarchy, the historical context and gender of this proto-voice failing to constitute itself as subject is quite specific for Beckett, even if difficulties in constituting the subject are neither gender-confined nor culture-confined: the difficulties that engaged his imagination were those of a woman (though *not* one single woman), in Ireland.[16] If we re-vise the Narcissus myth in the light of the foregoing analysis, we can see the possibility for creating such a space in the future. Outside of the received myth, there is no need for Echo's voice to become disembodied, nor for Narcissus to fall in love with an ideal that cuts him off from the material. No matter how "true" we may find the position of the three women in Beckett's plays in relation to personal experience so far, there is no need for women's voices to continue to be disembodied as they are there, nor for their autobiographical impulse to be curtailed. Such mythologizing is male-authored, although Beckett's scrupulous honesty caused him to repeatedly deny that there is any truth-value in his work, which is a gesture towards pre-empting attempts at mythologizing it.

Notes

1 Beckett's attachment to generic difference prompted him to repeatedly refuse to allow *All That Fall* to be produced as a stage play or film: even when Laurence Olivier went specially to Paris in 1968 to try to persuade him to let him stage it for the opening of the new National Theatre in London, he refused (Curnow 64, fn. 11).

2 Blazing light, with a maximum of simplicity and symmetry are indicated in the stage directions (*Happy Days* 9). The light was intensified in the course of revisions of the text, and in overseeing the staging for the first Berlin production, Beckett wanted absolutely no shadows cast on the stage (Knowlson 129).

3 See also Lacan, *Écrits* 110–20.

4 See "The Blind Spot of an Old Dream of Symmetry" in *Irigaray*.

5 *All That Fall* 35. The phrase "safe to haven", which gives rise to Mr Rooney's criticism, is an echo from the hymn "Jesus, Lover of my Soul" by Charles Wesley, thus an approved patriarchal text.

6 See the different versions of Jesus' riding into Jerusalem in John 12:15 and Matthew 21:5.

7 For instance, in such texts as Chaucer's "The Clerk's Tale", Ben Jonson's *Epicoene or The Silent Woman*, and Tennyson's *Idylls of the King*. See Coates 31–4.

8 For instance, "Is that not so, Willie . . . Is not that so?" (*Happy Days* 20); and "Yes, something seems to have occurred, something has seemed to occur" (30); or "What is a hog exactly . . . What exactly is a hog?" (35).

9 This shattering of the mirror is theatrically self-conscious, since it is the actress who takes it up, shivers it, and then says "it will be in the bag again tomorrow, without a scratch, to help me through the day" (*Happy Days* 30).

10 This unrecognizability is emblematized on the occasions when she puts on her spectacles to read, for this gesture, which is necessary for her to become the seeing/reading subject, alters her as object of the audience's gaze. In the second act, when only Winnie's face is visible for recognition, she can perceive herself only in fragments, like the infant before the mirror phase: the nose, a hint of lip, and the tip of the tongue that has been so well used (*Happy Days* 39).

11 However, the longer the audience looks at Winnie, the less of her it sees, and the nearer it comes to the end of the play.

12 In early drafts of the play, Winnie had been called Mildred (Gontarski 75), and there is only one phoneme different between Millie, the diminutive of Mildred, and the Minnie of *All That Fall*, as well as between Millie and Willie.

13 All the modes of transportation in the play are attributed the feminine gender, thus associating the female in English to a beast of burden: the hinny, the bicycle, the train and Mr Slocum's car, which he talks of in the following terms: "All morning she went like a dream and now she is dead. That is what

you get for a good deed. (*Pause. Hopefully.*) Perhaps if I were to choke her" (*All That Fall* 15).

14 For instance, this internalized voice insists that the age at which the motivating incident occurred was 70, not 60; and it adds to the number of positions in which this incident might have occurred.

15 See Lacan, *La Séminaire* 68 for a specularizing male's assertion that women do not know what they are saying, which is all the difference between him and them, and also Heath's discussion of it in "Difference".

16 Beckett is clearly exploring the division or plurality of the male subject in *That Time*, which he has called "a brother to *Not I*" (Pountney 92).

6

"Bog Queens": The representation of women in the poetry of John Montague and Seamus Heaney

Patricia Coughlan

I

This essay investigates the construction of feminine figures, and the vocabulary of roles allotted to them, by two prominent contemporary Irish poets, John Montague and Seamus Heaney. Feminine figures and more or less abstract ideas of femininity play a major role in the work of both: how should this centrality of the feminine be interpreted? Is it, as it most usually announces itself, to be taken as a celebration? Or does it flatter to deceive, as has been remarked about Matthew Arnold's perhaps analogous celebration of the alleged Celtic virtues of passion, sensuousness, non-rational insight? (see Cairns and Richards, "Woman"). I have chosen to discuss the work of male poets, believing strongly that both "gynocritics" – the "naming", recovery and revaluing of women's writing – and the persistent demystifying of representations of women in men's work must continue in tandem. The social and cultural construction of gender is a continuously occurring process, in which it is certainly not yet time to stop intervening. I shall argue that even able and serious contemporary work is deeply and dismayingly reliant upon old, familiar and familiarly oppressive allocations of gender positions. Our celebration of this work must therefore be inflected by this question as to its effect: can poetry's implicit claim to universality of utterance and to utopian insight be upheld in the face of a reader's awareness of its gendered and therefore (perhaps unconsciously) partial perspective?

The representation of femininity which occurs most insistently in this material takes the form of dualistically opposed aspects: beloved or spouse figures versus mother figures, which are in turn benign and fertile or awe-inspiring and terrible. Very much as in the actual social construction of femininity, the various feminine functions are sometimes made to coalesce bewilderingly, sometimes set in opposition to one another. In Heaney, for example, the nature-goddess is simultaneously spouse, death-bringer and nurturer. This invocation of a *magna mater* figure is celebrated by some readers as an empowerment of women, but it is only dubiously so if the agency described is a death-bringing one; such representations of feminine power ultimately arise from a masculine psychological difficulty in acknowledging woman's subjectivity as a force *in itself*, and not merely as a relation to man's (see Dinnerstein).

My discussion will attend particularly to the invocation of such allegedly immemorial archetypes of femininity and the various strategies by which that invocation is sustained. Especially important among these strategies are the attempt to reinvest with imaginative energy figures such as the sovereignty goddess from early Irish literature and myth as well as *magna mater* figures from other European contexts, and the projected conjunction in such figures of a neo-Jungian "feminine principle" with the physical territory of Ireland. This combined representation is also merged with the imagery of woman-as-land-and-national-spirit from the tradition of Irish nationalist political rhetoric. In this poetry, such mythic representations are often projected, with varying degrees of explicitness, upon a repertoire of female figures presented by a lyric speaker as autobiographically given.

One must question in general the elision of history which is involved in this smooth passage from memory to myth – an elision which precludes the possibility of understanding history as the product of human actions and not merely as a fated, cyclical natural process. It is also necessary in particular to interrogate the notions of essential femininity and immemorially assigned female functions as the vehicles of this myth-memory passage, and to notice that it requires an implicit assumption of the inescapability of a gendered allocation of subject-positions, by means of which rationality, speech and naming are the prerogatives of the autobiographically validated male poet, and the various female figures dwell in oracular silence, always objects, whether of terror, veneration, desire, admiration or vituperation, never the coherent subjects of their own actions. This reification of traditional modes of perceiving feminine identity is also supported by tactics such as recalling the Irish *aisling* form, which invests a potentially amorous encounter with allegorical political content.[1]

A particular contradiction is discernible in Montague and Heaney between the project of speaking for a politically oppressed and therefore hitherto unspoken group, Northern Catholics – a project important both intrinsically and to the reception of these poets – and their failure, in general, to perceive their own reliance upon and tacit approval of the absence of women as speaking subjects and of female disempowerment. Their female figures function as crucially important forms of validation-by-opposition of the individual poet's identity, in a (sometimes almost comically blatant) neo–Oedipal struggle. In Heaney, this wresting of a speaking ego from the *magna mater* which is also the land is interestingly complicated by specifically political Irish/English stereotyping: the (necessarily, if self-expressing) male poet (phallically) digging and ploughing like his ancestors becomes the culturally female voice of the subjugated Irish, about to inundate the "masculine" hardness of the planters' boundaries with "feminine" vowel-floods (see "A New Song", *Wintering Out* 33; and "Undine", *Door into the Dark* 26).

Irish ideology tends to an idealization of rural life. This is often centred on female icons of ideal domesticity, especially mother-figures, who are associated with unmediated naturalness. The feminist critique of this ruralist ideology must investigate the designation of spheres and human subjects as natural or cultural and their respective valuation. It is also necessary to bear in mind the way ideology has effectively denied women the freedom to develop a fully self-conscious ego and therefore to participate in civil society by allocating them a fixed position within the domestic sphere, and by the celebration of domestic virtues as constitutive of femininity. Feminist psychoanalytic demonstrations of the construction of human subjectivity as male and Oedipal also afford a perspective on which I have drawn.[2]

In the poetry I discuss, as in the culture which produces it, women are typically associated with that which is material, and defined in opposition to mind. They are nevertheless seen as possessors of a form of knowledge hidden from the masculine speaker; but this they mutely embody and cannot themselves expound. In Montague's and Heaney's lyrics each masculine speaker characteristically celebrates the domestic as immemorial and relishes it as sensually and emotionally satisfying, but defines himself in the performance of his most characteristic activity, poetry, in contradistinction from it. Woman, the primary inhabitor and constituent of the domestic realm, is admiringly observed, centre stage but silent. She is thus constructed by a scopic gaze, her imputed mental inaction and blankness being required to foreground the speaker's naming and placing of her.[3] What ostensibly offers itself as a celebration may rather be read, then, as a form of limiting definition, in which certain traditional qualities of the feminine are required to persist for a fit wife, mother or Muse to come into being. The constant naming of autobiographical "originals" for these figures effectively masks this nearly ubiquitous blotting out of the individual qualities of *actual* women by the dominant – and stereotyped – *ideal*.

The reader may feel a general resistance as such to the mythicizing mentality this exemplifies: that is, to the dehistoricizing effect of discerning, in some notional way as a truth *beneath* the actualities, an immemorial status quo which is represented as implicitly superior to modernity; and further,

to the accompanying aestheticization by the observer of the actual deprivation, suffering and hard work of others in the name of celebration. This
objection applies whether it is farming life, Irish political violence or gender
roles which are in question, and indeed in Montague and Heaney all three
of these are, in fact, intimately bound together. Such mythicizing moves
are discerned as false ones by Montague himself in a moment of the
"Epilogue" of *The Rough Field* in the lines "Only a sentimentalist would
wish / To see such degradation again . . .", and Heaney's work is perhaps
more open to this charge that Montague's own. Yet Montague falls back
upon just such sentiment later in the poem, when agricultural labour is
once again interpreted as part "of a world where action had been wrung /
through painstaking years to ritual" in apparent nostalgia for the imputed
absoluteness of such humble lives. The poem's ending stresses the poet's
"failure to return" for all his "circling" round his rural origin (*The Rough
Field* 82–3). The point is the necessary exclusion of the speaker *as* poet from
this rural scene – even if it had not been "going". The very practice of
cosmopolitan literary expression marks off the poet-figure from his material
throughout Montague's – and indeed Heaney's – work, however much
rural *pietas* it shows. This self-exclusion from the whole rural world as it
might be understood on its own terms is particularly focused in the female
figures this poetry constructs, who cannot even be manipulated, as the men
can, into role-models for the apprentice to poetry-making, divided, as they
are by gender and its assigned functions from the son-figures who construct
them. Heaney's digging and ploughing ancestors can be, however tran-
siently and superficially, nominated as ur-makers, but baking, praying,
home-making women – icons of domesticity whether vibrant (mothers) or
ruined (spinsters living by wells) – are set apart from and by the poet who is
concerned with conscious self-definition: an activity which must be pursued in explicit opposition to the encompassing space of a home.[4]

Heaney's attempt, in "The Seed Cutters", to sink the sense of self into
the immemorial betrays its own static quality, its relinquishing of the possibility of any significant action or change in its freezing into a final pose:

> O calendar customs! Under the broom
> Yellowing over them, compose the frieze
> With all of us there, our anonymities. (*North* 10)

The formal qualities of this poetry require particular analytic strategies from
the critic. It is very largely autobiographical and takes its claim to authen-
ticity from that familiar covenant between reader and poet which tacitly
agrees the immediacy and authority of such experience.[5] This fiction of
autobiography is perhaps a necessary and enabling one for lyric poets not
always exactly choosing to take up the challenge to the notion of a unitary
self offered by the "high" Modernists. But where the fictionality of the
poetic speaker is routinely concealed, a responsible criticism must seek to

recover the moment of his construction (it almost always is "his"). If this work were to be read primarily as unmediated transcription of the experience of historical individuals, it would become impertinent to question the constitution of the emotionally pivotal female figures – beloveds, wives, mothers, grandmothers – in it. My comments about these female figures, then, as about the central male ones, concern fictive beings whose status is virtual, not actual.

II

Each of the two poets inflects this conventional material with a slight difference. Let us take Montague's version first, starting with the crone-cum-chthonic mother. Hag-figures recur many times in his work, from "The Sean Bhean Bhocht" in his first collection to "The Music Box" in *The Dead Kingdom* (1984). The title of that first poem in which such a figure appears links it openly with popular historical representations of Ireland, by means of the 1798 ballad beginning "Now the French are on the say, says the Shan Van Vocht". In this first version, the link lies relatively inert; the description in the poem is heavily freighted with realistic detail: ". . . bread soaked in brown tea / And eased between shrunken gums. / Her clothes stank . . ." (*Poisoned Lands* 12). But nevertheless the two essential elements of what will become a familiar conjunction are present: the distaste of the observer for what he has found physically repulsive and even terrifying, and the sense nevertheless of the old woman's access to some form of knowledge which is by definition hidden from him. In "The Sean Bhean Bhocht", this secret knowledge is explicitly rendered as "racial memory", curse stories and legend retellings, and in the last stanza the physical abjectness of the woman's material existence is almost cancelled by a glorious landscape vision re-situating her tales in the bright freedom of a natural setting:

> But in high summer the hills burned with corn
> I strode through golden light
> To the secret spirals of the burial stone
> The grass-choked well ran sluggish red –
> Not with blood but ferrous rust –
> But beneath the whorls of the guardian stone –
> What hidden queen lay dust. (*Poisoned Lands* 13)

A hag or witch figure plays a role too in "Like Dolmens Round My Childhood, The Old People", in the same collection: an Old woman living "surrounded by animals", described as a "well of gossip defiled" and "Fanged chronicler . . ."; and once again she and the remaining "old people" listed in the poem are mysteriously elevated to "that dark permanence of ancient forms" by the conceit named in the title's simile. Later, in "The Wild Dog Rose", "The Music Box" and "Procession", the same lineaments recur to compose further solitary old women, though the implicit evocation of the Cathleen Ní Houlihan figure sometimes plays a more muted role (*The Rough Field* 77; *The Dead Kingdom* 36, 84).[6] In "Procession", the woman is the poet's grandmother, and once again distaste ("Hawk nose, snuff stained apron") mingles equivocally with a compassionate vision of her victim status ("Still hatred and division / stain that narrow acre / from which you sprang").

Mythical appropriations play an increasingly important role in Montague's work in the mid-1970s and early 1980s. The very tentative mythicization of "The Sean Bhean Bhocht", giving only a rather vague indication of her access to wisdom, which seems to be something not very precise to do with an earlier Ireland (spells, legends, a buried queen) becomes more insistent. In *The Dead Kingdom*, for example, with its Sheela-na-Gig prominent on an opening page, "The Music Box" rehearses the speaker's childhood memory of an old and frightening woman who lived beside a well which she kept clear of leaves and insects and of which she is described as the guardian. The epigraph of this sequence specifically signals the use of Old Irish material:

> I cast a pebble down, to
> Set the well's walls echoing.
> As the meniscus resettles
> I see a strange face form,
> A wrinkled female face,
> Sweeney's Hag of the Mill,
> The guardian of the well,
> Source of lost knowledge. (24)

This hag is from the Irish tale *Buile Suibhne*. She is a rather puzzling figure who challenges the mad Suibhne to a leaping contest, harries him, and is eventually destroyed by overleaping herself off a cliff.[7] One might suggest that this hag has a role in relation to Suibhne resembling the Sphinx's to Oedipus, with leaping in place of riddles, and the same result, the defeat of an earlier, baleful and originally divine female presence by the male hero. The oedipal parallel contributes to my general argument that an intense urge to self-definition in contradistinction to a feminine principle, cloaked as admiring celebration of women, is a main motivating force in these poets' work. In any case, the Hag of the Mill is evidently intended here to stand behind the poet's memory of old "Mary Mulvey", thus making her a challenger to be defeated, according to the legendary allusion. When we look at the poem, we find the blend of half-guilty retrospective compassion and mild disgust familiar from the earlier hag-poems; the woman is ". . . cramped / and horrible as some toothy witch. / We clattered stones

on your roof . . ." (*The Dead Kingdom* 36). Her one "secret", a music box
with a silver dancer swirling on top, which delighted the children, becomes
her moment of "grace", just as the dead-queen tales were that of the "sean-
bhean bhocht" in the earlier poem: the challenge to the remembering
masculine persona is to discern that grace underlying the woman's alien
terrifying presence. A further legendary resonance in "Mary Mulveys' "
living by the well clarifies this challenge: it may recall the Irish tales about a
young man being challenged by a crone for a kiss when he comes to draw
water. This crone turns, once her desire is granted, into a young and
beautiful woman, and espouses him. This female figure, with her two
conflicting aspects of ugliness and beauty, is a sovereignty-goddess, and in
espousing her the man can become king of the land. Her association with
water links her with the idea of perpetually renewed fertility.[8] Thus Montague's poem attempts to establish a connection between the circumstantial
detail of the actual old woman, autobiographically validated, and an immemorial legendary event, whose metaphorical recurrence is implied by such
means: the poet standing, presumably, for the young king-figure, and the
twin aspects, horror and grace, of the woman being represented by her age
and her music-box. How should we read this palimpsest of actual and
mythical?

It may help to examine the route by which the mythical and legendary
material comes to Montague. Two likely sources are Robert Graves, for
whose work he has frequently expressed admiration, especially *The White
Goddess* (1949), and Joseph Campbell's *The Hero With a Thousand Faces*
(1975). Graves's work makes an oppositional sexual encounter with a
potentially lethal female principle constitutive of the poet-figure, and both
Graves and Campbell treat the hero's biography (automatically masculine)
in a universalizing perspective. Campbell grafts his culturally heterogeneous
material onto a Jungian archetypal understanding of all mythologies, closing
effortlessly the various gaps which would appear to yawn viewed from a
non-idealist perspective: between the individual material moments of each
culture's myths and legends, between those ancient or folk worlds and
modern life, and, needless to say, between male and female experience. The
sovereignty-figure at the well, "before her marriage . . . a hag or a woman
whose mind is deranged" (Rees and Rees 74), is in Montague an enabling-
figure for his imagination to work: the reader may conclude that like the
young prince at the well he acquires sovereignty in his craft by his brave
attention to such ugly and unpromising women. The encounter is always
one-sided, however; the shape of the myth guarantees that the female
figure is there to be kissed and transformed (like Sleeping Beauty, with
whom she is linked by Campbell): her passivity is part of the prescription,
like the ignorance, deprivation and gendered speechlessness of the women
in the poems. One ought to point out that in this respect the rewriting of
the legendary material is not necessarily faithful to its original: Suibhne's

hag of the mill, for instance, has quite a lot to say, and the sovereignty figure in the tale directs operations, in keeping with her divine status, from a position above that of the prince. It might be a mistake to assume that the inherited material itself offers only irremediably disempowering representations of women, however evident such disempowerment is in current masculine *uses* of it.

Montague constructs other female figures as guardians and sources of wisdom also, particularly his kinswomen: his aunts, foster mother and mother. Such figures are associated paradoxically in his work both with death and with origins. This contradiction is not, of course, peculiar to his work, nor indeed to Heaney's, but it is focused with peculiar and intriguing clarity in it. Montague's collection *The Dead Kingdom*, for example, represents on the level of realistic narrative a journey to the North of Ireland for the funeral of the poet's mother.[9] But it also rehearses a penetration of an under- or other-world, which is simultaneously the past, Ulster; the earth, nature; and, as we have seen, the well of knowledge. The dead mother in the poems (who is bitterly accused on a personal level of inflicting a "primal hurt" in giving away her son, the future poet, to be fostered) is also death as mother, and mother as death, part of the general *topos* in literature of the destroying mother.[10] This is ultimately a metaphorical way of understanding creation and destruction as unified; it is important to notice, however, that it depends upon a projection of woman as *necessarily* contradictory.[11] In *The Rough Field* (1972), "The Leaping Fire" marks the death of another maternal figure, the poet's foster mother, who like the earlier hag figures arouses mingled distaste, fear and compassion in the poem's persona. The constellation of her features is significant. She possesses a quasi-magical skill, to do with renewing and sustaining life, which is shown in her daily rekindling of the fire:

> "Each morning, from the corner
> of the hearth, I saw a miracle . . .". (19)

Her distance from sexual activity and her religious devotion are stressed and linked with her physical grotesqueness in the speaker's mind:

> a frail body grown monstrous,
> sighing in a trance
> before the gilt crucifix. (21)

And his anxious distance from such an existence is registered in his apotropaic assertion of his own sexual drive by masturbation ("The sap of another generation / fingering through a broken tree"). The "broken tree", however, is numinous: at the end a bird-cry over Paris is read as the announcement by a spirit voice, banshee-like, of the woman's death, arousing a momentary reinhabiting of her thought-world by the adult, secularized, metropolitan speaker: "I crossed myself / from rusty habit. . . . / A hollow note". In this poem, the neo-mythicizing impulse is salutarily opposed by the accidence of memory, so that the image of an actual woman at least impedes the totalizing projection of a notional female spirit as immemorial adversary. Though this representation remains one from the outside, and despite the narcissism of the masturbation scene and the allocation of rootedness and domesticity to the female and cosmopolitan secularity to the male realm, it retains a certain grace in the poet's acknowledgement of the mystery attending another existence, a rival autonomy.

Such complexity deserts Montague at his more Gravesian moments, which are frequent in the 1975 collection *A Slow Dance*. Two poems in the title sequence of the collection (beginning: "I: Back. Darkness, cave / drip, earth womb . . ." and furnished with prehistoric monuments and early Irish references) explicitly employ the conceit of landscape as female body. One is the litany-like "For The Hillmother", which invokes a benign chthonic presence as sexually welcoming and fertile:

> . . . Moist fern
>   Unfurl for us . . .
> Freshet of ease
>   flow for us
> Secret waterfall
>   pour for us
> Hidden cleft
>   speak to us
> Portal of delight
>   inflame us
> Hill of motherhood
>   wait for us
> Gate of birth
>   open for us. (10)

The other poem is "Message", which constructs a more unsavoury and threatening female figure ("her secret message, shaped / by a wandering wind / puts the eye / of reason out "), but nevertheless ends with a form of self-insertion into a scarcely metaphorized vaginal crevice:

> ease your
> hand into the
> rot-smelling crotch
> of a hollow
> tree, and find
> two pebbles of quartz
> protected by
> a spider's web:
> her sunless breasts. (10)

This passage neatly manifests a disassembly and arbitrary redistribution of the female body characteristic of fetishization, of which these poems, and also Heaney's bog-goddess poems, especially *North*, are good examples. It is difficult to know how readers with a different, non-fetishized or unobjectivized understanding of women's being – female readers, and surely many male ones – should interpret these poems, whose perspective must strike them not merely as gendered, but as disturbingly close to a figurative dismemberment.[12] In the same collection, whose title sequence is said by the publisher's cover copy to "mime a deep psychic experience of intimacy with the earth", the poem "The Hero's Portion" grafts onto a Roman description of Celtic feasting customs a strikingly brutal passage. The hero summons a waiting woman "to squat across his lap": his harper mauls a feminized instrument ("pulled / his long curved nails / through the golden hair / of his harp . . .". The harper's song ends:

> *sing the sword*
> *so fierce and tall*
>
> *sing the ladies*
> *whose bowels crave*
> *its double edge*
> *of birth and grave.* (*A Slow Dance* 36, 37)

The poem lacks any indication of ironic distance from these sentiments (such as is evident in the late Yeats work which it recalls), and indeed is admiringly described by the publisher, presumably with the author's sanction, as displaying "elemental energies".

Not all of Montague's middle and late work is as blunt as this. A less disturbingly invaded and less limitingly gendered version of a chthonic being is later invented in "The Well Dreams".[13] Based on a discreet and witty personification, this poem has all the tact and inclusiveness lacking in the rather bruising writings I have been discussing. The well "recomposes" itself after water is drawn there, supporting an "unpredictable ballet" of water-spiders and washing a coin thrown in. A site of votive offerings, it is metonymically associated both with the saint whose cult it represents and with the "neutral realm" of midland Ireland where it is set. The coin it renews is "queen of the realm, made virgin again", and above all it has a self-sufficient life, expressing in "small intensities of mirth, / the hidden laughter of earth' (*The Dead Kingdom* 38–40).

The other main strand in Montague's work has consisted of personal love and erotic lyrics. Some of the former, particularly in the collection *The Great Cloak* (1978), have been concerned to construct a female spouse-figure who takes the form of an icon of domestic attachment, comforting and anchoring the hitherto wandering male figure. The ecstatic celebration of this figure does not, however, dispel the reader's impression of her as

predominantly an aspect of the speaker's lyric autobiography and an adjunct
to his self-investigation. It may be because she, somewhat like the mother-
figures we have been discussing, is imaginatively constituted *in the poetry*
through mythological and legendary parallels, and also because she is
praised as a consumable item, like sumptuous fruit. "A Dream Of July"
merges these two procedures with particular clarity:[14]

> Like a young girl
> Dissatisfied with
> Her mythic burden
> Ceres, corn goddess . . .
>
> . . .
>
> Her abundant body is
> Compounded of honey
> & gold, the spike
> Of each small nipple
> A wild strawberry. (*The Great Cloak* 44)[15]

Beauty and seductiveness may be lavishly bestowed on this figure, but not
rational distance or self-determining will; she is described as "Fulfilled in /
Spite of herself", underlining the division of labour between understanding, naming and empowerment on the part of the male, and intuition and
embodiment on the part of the female. A later poem, "The Well-
Beloved", shows a conscious recognition of the process of mythologizing
projection upon women which has been constitutive of so much of
Montague's work, but does not forego its continuance, perpetuating the
categories of that process even in the moment of recognition.

Despite the first line of the stanza, this passage leaves the reader with an
unmistakable impression of the poet's belief in the objective existence of
these "disguises":

> Raised by the fury of our need,
> supplicating, lusting, grovelling
> before the tall tree of Artemis,
> the transfiguring bow of Diana,
> the rooting vulva of Circe, or
> the slim shape of a nymph,
> luring, dancing, beckoning:
> all her wild disguises! (*Mount Eagle* 46)

Montague's other autobiographical erotic poems also represent a fetishized
female body. Though without pastiche mythology, they too offer a vision
of woman as landscape, spatially organized: "Snowfield" reads her as a
"white expanse" over which the male lover makes "warm tracks" at which
afterwards he "gaze(s) happily" (*The Great Cloak* 11).[16] In "Don Juan's
Farewell", the hero recalls multiple female partners, who are again

objectivized and discounted as separate selves by their synecdochic representation as "sweet shudder of flesh / behind shadowy blinds" and as "warm mounds of / breathing sweetness". They are also marked, almost in a Sadean sense, as erotic objects by "long bars of light / across tipped breasts". The poem emphasizes the existential isolation of the Don Juan character, who at the end tells himself that he has been "searching through / another's pliant body" for "something missing / in your separate self" (*The Great Cloak* 19). Here in the erotic, as elsewhere in the domestic interior, women are the silenced attendants of a masculine quest. Such poems seem to proclaim a moment of sexual liberation, but the erotic subject-positions they represent may be seen rather to offer a mere continuance of consuming masculine passions, and quite fail to encompass a mutually liberating sexuality.

III

Turning to the representation of gender roles in Heaney's work, we find that he tends towards two opposing and possibly complementary representations of gender interaction. One constructs an unequivocally dominant masculine figure, who explores, describes, brings to pleasure and compassionates a passive feminine one. The other proposes a woman who dooms, destroys, puzzles and encompasses the man, but also assists him to his self-discovery: the mother stereotype, but merged intriguingly with the spouse. Members of the first group, representing masculine domination, are "Undine" and "Rite of Spring", in which the man's victory is achieved in agricultural terms; "Punishment" and "Bog Queens", which combine an erotic disrobing narrative (as in Renaissance and other love poetry) and a tone of compassionate tenderness, with a very equivocal result; and the political group including "Ocean's Love to Ireland", "Act of Union" and "The Betrothal of Cavehill", which usually rehearse narratives of rape and sexual violation. The second group contains "The Tollund Man", "The Grauballe Man" and the intense and intriguing "Kinship", which merges mother and spouse as well as active and passive and, I shall argue, functions primarily as a masculine-identity myth, despite its political ending and the political criticism it has chiefly attracted.

In Heaney's first two collections, the most prominent form of attention to gender roles is what may be termed vocational: an allocation of special domains to the masculine and feminine, of a triumphantly traditional kind. Masculine actors find the greater space: in *Death of a Naturalist*, the very first poem "Digging" foreshadows later, explicitly sexual, bog poems, with its all too relevant succession of phallic surrogates – pen, "snug as a gun", spade – and its sensuously rich material which waits passively to be "dug" ("He . . . buried the bright edge deep", in the "squelch and slap / Of soggy peat" (12)). The active prowess of the speaker's male ancestors is stressed, and he is concerned to present his own displacement to intellectual performance as not interrupting his place in that succession.[17] Parallel to this insistence on inheritance, however, these early poems also rehearse the construction of an individuated masculine self: in the title poem "Death of a Naturalist", the croaking bullfrogs – "croaked on sods" – may be perceived as an invasion of maleness into the child's pre-pubertal feminized world, governed by "Miss Walls" the teacher, whereas two poems later in "An Advancement of Learning" the boy successfully faces down the slimy, "nimbling" rat in a test of courage which confirms his own masculinity (15, 18).[18]

With increasing definiteness in the successive collections, the memory of an essentially unchanging rural world is rehearsed, with its traditional crafts and trades; and as a central part of that dispensation, male and female subject-positions are also construed as immemorially fixed. Once natural threats such as those represented by the rat, or by the eel-nits in "Vision", (*Door into the Dark* 45) have been overcome, the speakers of the poems identify admiringly with active natural creatures such as the bull in "Outlaw" (16), and the trout which is rendered in strikingly phallic terms – "Gun-barrel", "torpedo", "ramrodding" ("Trout", *Death of a Naturalist* 39). The trout's ballistic activity is contrasted with the neighbouring "Cow in Calf" (38), where bulk, slowness and recurrence of the same are stressed: "Her cud and her milk, her heats and her calves / keeping coming and going" (38).

There are human versions of such continuities: "The Wife's Tale" with its rare female speaker is typical in celebrating, without obvious intentional irony, the separate spheres of farm and home labour: "I'd come and he had shown me / So I belonged no further to the work".[19] But Heaney's imagination is already dwelling more intensely on metaphors of *nature* as feminine than on the human version. Other strongly conventionalized female figures do also appear, especially mother figures signifying domesticity, intermittently from the earliest poems. But the centre of imaginative intensity is undoubtedly his curious and compelling construct of the land-cum-spouse-cum-deathbringer, with its active and passive aspects.

The hags and goddesses, classical and Celtic, of Montague's poems are replaced in Heaney's by this figure. Its more politicized version, as it appears tentatively in *Wintering Out* and assertively in *North*, represents a merging of the north European fertility goddess, whom Heaney found described in P.V. Glob's study of Iron Age bog burials, with the rather vaguely realized notion of the land of Ireland as seeker of sacrifices, from nationalist political tradition.[20] In his bog poems Heaney sexualizes the religious conceptions of Celtic and north European prehistory. [21] Gender in Celtic and other early mythologies was a metaphysical concept, one of several dyadic means of cosmic organization (male : female lining up with black : white, left : right, north : south, and so forth); a proper service to male and female divinities of earth and air was connected with successful cultivation.[22] This is, of course, markedly different from the predominantly *sexual* interpretation of gender in our culture, which sees it as inextricably bound up with individual personal identity and affective fulfilment, an understanding deriving from Christian theology, the European tradition of courtly love, and the insights of psychoanalysis, among other sources. Heaney's archaizing projection of specifically sexual feeling on to agricultural practices ("Rite of Spring", "Undine") (*Door into the Dark* 25, 26) and human sacrifices to a fertility goddess (the bog poems) seems to be a bid to reach past urban and intellectual social forms and their accompanying thought-world, which are implicitly judged as wanting, to a notional state of physical naturalness and "anonymities" whether folk or prehistoric. An obvious casualty of this attempt, were it to succeed, would be the impulse to individual self-determination and reflexivity. This is an impulse noticeably present in the self-construction of poets, but it is its assumed absence as a defining figure in the lives of Irish rural people and Iron Age Danes which seems to be being celebrated. Thus a disjunction appears between the speaking subjects of these writings and their unspoken objects. In particular the female figures in this conjured world are the epitome of a general silence, at the opposite pole from the describing, celebrating, expressing poet. Whether active or passive, these figures are spoken for, and this division is a highly problematic one.

The two sucessive poems, "Rite of Spring" and "Undine" are perhaps the first examples of an attempt to project sexual feelings into a landscape (*Door into the Dark* 25, 26). They are therefore ancestors of the more famous bog poems, but differ from them in using the second model I have outlined at the outset, one of male activity and female passivity. They project onto a water-pump and a stream respectively the figure of a sexually willing woman, who waits to be coaxed into satisfaction by farming skill: "It cooled, we lifted her latch, / Her entrance was wet, and she came" (25). This masculine narcissism is even more apparent in "Undine", which ventriloquizes the water-nymph's voice:

> . . . And I ran quick for him, cleaned out my rust.
> He halted, saw me finally disrobed . . .
> Then he walked by me. I rippled and I churned . . .
>
> He explored me so completely, each limb
> Lost its cold freedom. Human, warmed to him. (26)

It is difficult to read these pieces as other than classic fantasies of male sexual irresistibility: the moist pump-entrance, the flowing irrigation drain ("he dug a spade deep into my flank / And took me to him") seem almost like a parody of the narrative of erotic wish-fulfilment, in which the frigid female gladly warms to an expert and forceful man.[23] In one sense, the guise of a representation of rural life scarcely survives this sexual excitement, though in another it is being mobilized to legitimize the work, as eternal fact. One might read this conjunction of rural and sexual utopianism, foregrounding pleasure and promising a notional return to an earlier less repressed state; but the obliviousness of most sexual revolutionaries of the period to their own masculinist understanding of pleasure also marks Heaney's version, and hinders such an interpretation.[24] The pump and the stream are (preposterously, when one puts it like that) each imagined as "fulfilled in spite of herself", like Montague's Ceres-figure, which is to say disempowered; hence the real resemblance to pornographic fantasy. They cannot choose but be played upon, like the "Victorian Guitar" which like its gentlewoman owner needs to be "fingered" into pleasure (*Door into the Dark* 33).

There is a further recurring feature of Heaney's work which connects with this nexus of ideas. This is the conceit of language as erotically enabling, joined in the following passage from "Bone Dreams" with the female-body-as-landscape in a political conceit. The Irish poet "colonizes" with his charm – or force of language – the "escarpments" of a female England. He projects himself as the phallic "chalk giant":

> carved on her downs.
> Soon my hands, on the sunken
> fosse of her spine
> move towards the passes. (*North* 29)

The lover-speaker "estimate(s) for pleasure / her knuckles' paving", and begins "to pace" her shoulder: all usual amorous activities in which, however, the explorer's, "estimator's", evaluator's position is the man's. This is blood brother to the fetishizing erotic persona of Montague's work.[25] Other instances of the association of speech with eros and energy or force in Heaney help to elucidate the topic. In "Midnight" the eradication of wolves in Ireland is made the sign both of the seventeenth-century conquest and of emasculation. The poem ends:

> Nothing is panting, lolling,
> Vapouring. The tongue's
> Leashed in my throat. (*Wintering Out* 46)

making a symptomatic equation of phallus, speech, predation and national strength almost too obvious to mention. "Come To The Bower", which echoes the title of a favourite Irish parlour patriotic song, combines the traditional topos of disrobing with the richly sensuous apprehension of the landscape which is one of Heaney's most characteristic features:

> My hands come . . .

> To where the dark-bowered queen,
> Whom I unpin,
> Is waiting . . .

This land-spouse is herself rendered as a bog body, wearing the necklet or torc which stood for the goddess:

> A mark of a gorget in the flesh
> Of her throat. And spring water
> Starts to rise around her. (*North* 31)

The welling water indicates her fertility. The unpinning and marking encode her female disempowerment (precisely as pornographic texts do, since social life and the aesthetic utterances it produces form a symbolic continuum) and thus fix her role as an erotic object. At the end of the poem, she is further named, as wealth: "I reach . . . to the bullion / Of her Venus bone". Here the reality of the ritual murders Heaney found recorded in Glob is metaphorized and explicitly eroticized, in a striking and disturbing mental transformation.

"Punishment", the poem describing Glob's "Windeby girl" – the drowned body of a young woman with a halter round her neck – has attracted much commentary, chiefly about the analogy it makes with tarring and feathering in Northern Ireland. The speaker of it does to a certain degree interrogate his own position, discerning it as that of "the artful voyeur", but the words' overt application here is to his sense of his political ambiguity: he would "connive / in civilized outrage", but understand the "tribal, intimate revenge" being exacted (*North* 38).

The publicly expressible "civilized outrage" belongs to a language which the persona of all these poems feels is denied him and his ethnic group; he constructs Northern Irish Catholics as, like Celts to the ancient Romans, a race mysterious, barbarous, inarticulate, lacking in civility.[26] But, one might argue, the result of this expressed sense of marginalization by the speaker is to make the girl seem doubly displaced: the *object* of equivocal compassion by a *subject* himself forced to be covert, himself the *object* in turn of others' dominant and therefore oppressive civility. Thus the fascinated details of the description which composes the girl as passive and observed object have the effect, whatever the intention, of outweighing the initial assertion of a shared subjectivity ("I can feel the tug / of the halter at the nape / of her neck . . ."). The compassion is equivocal not just because of the half-sympathy with the punishers, but because of the speaker's excitement (can we not identify it as specifically sexual?) at the scopic spectacle of the girl's utter disempowerment ("It blows her nipples / to amber beads . . ."). Hence the usual sense of the word "voyeur" must suggest itself strongly.

Turning to the active feminine, Heaney's engagement with a female destructive principle is particularly intense, as an examination of his Ireland-spouse poems "The Tollund Man" (*Wintering Out* 47) and "Kinship" (*North* 40) shows.[27] In the "Tollund Man", the sacrificed corpse is described as "bridegroom to the goddess", who is credited with a murky amalgam of lethal and sexual acts:

> She tightened her torc on him
> And opened her fen,
> Those dark juices working
> Him to a saint's kept body . . . (*Wintering Out* 47)

This, like "Punishment", aestheticizes the horror of a murdered corpse and presents it as a natural phenomenon ("The mild pods of his eye-lids, / His pointed skin cap"). But here it is also made an effect of erotic absorption and incorporation by a female energy conceived as both inert and devouring.[28] If one turns the motif this way round, for the moment understanding it primarily as a way of thinking about woman rather than about Irish political murder, it reveals an intense alienation from the female. Eros–Thanatos pairings generally do seem to rely on a perception of woman as channel for masculine fear and desire, and this is no exception.[29] When one readmits into one's mind the poem's parallel between Stone Age sacrifices to the fertility goddess and Irish political murders in the 1970s, one's increased awareness of the erotic–aesthetic frisson in the first section makes the analogy seem all the more shaky and difficult to assent to. Can this sexual thrill really have anything other than mischief to bring to our thought about the actual perpetration of torture and murder?[30]

"Kinship" at the dead centre of the collection *North*, also represents a centre of Heaney's project. Developing a hint at the end of the earlier "Bogland" ("The wet centre is bottomless" *Door into the Dark* 56) it presents Ireland's bogland as above all an encompasser – ruminant, storer, embalmer, "insatiable bride", swallower, mideen, floe. At the end of the passage is a disrobing moment: the ground "will strip / its dark side" as if undressing. As the poem's hero pulls out, then replaces, a turf-spade in the bog, "the soft lips of the growth / muttered and split", leaving the spade-shaft "wettish / as I sank it upright . . ." (*North* 42). Following this moment of phallic discovery (evidently granted with some reluctance by the bog) and reinsertion, recalling Heaney's many earlier digging and ploughing passages, there is an explicit merging of birth and death – "a bag of waters / and a melting grave" – in this personified ground, a "centre" which, unlike Yeats's, "holds" (*North* 43). The poet identifies himself as having grown out of this bog "like a weeping willow / inclined to / the appetites of gravity". In a turn to the overtly political at the end of this poem, he addresses Tacitus, Roman describer of Celtic Europe, wryly acknowledging the practice of "slaughter for the common good" (which presumably represents both the ritual human sacrifices described in the *Germania* and Northern Ireland's deaths):

> Our mother ground
> is sour with the blood
> of her faithful,
> . . .

report us fairly,
. . .
How the goddess swallows
our love and terror. (*North* 45)

First, taking this passage politically, one might argue that the evident irony in the expression "slaughter for the common good" does not solve the more general problem of a projection of the mythic and ritual onto history and the resulting blockage of rational understanding and possible action. The poet compulsively predicates his claim to intuitive identification with his landscape on personifying it as feminine and equating it with death ("The goddess swallows / our love and terror"). As others have suggested, this further entangles the gloomy facts of Irish political history with the heady rhetoric of nationalist ideology instead of interrogating them.[31] My second point concerns the poem's real priorities. It privatizes and sexualizes the political. Its early sections show much greater intensity than the later (which has probably contributed unnoticed to critics' questioning of the ending): the charged personal ode to the bog as mother and partner – giver and receiver of the spade-phallus – is no more than tenuously related to the political references at the end, which risk seeming merely dutiful. I think the real focus is on the speaker's private myth of identity formation, on wresting a self from the 'feminine' unbounded indeterminacy of the bog. This poem attempts a synthesis of the stereotypes of femininity: the bog-goddess is imagined as both mother and spouse, and as destroyer and provider, but it is still persistently (and in both senses) the *ground* on which the speaker's self and his very identity is predicated. The feminine is thus once again an Other but not really envisaged as an alternative subject or self: a relation of complementarity, certainly, but not of equality, and one which enshrines difference in the oppressive sense of that word.

Following the privatized and sexualized bog-Ireland poems, there is also a series of poems in *North* which mount a specifically political gender-historical narrative of English conquest and colonization in Ireland. This series includes "Ocean's Love to Ireland" and "Act of Union". Both these poems employ the conceit representing political conquest by acts of sexual possession, and "Act of Union" makes the male/English violator its speaker; and/or: it is a love poem to a pregnant spouse. There is a crucial ambiguity about the sexual act in both poems: rape (indicated by a reference to Elizabethan massacres) or seduction by a male force whose energy is attractively irresistible? The language of "Act of Union" strongly recalls that of the exploring lover in "Bone Dreams":

. . . I caress
The heaving province where our past has grown.
I am the tall kingdom over your shoulder

>   That you would neither cajole nor ignore.
>   Conquest is a lie . . . (*North* 49)

Her mutuality is said by the male speaker (England) to have supplanted
violation of an unwilling woman (Ireland). How ironically is that speech to
be read? Does not the tone strongly recall the gender triumphalism of "Rite
of Spring", which, after all, enthusiastically celebrated the farmer's sexualized thawing of the pump? The speaker in "Act of Union" regrets the
pain of his partner's imminent childbirth ("the rending process in the
colony, / The battering ram") but also reads it as the promise of a forth-
coming Oedipal struggle: "His parasitical and ignorant little fists already
. . . cocked / At me across the water". One can credit Heaney with a vivid
rendering of the complications, the tangled intimacy, of Anglo-Irish political relations. But one might also feel that to rehearse the narrative of these
relations in these terms is to re-mystify rather than to attempt an understanding of the phenomena. What is especially questionable is the apparently unconscious equivocation in Heaney's deployment of gender. The
application of force in the agricultural handling of nature, imagined as male
sexual domination, is felt as deeply right. But the occurrence of the same
structure in political relations is (presumably, in the work of a poet of
Catholic nationalist origins) to be taken as reprehensible and grievous.
Further, in the structure of *North* the death-bringing goddess's claiming
helpless victims (female force) in the bog poems is matched with the rape-
narratives in the pendent colonization series (male force). The symmetry of
this deepens the sense of inevitability generated by the whole project of the
mythicization of history. The social, economic and constitutional conditions of modern Ireland are elided in this reductive narrative which
merges the chthonic personifications of the Iron Age with a presentation of
gender roles as immemorial.

The brief lyric "The Betrothal of Cavehill" closes the series with a
quizzical moment:

>   Gunfire barks its questions off Cavehill
>   And the profiled basalt maintains its stare
>   South: proud, protestant and northern, and male.
>   Adam untouched, before the shock of gender.
>
>   They still shoot here for luck over a bridegroom.
>   The morning I drove out to bed me down
>   Among my love's hideouts, her pods and broom,
>   They fired above my car the ritual gun. (*North* 51)

In the second stanza, the familiar moment when the land is taken as spouse
(". . . to bed me down / Among my love's hideouts, her pods and
broom") allows us to identify the "bridegroom" equivocally in three

possible ways: either as an autobiographical splinter of the poet, or as an IRA man on the run and living rough in the countryside, or as the rock itself "marrying" the prone land it surveys so dominantly. So the familiar reprise of nationalist attachment to the land as a betrothal to death is complicated by the ethnically double male presence in the poem: the "Adam untouched" figure of Cavehill, which is made to represent the culturally masculine intransigence of northern Protestantism, disdaining converse with the land-as-Eve; and the presumably Catholic "bride-groom", who "beds down" in the land. Even the *culturally* feminine Catholic/nationalist figure is *biologically* male: may we read this as a discreet Utopian moment in which all (males) may merge their differences in a general bedding down in the (female) land? As to politics, this may be an improvement; but as to gender, it is the status quo as in all the other poems: politics is seen in terms of sexuality, but not the reverse. The mildly humorous characterization of the rock as phallic stops short of demythicizing Genesis, however wry it is about northern Protestant no-surrendering: the gender *there* was before gender was already male.

It may seem that I am ignoring one of the prominent developments of Heaney's later work, namely his "marriage poems", particularly in *Field Work*, and indeed the sprinkling of earlier personal love poems. I believe, however, that these poems are mostly also recuperable to this broadly dualistic active–passive pattern I have outlined.[32] Poem VI in the sequence *Station Island*, for example ("Freckle-face, fox-head, pod of the broom"), is motivated by an autobiographical "plot", but centres on the constitutively masculine gestures of watching and actively desiring an uncommunicative and mysterious female figure, who is associated with bags of grain, like the sheela-na-gig in *Station Island*:

> Her hands holding herself
> are like hands in an old barn
> holding a bag open (49)

and what one might term a genial voyeurism is typical of the love poems in general: "The Skunk" is a classic example (*Field Work* 48).[33] "Polder" (*Field Work* 51), one of the "marriage poems", is a kind of psychologized reprise of "Kinship", shorn of political extrapolation. It retains the land–woman metaphoric equation: in the combined metaphor of possession and origination re-employed from "Kinship", the woman is the territory where the man, "old willow", has his "creel of roots", and "I have reclaimed my polder, / all its salty grass and mud-slick banks". One might read the sequence *Field Work* itself, and its stress on the erotic excitement of retracing physical marks and stains on the spouse's limbs, as working to fetishize woman's body in much the same way as Montague's *The Great Cloak* does.[34]

So must we not conclude that the poetry of Montague and Heaney as a whole is insistently and damagingly gendered? Its masculine personae, whether in the narrative of personal identity, or that of nationality, must, it seems, possess or be possessed by a counter-force personified as feminine: an encounter of the genders as of aliens – dog eat dog, possess or be swallowed up – is forever occurring, even within and beneath politics. On this evidence, it remains very difficult for men, when they imagine self-formation as a struggle, to escape conceiving that struggle, however meta-phorically or virtually, as *against* the feminine. The integral self counted as so precious to the capacity for expression of these poets is won against a necessarily subordinated ground of merely potential, never actual feminine selves. In Lacanian terms, they seem to be stuck in the self/not-self dualism of the mirror stage, failing to arrive at an acknowledgement of the existence of an autonomous subjectivity in others: a structure common to sexism and racism.[35] Just as "every document of civilization is a document of barbar-ism", in Benjamin's phrase, so one is tempted to conclude that every feat of self-discovery by these masculine poets entails the defeat of a feminine ego. Or as Irigaray puts it:

the/a woman fulfills a twofold function – as the mute outside that sustains all systematicity; as a maternal and still silent ground that nourishes all foundations – . . . (365)

Notes

1 Paul Muldoon's "Aisling" which parodically refuses its due of reverence to this icon, substituting "Anorexia" for Aurora and Flora, merely replaces a falsely idealized feminine figure with a self-destructive one arousing masculine distaste – inadequate as demystification (see *Quoof* 39). See also Longley, *Poetry in the Wars* 207, for an approving view.

2 For the debate in feminist anthropology on the applicability of the nature–culture opposition to gender, see Ortner; Brown and Jordanova; MacCormack and Strathern; and Ardener. On the limitation of woman to domesticity, see Mills; and on Freudian Oedipal dogmatism, Irigaray. More specifically, I have been helped by Goodby, whom I wish to thank for kindly showing me his research. Trevor Joyce's discussions with me on theoretical issues and his suggestions about drafts of this paper have been invaluable.

3 The phrase in Heaney's poem "Punishment" (*North* 38) describing the poet as "artful voyeur" is only an explicit crystallizing of a very general subject-position in his work, as I shall try to show. Laura Mulvey's classic discussion of the male gaze and the scopic is helpful here.

4 For baking, see "Mossbawn 1. Sunlight" (*North* 8); the ploughing and digging fathers are enlisted in "Digging" and "Follower" (*Death of a Naturalist* 13, 34).

5 Even the sequences of Montague and Heaney tend to be predicated as narrative on the personal experience of the poet.

6 This is in contrast with Heaney's deployment of this type, as we shall see. On spousal and maternal versions of Ireland-figures, see Hawkins, who finds in the Emmet-Curran plot an instance of the Venus-Adonis or Ishtar-Tammuz myth, in which a son-cum-lover dies seasonally for the Great Goddess who represents natural continuity. See also Wills.

7 See O'Keefe 61–3, 73–5, 83. I am indebted for useful discussion of this and other Old Irish matters to Máire Herbert.

8 See Rees and Rees 73–4; Gose 152–64; and Campbell 103–4. Heaney also mobilizes these associations in his version of old woman and well, "A Drink of Water" (*Field Work* 16).

9 This journey is significantly framed by the haven-like domesticity of the adult poet's marital home, where "a woman is waiting" (*The Dead Kingdom* 11, 59, 94, 96).

10 Heaney's sequence "Clearances" is in a sense also part of this dead-mother literature, with its limitations of caution and distance within the framework of gracefully expressed affection. See, in particular, the endings of poems no. 3 and 4 (*The Haw Lantern* 27, 28).

11 There is an encyclopaedic mythological literature on this subject, and several recent demystifications of it by feminists. See Eliade 418–19, and Campbell 102–66, for examples of the former; and Mills 157ff., for some of the latter. There are fairly routine instances of the rendering of the feminine as death-bringer in Montague. In "O Riada's Farewell" a death-goddess appears in several guises: as "Miss Death" in evening dress, as a musicianly "mistress of the bones", and as a wrecker: "The damp haired / seaweed stained sorceress / marshlight of defeat" (*A Slow Dance* 59–60). See also his borrowing of Spenser's Mutability goddess: "dark Lady of Process / our devouring Queen" (*The Dead Kingdom* 19, 22).

12 The effect is similar to that of some erotic poems in earlier literary tradition, such as Donne's *Elegy XIX*: "To His Mistress Going to Bed", or *blazon* poems in general. For the general structure of fetishization, see Freud; for an argument linking this with forms of objectivization and dismemberment in colonial discourse, see Bhabha.

13 One must point out, however, that Montague's more recent collection *Mount Eagle* returns dismayingly to the earlier fetishizing perspective in the voyeuristic "Sheela na Gig" (31); and when the vocabulary of the earlier well-poems recurs, it is with a far less delicate touch: "from the spring well / with a brimming bucket; its trembling meniscus, / water's hymen" ("Peninsula", *Mount Eagle* 64).

14 See also "A Meeting", "Sunset", and "Waiting" (*The Great Cloak* 43, 55, 56).

15 Compare "Harvest" (*Mount Eagle* 43). Heaney also constructs a Ceres-figure, but uses it as an icon of healing fertility in a poem about political murder ("After a killing"; *Field Work* 12).

16 See also the following poem, "Tracks" (*The Great Cloak* 12).

17 See also "Follower" (*Death of a Naturalist* 24).

18 See Roe's argument that this poem reveals what he calls Heaney's "mythic wish" in an early form. Roe says that the female teacher who explains the natural history of frogs "appears as external author of guilt – perhaps a sexual

awakening –" and represents "a sort of primary school Eve who bears responsibility for the . . . child's lost innocence" (169).

19 Though, of course, a feminist reader might not be able to avoid giving an
    ironic *reading* to such a poem: "I gathered cups . . . / And went. But they still
    kept their ease / Spread out, unbuttoned, grateful, under the trees" (*Door into
    the Dark* 27). I am grateful to Mary Breen for discussion of the issue of the
    masculinist representation of domesticity.

20 See Heaney, *Preoccupations* 57–8, for his own account of his inspiration by
    Glob. The modern political half of the construct finds perhaps its most popular
    and familiar expression in the writings of Patrick Pearse.

21 The most sustained account of Heaney's whole bog complex is Jacqueline
    Genet's, which crisply notices the poems' sexual emphasis and meanings, but
    foregoes interrogation of them.

22 See Alwyn and Brinley Rees; Berger. See also Mac Cana, *Celtic Mythology* 49–
    50, 85–94: "the mythological role of love . . . is of its nature functional or
    ritual rather than personal" (85).

23 Neil Corcoran severely understates the case when he says "the poem has, like
    'The Wife's Tale', its element of male presumption" (58).

24 See Mills on the inadequacies of Marcuse's sexual libertarianism in *Eros and
    Civilization*, which greatly influenced thought in the 1960s. In the Irish context, Heaney is also revising the rural vision of Patrick Kavanagh, one of his
    primary enabling figures, to include sex, but sex neither as ideal romance nor as
    frustration, its two guises in Kavanagh. The crucial moment in earlier Kavanagh, of critique of the emotional and other deprivation attending Irish rural
    life, is, however, elided in Heaney.

25 With it may also belong the conjunction in the later "La Toilette" of dressing,
    sacredness and language ("But vest yourself / in the word you taught me / and
    the stuff I love: slub silk") (*Station Island* 14).

26 See "Freedman" (*North* 60); "The Toome Road" (*Field Work* 15), with its
    British tank crews as "charioteers"; and also "Kinship", discussed below.

27 It may be worth remarking that his sense of this identification seems quite
    different from that in early Irish mythology, in which several female war- and
    death-divinities appear: the hero or king must couple with them so as to ensure
    his victory or continued rule, but they – the Morrighan, the Badhbh, and
    Macha – are actively characterized as speaking figures. The territorial goddesses
    such as Anu dominated an area but were not especially thought of as murderous. Heaney's version seems a modern and hybrid construct. See Mac Cana,
    Celtic Mythology 66, 86.

28 See Corcoran 96ff., for an informed and intelligent commentary from a general
    point of view on these poems. Longley, *Poetry* 140–69 gives a trenchant discus   •
    sion which makes some good demystificatory points, but insists on a formalist
    and depoliticizing understanding of poetry which is itself open to question
    ("Poetry and politics, like church and state, should be separated" (185)).
    Andrews is sensitive and painstaking, but his formalist approach tends to perpetuate the reification of gender-roles.

29 See Mills 157ff. on Freud, Marcuse and the notion of the "primal horde":
    "Because woman was Eros/Thanatos/Nirvana in 'immediate' union she

represented the threat of 'mere nature' – 'the regressive impulse for peace which stood in the way of progress – of Life itself' " (157, quoting Marcuse's *Eros and Civilization* (1972)). One might add that Heaney's repeated meditations on the bog bodies are, of course, not at all concerned to open the enquiry anthropologically towards a rational investigation either of stone age religious and agricultural behaviour, or of Irish politics, but to make "offerings or images that were emblems" (Heaney interview 1977, quoted in Corcoran 96).

30 As Edna Longley has well said: "Heaney does not distinguish between involuntary and voluntary 'martyrdom', and the nature of his 'archetype' is such as to subsume the latter within the former" (*Poetry in the Wars* 151).

31 On the irony in the last section of "Kinship", see Corcoran 119, against other commentators who accuse Heaney of a crude nationalism (Longley, *Poetry in the Wars* 185–210 and Morrison, *Seamus Heaney* 68, 81).

32 With the exception of the early "Lovers on Aran", in which for once the stress is on a quality of mutuality and indistinguishableness in the lovers' relation: "Did sea define the land or land the sea? . . ." (*Death of a Naturalist* 47), and occasional other poems such as no. X of the *Glanmore Sonnets* ("I dreamt we slept in a moss in Donegal . . .") (*Field Work* 42).

33 The engagingly self-mocking "Sweeney's Returns" even discerns that voyeuristic structure as a comedy, but scarcely to the extent of dismantling it (*Station Island* 114).

34 It is fair to say, however, that Heaney's *The Haw Lantern* marks a general turn away both from mythicizing in the earlier manner, and from sexual stereotyping in love poetry; but it is not yet clear whether this does signal a new politics in the most general sense.

35 As Bhabha says: "Colonial power produces the colonized as a fixed reality which is at once an "other" yet entirely knowable and visible' (156). On the mirror stage and entry into the symbolic order as a passage beyond dualism, see Mueller and Richardson 136. I thank Nick Daly for discussion of this point.

7

Jennifer Johnston's Irish troubles: A materialist–feminist reading

Christine St Peter

Jennifer Johnston ranks at this moment as one of Ireland's most successful novelists. Although the first of her novels appeared as recently as 1972 when she was already 42 years old, she established within a few years a very large readership in Ireland, the United Kingdom, the United States, Canada and Western Europe. At the time of this writing, she has published eight novels, receiving for them three important prizes.[1] The appearance of each new novel now merits respectful, even enthusiastic, notice in the reviewing columns of major newspapers in the English-speaking world, but there is relatively little interest in Johnston's work among academic critics. To date, only 10 articles have been published on her work in scholarly journals, a somewhat surprising fact given the amount of attention paid twentieth-century Irish writing in these publications.[2] It is possible that academics have not yet discovered her; that they have discovered and dismissed her; or perhaps that they do not know precisely what to make of her. Judging from the critical studies that do exist, this last explanation is plausible, since we find in them quite contradictory accounts of her "meaning". But for the feminist critic intent, as I am, on including Irish women writers in the formidably male canon of Anglo-Irish literature, Jennifer Johnston offers some very perplexing problems indeed.

I am not the first feminist critic to stumble over these problems. In 1982, Shari Benstock wrote an elegant and subtle article on Johnston entitled "The Masculine World of Jennifer Johnston". At the beginning of her discussion, Benstock warns us that she intends to avoid the most obvious avenues of approach to this writer; she does not wish to consider Johnston as "either a Woman writer or an Irish writer, although obviously she is both" (192). Given the title of the essay, Benstock would seem to be leading us towards an evaluation of Johnston as a male-identified woman writer with a presumed audience of men or male-identified women. But she refuses us this simplistic reading, rejecting as misleading the assumption that because Johnston's "thematic and metaphoric elements" are the traditionally male subjects of "hunting games, chivalric and heraldic codes, puberty rites and the [Big House] law of primogeniture", her novelistic world is a masculine one. In fact, towards the end of the article, Benstock states that the title of her essay "is entirely inappropriate to [Johnston's] subject": this world is not masculine, not open, accessible, social, a world of action, but rather specifically feminine: closed, suffocated, lonely and inward-turning (216).

Then in another strategic feint, Benstock refuses the feminine reading, arguing that the novels seem to "hold as a kind of statement about the survival of human beings in general and of the literary artist in particular". Johnston's stories are "socially remote commentaries on the fictive process itself":

> Against the myth of Irish storytellers, the ebullient, social beings . . . Johnston posits another kind of Irish voice – one that is not clearly even Irish but rather transplanted and misplaced, one that is neither male nor female . . . one that is distinctly separate from and aligned against its origins and impetus. (193, 216)

Finally, then, she considers Johnston's novels to be "tales of the lonely individual as storyteller" located at "the furthest reaches of artistic alienation" (216–17). Why, then, one wonders, the title?

Benstock's article was written after the publication of Johnston's first five novels: *The Captains and the Kings* (1972), *The Gates* (1973), *How Many Miles to Babylon* (1974), *Shadows on Our Skin* (1977) and *The Old Jest* (1979). Since then, Johnston has published another three: *The Christmas Tree* (1981), *The Railway Station Man* (1984) and *Fool's Sanctuary* (1987). The subjects of these later novels provoke the reading that Benstock avoided – the consideration of Jennifer Johnston as both an Irish writer and a Woman writer.[3]

I have three reasons for this. The first, and most obvious, is that in all three of these novels, unlike the earlier five, Johnston places an adult woman at the narrative centre of the novels, each of them telling the gender-marked story of her life. In this Johnston could be said to be writing as *a* woman, about women, for a predominantly female audience. The second reason for this consideration is that, with the exception of *The Christmas Tree*, Johnston uses Ireland's tempestuous political history as a primary focus in her books, and her obsessive and compassionate concern demands our acknowledgement of her political and cultural awareness. The third reason has to do with reader response: in virtually all the responses we find a significant focus on her writing as feminine and apolitical. Is this why *The Railway Station Man* which, along with *Shadows on Our Skin*, is Johnston's politically most challenging novel, is the novel that has had the worst sales, the least enthusiastic reception?[4] This focus on Johnston as both an Irish and Woman writer insists on the political nature of her texts. This is not an easy stance for her since, as we shall see, she has an idea that the Irish writer has a particular form of responsibility to her society. And yet even granting her political awareness, we find that nowhere in these novels does she manage to resolve the ideological contradictions in her depiction of Irish social and political life.

Foci such as these, including that on reader response, are characteristic of materialist-feminist criticism. Although I do not have space here to do justice to the complexity of the method or the scope of Johnston's eight novels, I will in the course of this chapter consider briefly a number of other questions also based on a materialist-feminist perspective: what kinds of myths or narratives of Irish history does Johnston draw upon in producing her novels? How does she reproduce the material conditions, especially class or caste relations, of twentieth-century Ireland in her writings? How do her female characters function within her historical narratives? Can we discover in the collision of divergent meanings within her texts a critique of their inscribed values or do the texts endorse, too comfortably, the incompatibility of these values? All of these questions rest upon the assumption that every literary text functions as a site of political activity, and that the ideologies in the text help maintain or subvert a particular set of social and economic relations at a particular juncture in history. But before turning to the novels with these questions in mind, I will continue my examination of the critical response to the works, since here we discover contradictions that correspond to those in her texts.

As Lillian S. Robinson points out in a general analysis of reader response, it is no accident that certain groups benefit socially and institutionally by the perpetuation of certain literary interpretations, and that other groups are oppressed by them ("Dwelling in Decencies" 10). Or, put slightly differently, this time by Catherine Belsey:

> Having created a canon of acceptable texts, criticism then provides them with acceptable interpretations, thus effectively censoring any elements in them which come into collision with the dominant ideology. To deconstruct the text, on the other hand, is to open it, to release the possible positions of its intelligibility, including those which reveal the partiality (in both senses) of the ideology inscribed in the text. (58)

When Shari Benstock declares Johnston's focus to be the tragic isolation of an individual storyteller, she does not consider the political implications of her critical dismissal of alternative concerns. Yet one might point out that a fundamental precept of bourgeois aesthetics is that good art celebrates that which is unique or eccentric in human experience and that individual achievement or its obverse, individual failure, combined with the subjective isolation of artist or character, are the artistic norm in Western literature.[5] So "natural" is this view that critics refer unselfconsciously to "art" as though it were possible to assume the transhistorical independence of aesthetic judgement. Among Johnston's critics, for example, we find an almost univocal agreement on the perfection of her "art", yet very little sense of what the concept "art" means except perhaps an intelligent, precise rendering of "reality".

This suggests a comfortable fit between Johnston's depiction of a self-coherent "world" and her audience's prior expectations on that subject. A droll review of Johnston's early novels by Auberon Waugh gives us a picture of what these expectations might be. Describing Johnston's subject as the "decline and decay" of the formerly great Big House, with its memory-tormented, ineffective Anglo-Irish landlord and his feckless, charmless, poor, stupid and dishonest Irish tenants, Waugh tells us (who is this "us"?) that Johnston gives us "the Ireland we all know and love . . .".

Anthony Burgess, another critic who compliments Johnston's art, is quoted thus by Mary Rose Callaghan in the concluding lines of the Jennifer Johnston entry in the *Dictionary of Irish Literature*: "This is a unique and perfect art, born of a time and place and temperament, not contrived against their grain. It represents no movement, and one can learn nothing from it except the ancient virtues of human concern and verbal economy" (316). However oracular this may sound, Burgess has really told us nothing of her work except that it fits with a dominant ideological mode or "grain" and can therefore paradoxically transcend that "grain" into some realm of the perfect. And yet even as he grants her this perfection he condescendingly deprives her of seriousness and scope since she teaches us nothing but lessons learned long ago.

The critics who eulogize Johnston's perfect art often go on to describe her "world" as both tiny and limited, isolated from significant history either by the narrative reliance on nostalgic retrospection or by the marginality and isolation of her characters. Here is a characteristic example, positive yet patronizing: "the careful crafting of scene and character has a quality associated with the past, another life. The careful reader can cherish the images and textures of the portraits that compose the restricted world of which she writes" (Connolly 124).

The critical juxtaposition of "restricted" and "craft" drifts inexorably towards an interpretation of the novels as "restricted craft". The "miniature novels" and "little tales" reveal "limited compass" (Dunn; Blythe; Tuohy). Wisely restricting herself to the small confines of her experience and vision she can, we are assured, within those constraints write beautifully, like her famous predecessor Jane Austen. In other words, one can grant the artistic achievement as long as one can refuse other claims to greatness. Undergirding this reading would seem to be the reassuring patriarchal assumption that a woman writer cannot, perhaps even should not, know of the larger world that is the sphere of the male writer of comparable "artistic" achievement. This assumption can take very odd turns and it is here that the Jane Austen reference demands a moment's attention.

Mark Mortimer, in an article entitled "The World of Jennifer Johnston", undertakes to define what he calls her "field". Having pointed out that "more than half of *How Many Miles to Babylon* takes place in the North of France during the first World War" and that both this novel and *The Gates* rely on historical re-creation of earlier periods, he then goes on to draw these conclusions:

> In these novels the exclusion of the outside world is almost as sweeping as with Jane Austen. And as wise; for like her famous predecessor, Jennifer [!] knows her limitations; concentrates on the scene she is familiar with; restricts herself to the milieu she has experience of. This segment of society is her "little bit of ivory, two inches wide." [*sic*] (91)

At the conclusion of his essay, Mortimer reiterates his praise for her decision to "concentrate, like Jane Austen, on a "little piece of ivory" [*sic*] . . . on the deliberate narrowing of her field to the people, the places, the way of life she knows so well" (94).

In another academic article, we are offered once more the disparaging, inaccurate, and again misquoted application of Jane Austen's ironic self-description[6] to Johnston's novelistic universe: "A Little Bit of Ivory. Two Inches Wide: The Small World of Jennifer Johnston's Fiction". The author of this essay, Rudiger Imhof, offers a literal reading of Johnston's prose – that misses her use of irony, humour and understatement. He then crowns his attack on Johnston's technical "ineptitude" with the oblique suggestion – can I possibly be reading correctly? – that the 50-year-old author, like her 19-year-old female protagonist in *The Old Jest*, deserves a "good spanking" (142–3).

This, of course, is an extreme example of splenetic misogyny. Most of Johnston's critics, male and female, academic or journalistic, praise Johnston's achievement even if in so doing they often reveal an all too familiar unconscious gender bias that gently dismisses the female writer, her subject matter and her female characters. One could produce a number of disconcerting examples, as in the description of bike-riding, marathon-walking Helen Cuffe in *The Railway Station Man* as "50-year-old female flab", while her 50-year-old male lover, definitely not the artist of the two, is described by Grace Ingoldby as "Merrick-like".

I do not intend to gather here idiosyncratic little displays of sexist aversion, nor do I intend to focus exclusively on the ways in which gender bias in Johnston's readers reproduces the unequal power relations in the communities now reading her works. But it is curious that when Johnston's critics see her as transcending her feminine enclosure, this achievement is marked as masculine by Charity Blackstock – "A formidable novelist, Miss Johnston who writes like a man with the sensitivity of a woman" – and by William Cole – "If you want to know what's happening in the Irish novel today, Miss Johnston is your man (as the Irish would say)." One fears they might; that is no country for women writers.

And yet even as I castigate Johnston's critics for reducing her to some notion of the genteel female writer or a male *manqué*, we find Jennifer Johnston doing this to herself. In an interview from 1984, Johnston was asked the inevitable question about her relationship as Irish writer to the achievement of James Joyce. Her response was this self-deprecating one:

> I'm working on a very, very small canvas. I would not ever have felt under the shadow of Joyce at all because my own way of looking at my work and looking at what I'm trying to [do] was so minuscule. I would look at myself much more in terms of somebody like E.M. Forster or Jane Austen. (Johnston, "Q and A" 26)

Lamenting that most of Ireland's writers are "not what you call socially concerned", she then went on to describe her work-in-progress, *The Railway Station Man*, as a novel "about a woman, and the North comes into it peripherally. The whole violence of the country in general" ("Q and A" 27). This "peripherally" may be a sort of wry understatement, but it feels more like an unwillingness to credit her own remarkable ability to use an individual life as emblem of national catastrophe. If so, this seems to me a disappointing failure to challenge the dominant perception that male authors are pre-eminently the ones who have depicted the nightmare of twentieth-century Irish history, even where their subject is the effect of the nightmare on women's lives. One wonders at an author in the same breath talking of "the whole violence of the country in general" as her subject, yet describing her canvas as "minuscule"? With such questions in mind, I shall return at the end of this study to a closer look at this novel, and to Johnston's remark about social concern.

I would assert that the canvas of Johnston's *oeuvre* is unusually large for an Irish writer: her Ireland includes the whole island, Protestant and Catholic, female and male, young and old, urban and rural, and it chronicles events from before the First World War to the present "Troubles". Only one other critic seems to find apposite an insistence on the historical scope of Johnston's novels. Heinz Kosok states: "If one disregards for a moment their chronology of publication, Jennifer Johnston's novels present a continuous comment on the history of Ireland from the beginning of the century to the present day" (102). But Kosok later suggests that if "these

novels can be seen from one angle as chapters in the recent history of
Ireland, they are also, and perhaps in the first place, individual stories for
which the Irish background provides no more than an accidental setting"
(106). Here he withdraws from what I consider his more striking insight.
An Irish "setting" is hardly "accidental" in these novels that record with
great care the ways in which individuals recoil from, or attempt to meet,
the political, economic and cultural exigencies that impinge so crucially,
and so damagingly, on their lives.

The tragic stories of isolated individuals serve as emblems of Irish political
and social life. But in her treatment of these stories I think we find paradoxically both a desire to create, and an ideologically based refusal to maintain,
the possibility of the egalitarian, cross-caste relations Ireland needs to survive.
In every one of her novels, she explores the possibility of such communion,
always between two lonely individuals who take risks to reach across class/
age/sexual/religious divisions. Yet in every novel, except *The Railway Station
Man* and perhaps *The Christmas Tree*, she ultimately rejects the promise.
Private accommodations between individuals cannot withstand the massed
social resistance they meet, nor are the individuals able to risk enough to
make the communication effective. This may reproduce very accurately the
contemporary Irish experience, but it also inscribes, and thus promotes, a
sense of despair about finding "solutions" to the Irish Troubles.

I earlier asked what kinds of myths or narratives of Irish history Johnston
draws upon in producing her historical novels. Obviously, the lingering
drama of the Big House and its Protestant owners is one such element,
leaving its traces in five of her eight novels, although with uneasy am-
bivalence. The myth has many versions, most famously Maria Edgeworth's
Castle Rackrent. Yet for readers of twentieth-century Irish literature, the
dominant version of the myth is the one wrought in the gorgeous poetic
creation of W. B. Yeats:

> How should the world be luckier if this house,
> Where passion and precision have been one
> Time out of mind, became too ruinous
> To breed the lidless eye that loves the sun?
> And the sweet laughing eagle thoughts that grow
> Where wings have memory of wings, and all
> That comes of the best knit to the best? Although
> Mean roof-trees were the sturdier for its fall,
> How should their luck run high enough to reach
> The gifts that govern men, and after these
> To gradual Times's last gift, a written speech
> Wrought of high laughter, loveliness and ease? (*Collected Poems* 106–7)

If Yeats believed that in the Big House the "best knit to the best", Jennifer
Johnston's novels do not endorse such a notion. Nor do they subscribe to

the fabrication, so skilfully wrought in Yeats's poem, that in this historical phenomenon "passion and precision have been one / Time out of mind". On the contrary, Johnston takes considerable pains to demonstrate precisely when and how the "high laughter, lovelines and ease" were built on the exploited needs and alienated labour of the serf-like peasants. She shows as well how the landlords' control, sometimes meshing with the interests of the Catholic clergy, combined where necessary to keep subject the "[m]ean roof-trees", whose lowliness seems part of organic nature in the Yeats poem.

Johnston presents her moral position most baldly in *The Gates*. In a remarkable, Flaubert-like scene, she juxtaposes the eviction of destitute tenants with the quarrelling for candy between the young sons of the landlord who happen to pass by the scene of the eviction with their governess:

> A dazzle of sunshine danced on the flailing picks as six of his father's men ripped the roof off a cottage. His governess had let the reins go slack and the pony cropped the grass. The brass trappings glittered. A lark's song faded above them. Hunks of greying thatch slithered into what had been someone's living room, bedroom, kitchen. Beams cracked like the gun shots of later years. Bertie pulled a paper bag out of his pocket and shoved a sweet into his mouth. (96)

This 50-year-old image in the fuzzy mind of Major MacMahon is immediately preceded by the Major's resentful reading of the morning newspaper: "A black-coated politician smiled genially at him. . . . Rapscallions, rascals, crooks, every one of them. Jumped-up sons of grocers"; it is followed by the memory of the governess's dismissive assessment of the eviction:

> Your father's been too kind to them for too long . . . Give these people an inch and they'll take an ell. They refuse to understand that he has to live, too.
> . . . The Lark whirled down towards them again, unconcerned with anything but its own song."
> "Hail to thee, blythe spirit", said the governess. (96–7)

But in case we miss the narrative inscription of class discrimination, Johnston had chosen to instruct her readers directly by means of a rather awkward authorial intrusion earlier in the novel. In a chapter entitled "A Slight Explanation", she abandons her story to reflect for a moment about the foundations of this Big House wealth in the 1820s:

> The homeless people were rented (at what were, to the landlord, minimal rents) patches of mountainy land, on which to build their huts and scrape for themselves and their enormous families. "The Irish breed like rabbits," Mrs. MacMahon had said once to some London

friends, "I'm told indeed, when there's no food in the house they boil the baby." (35)

This is a clear example of what I have been calling contradictory ideology in the text: in one sentence so careful to establish the economic unfairness of Big House power, Johnston succumbs in the next to what Polly Devlin has described elsewhere as a characteristic verbal game of the Anglo-Irish: exchanging funny tales about the behaviour of that sub-species, the Irish tenantry.[7] There is little doubt that Johnston's cleverly wrought if cruel witticism is the feature that will remain lodged in our memories, especially as Johnston elsewhere in the novel describes the very fertile and brutish Kelly family as grotesque animals. And yet in the next paragraph, Johnston returns to her original indictment, telling us that the absentee English landlord received from his steward, "a most satisfactory employee":

> enough money each year to keep them in the style to which they were accustomed. No questions were ever asked as long as the money arrived at the appointed times . . . [supplied by the sale of Irish corn] that filled the autumn grain ships, that left the pier at Gortnaree for English ports, that filled hundreds of hungry English bellies, that filled the pockets of Mrs. MacMahon, his sons, and their hardworking conscientious stewards. (35–6)

Since this is the only direct authorial statement in any of Johnston's novels, we might assume it reveals her own moral and political position. And yet this trenchant condemnation is subverted narratively a number of times in this novel. For example, when Major MacMahon recalls the local eruption of the Civil War, it is the speciousness of the republicans' courage he – and Johnston – fix on, their anger more intent on punishing traitor republicans than the hated landlord to whom, in Johnston's novels, a begrudging respect is always due. Before the armed fury of the landlord, the republicans flee, daring only the quailing act of burning down the steward's lodge, not the Big House itself. One might resist this equation of author and character were it not that Johnston repeats this transaction in another text. In *The Old Jest*, set in the same period in Irish history, the fecklessness of the republicans is repeated, when a similar group flee before the authority of two fey old women, armed with nothing but their Bentley and the remnants of their former position. Where the insurgents are effective in their terrorist activities in *The Old Jest*, it is because these acts are performed by a glamourously portrayed political refugee from the Anglo-Irish Ascendency class, Major Angus Barry.

Johnston sees the injustice of the inequity but cannot shake a class prejudice that the "luck" of her Paddy's and her Sean's and her ubiquitous Bridie's cannot "run high enough to reach / The gifts that govern men . . .". The owners of the Houses, even in their contemporary derelict condition, may be drunken sots, but they can still wear their regimental ties properly; their drunken servants and peasants are merely bestial. The exception to this rule are the female nannies, an Anglo-Irish version of the faithful servant myth: these women support unwaveringly the privilege of the landed family in exchange for a measure of power over the physical lives of the privileged young. Stewards form an intermediate, separate class, and from this group can rise gifted individuals. The one instance in these Big House books where Johnston creates the possibility of gifted leadership among the lower classes is in the son of the steward, Cathal Dillon of *Fool's Sanctuary*. But even Cathal is obliterated by an act of noble self-sacrifice that perpetuates class privilege, and by a narrative necessity that demands punishment for two violent acts: belonging to the republican cause during the Civil War and daring to love a woman of the landed class.

Johnston's Big House myth is yet more complicated and conflicted. In *How Many Miles to Babylon?* and *Fool's Sanctuary* the male owners of large estates realize how unjust is their privilege. They are interlopers, and by the First World War they know their days are numbered; they maintain, none the less, a sense of stewardship toward the land they hold. In a scene of fatherly advice, young Alexander is told:

Here, the land must come first. You understand. It is this country's heart. It was taken from the people. We . . . I must be clear . . . We took it from the people. I would like to feel that it will, when the moment comes, be handed back in good order. (*Babylon* 42–3)

He speaks of the people but means only the land: "In this country the land is our most important asset. . . . Life can be very barren, my boy. Never forget that in these parts the earth is far from barren" (33). Yet four pages earlier in the text, the father had acquiesced in his wife's forbidding of any communication with Jerry, a tenant's child: "Chaos can set in so easily" (29). When Alexander eventually disobeys this class imperative, he pays for the transgression with his own death.

Mr Martin of *Fool's Sanctuary*, more enlightened and less a tool of his wife, devotes his life to drainage schemes and the "Bolshevist" redistribution of rural Ireland, a project he shares with his steward and "one true friend":

Servant, some people would have said; master and servant. But it never seemed like that to me.

They never called each other by their Christian names, that is true; nor ate formally in each other's houses. But their lives were so bound together, their dreams were the same dreams, their tragedies the same tragedies, they spoke a language to each other that none of the rest of us really understood. (35)

The partnership of master and servant in this novel serves to exonerate this landlord's continuing control of the countryside, since he is holding and

improving the land while waiting, not for the revolution, but the "demo-
cratic evolution" of the country (34–44).

Fool's Sanctuary, the latest of the novels discussed here, is the only one
that offers this kind of alternative, albeit fruitless, economic vision. The
novel offers another oddly unhistorical detail; after the father's death, his
daughter Miranda remains in possession of his estate until her own death 40
years later because her older brother chooses not to return to Ireland. *Fool's
Sanctuary* is, however, in many ways a disappointing repetition of
Johnston's earlier Civil War novels. Like the eponymous house itself it is,
textually, a "romantic ruin full of ghosts". It is as though in this novel the
author retreated from her more adventurous path and decided, like her
memory tormented protagonist Miranda, to play her play again (2, 132).
Miranda's solitude is completely without issue and depends for its particular
form of embalmed mourning on the unlikely chance of her retaining
tenancy of her brother's estate.

Fool's Sanctuary shares with Johnston's other Big House books a curious
slant on marital relations in a time when women had little economic or
legal power: the benevolent stewardship of the patrilineal heir is blocked
by, at worst a vicious, at best an unsettlingly restless, wife who subverts the
landlord's plans. In what must be at least to some extent a distortion of the
historical reality, the wives of the Big Houses are the "bloods", hunting and
riding and socializing while their gentler, put-upon husbands stay home to
mind the hearth and land. When the women are trapped at home in the
country they tend to play Chopin in a "black burning rage" or soulful
Brahms that haunts their progeny throughout a lifetime. In *The Captains
and the Kings* and *How Many Miles to Babylon?* the women actually destroy
their husbands and sons. Such ruinous actions co-exist with two other
features of Johnston's novels: a pathological obsession of sons with their
mothers and a striking misogyny among the married men as a result of
which they withdraw from their women's lives, pursuing not other
women, but all-male companionship. Thus does Johnston recreate
woman-hating myths about Woman the Devourer, or that familiar Irish
archetype, the cannibal Mother. Married women, especially those who are
mothers, are treated with considerable hostility by Johnston: even Mrs
Logan of *Shadows on Our Skin* is grotesquely unattractive, although in this
working-class novel a different set of social "verities" pertain, and Johnston
makes her the brutalized victim of a monstrous husband and inescapable
poverty.

Johnston's Big House myth is not asserting the power of women over
men, but the evil effects, on women, men and children, of female entrapment. So it is interesting to note that Johnston's three most recent novels
have female protagonists who choose to live apart from men. In the earlier
The Captains and the Kings, hapless Clare Prendergast rejoices quietly in her
daughter's double firsts at Cambridge:

"I suppose it means she'll have no difficulty in getting a good job."
"No problem at all. All sorts of doors open to her."
"She won't have to rely on getting married then." (130)

This baldly states the traditional economic necessities of women's marital choices. But with the publication of *The Christmas Tree* (1981), *The Railway Station Man* (1984) and *Fool's Sanctuary* (1987), Johnston narrates the possible effects of a different economic reality for women, the choice of remaining unmarried. Here female solitude is the *sine qua non* of women's survival and, in the first two, the source of their creative energy. Judging from various narrative moments in these novels, Johnston would have us believe that men living with women assume the right to exert authority, and expect as their natural prerogative, service from women.[8] Women who would be in any way autonomous must therefore escape from cohabitation. In none of Johnston's novels does she imagine the alternative of real community or even friendship with other women.

The Railway Station Man and *The Christmas Tree* present a dramatic shift in Johnston's choice of subject. (*Fool's Sanctuary*, as I said above, offers a disappointing return to an earlier formula.) In these two novels, for the first time, her protagonists are adult women, living in contemporary Ireland; they are middle-class, single, mothers and aspiring artists. Both are Protestant but learn to maintain effective ties with non-Protestants.[9] Again, Johnston is clear that such freedom depends on a particular material basis. In *The Christmas Tree*, Constance Keating's freedom is the result of a small inheritance from her grandmother. Widowed Helen Cuffe can finance her independence by virtue of state compensation paid at the death of her Provo-killed husband. Neither of these economic "opportunities" is widely available, of course, so presumably neither is this degree of freedom. Certainly in her only working-class novel, *Shadows on Our Skin*, Johnston is sensitively aware of how straitened and raw are the lives of the urban poor who cannot escape Derry's violence and poverty. So perhaps she implies a kind of judgement in her depiction of what Constance Keating and Helen Cuffe choose to do with their freedom. With their legacies, both women buy flight.

Flight is the characteristic movement in all of Johnston's novels.[10] In *The Captains and the Kings*, *How Many Miles to Babylon?*, *The Christmas Tree* and *The Railway Station Man*, the flight is an actual departure of the central character from the scene of life's previous suffering. In *The Gates*, *Shadows on Our Skin*, *The Old Jest* and *Fool's Sanctuary*, important secondary characters choose flight as their ineffectual solution to Irish-born troubles. Beyond these narrative events, however, we find the author choosing other forms of flight: the textual flight from the present into a nostalgically reconstructed past, or the use of marginal, powerless characters as our narrative window onto the novel's events. By choosing time past or characters distant from significant action, Johnston inscribes in her texts the impossibility of effective intervention in contemporary Irish society. Flight is the most prominent response Johnston offers to the intransigent Irish "Troubles". Yet what makes this movement striking – and the novels so interesting – is the tension the characters feel about choosing flight instead of engagement. This collision of divergent values functions as a critique of the narrative "resolution" that seems to glamorize solitude or flight.

At first glance, Constance Keating (*The Christmas Tree*) would not appear to be fleeing Ireland so much as fleeing a numbing bourgeois family and the Ballsbridge materialism that ensnare her mother and sister. By moving to England, she can attempt what is impossible to her at home, a career as a novelist. But England is virtually absent in this novel, an Irishwoman's desert. After a quarter of a century and three unpublished novels, she settles for another kind of immortality, having a child. But she ensures that the child will not be Irish, either genetically or culturally, another form of flight. Returning to Dublin to die, she finally writes a novel that will be published, the novel the reader is reading. This is the obvious narrative triumph. And yet another important element enters this novel for the first time in Johnston's work: the agent of the novel's delivery is an orphaned servant woman with whom Constance has managed to create a kind of rough partnership, admittedly a little matronizing, but the first "Bridie" in Johnston's fiction, capable of effective, intelligent partnership. Yet the inevitable pattern of flight recurs at the end after Constance's death when Bridie in her turn, and in the company of Constance's daughter and former lover, must depart Ireland for England.

All her life Constance Keating managed to avoid political awareness, and the Dublin of *The Christmas Tree* has no hint of the civil disorder or foreign wars that loom so importantly in the other seven novels. It is only when Constance ends up in Greece with a lover who is a survivor of the Jewish Holocaust that she is forced to inhabit a social reality larger than herself, and it is only at that moment that she has a story worth writing.

This pattern of avoidance and discovery Johnston repeats in the story of Helen Cuffe of *The Railway Station Man*. Like Constance, she has tried all her life to avoid unpleasant realities, not through active refusal but through a somnolent passive resistance. Her self-removal from Derry to the sleepy coastal village of Knappogue, Co. Donegal is meant to provide impenetrable insulation against the violence she had suffered in Derry. Early in the novel her son, a Political Science and Economics major at Trinity College, Dublin, sententiously attempts to provoke Helen into political awareness:

What on earth do you know about the truth of things? The actuality. You sit on the side of this hill and stare at the sea. Your house is warm, you have enough to eat, nobody bothers you. What have you ever known about anything. . . . It's one of the great enemies we have to fight against. Bourgeois complacency.

But she rejects his "slogans" with a weary rejoinder: "I don't have to listen if I don't want to. That's one of the things freedom is about. Anyway, when you've something new to say . . . oh God, when anyone has something new to say I will listen . . ." (32–3). The trouble is no one seems to have anything new to say, the Irish imagination numbed by blighting distinctions between Protestant and Catholic, IRA and RUC, violence and quietism.[11] When Helen's son and lover join her former husband as accidental victims of the "Troubles", she becomes obsessed with the political realities but has difficulty knowing how to act politically.

Helen suffers more "actuality" than any one person should bear. Like Mrs Logan of *Shadows on Our Skin*, another revolutionary's mother, she longs for a cessation of the violence and the chance to live one's life as one wishes. By the end of the novel, Johnston has demonstrated that one cannot flee far enough in Ireland to be safe from random violence. Helen has "freedom" but no peace. Mrs Logan has neither peace nor freedom, but still has a very definite view of what is needed for Northern Ireland:

> Is there a job for every man? And a home for everyone? Have all the children got shoes on their feet? Are there women down there scrubbing floors to keep the home together because stupid, useless old men are sitting around gassing about freedom? . . . . Take your bloody fairy tales out of this house before I . . .

At this point her husband forcibly reminds her of her reality:

> "Before what?" He taunted her. "I'll get out of my own house in my own good time and no befores or beafters from you." (154)

Mrs Logan earns the money that keeps the house going, but is not the head of the family that inhabits it. She is too beaten and helpless to work towards her vision of a just society. And yet her Utopian dream of "a proper job with a future, a bit of security, money to buy a nice wee house with a bit of a garden" (135) is the material reality of Helen Cuffe's life. From her financially more cushioned perch, Helen has concocted a blander political philosophy: "We all have a right to live the way we want" (*Railway Station Man* 97). This appeal to "rights" is more a fantasy than a plan, its libertarian basis no bulwark against aggressive evil. Voicing the dilemma of a decent person just wanting to live and let live, she is reassured by her lover: "Only in art, Helen, is there any approach to perfection achieved. In living there is none. There never can be. I sometimes think the man with the gun sees more clearly than we, poor tired creatures of good will" (152). Because of the authority Johnston gives this speaker and Helen's subsequent success as artist, one assumes this statement carries considerable authorial agreement. Needless to say, this is one of the world's oldest myths. And politically one of the most ineffectual. With such narrative interventions does Johnston fuel the attitudes of her critics who compliment her on her perfect, timeless art, with neither "movement" nor "lesson". But one can read another, political, subtext in this novel.

I pointed out earlier that in *The Christmas Tree* Johnston for the first time imagines a convincing if unequal partnership between a Protestant woman of independent means and a young, Catholic woman hired to help her. In *The Railway Station Man*, Johnston creates an even more remarkable partnership, this time between Helen Cuffe and a young Catholic odd-job man named Damian Sweeney. He, a former political revolutionary, she a multiple victim of terrorism, manage to create a friendship that bridges the cultural and personal chasm separating them. But this miracle of human understanding is possible only because both had, in their previous lives of self-chosen isolation, submitted themselves to a rigorous discipline of refusing any inherited Irish orthodoxies. Both were able to see with a new kind of vision that made possible, for them at least, a new kind of world. In other words, this novel, and to a lesser extent *The Christmas Tree*, move beyond Johnston's earlier character-as-prisoner-of-history model to a view of human isolation as prelude to liberation. When the novel ends, we are left with the hope – an important one – of this new form of relationship, the first successful cross-caste friendship that extends beyond the end of a Johnston novel. A small revolution, perhaps, especially since Damian's virtue depends, to some extent, on the fact that he, like Helen, has withdrawn from active political participation. And yet, in its limited way, their successful friendship can work against the "grain of the time and place" without being destroyed by the circumstances of the time and place.

In Johnston's Big House novels, we find a collision of ideologies: an acute sense of the evils wrought by religious, economic and caste distinctions, but always accompanied by a narrative subversion of her implied ideal of egalitarian justice. Moreover, in choosing subjects from the past, she perpetuates old failures in Irish history, gilding them in comforting melancholy that glamorizes their tragic endings. *Shadows on Our Skin* and *The Christmas Tree* move us into contemporary history, but create a sense of the multiple ways in which the problems exceed the will and the imagination of the Irish. The triumph of *The Railway Station Man* is that it hesitantly suggests the possibility of a different social and political future.

Earlier in this study, I quoted from an interview with Jennifer Johnston in which she claimed that Irish writers, with the exception of the northern Field Day writers, are not socially concerned. She laments this withdrawal, arguing that Irish writers should be not the "voice of the people" but the "conscience of the people":

> I think if you are going to be the conscience of the people, you've got to undermine the whole system so that all the people know what you're saying. There's no point in just intellectuals reading and agreeing and disagreeing. ("Q and A" 27)

She says she is "much too frightened" to aspire to this role of artist as conscience. The alternate vision of *The Railway Station Man*, the book she was writing at the time of the interview, suggests otherwise. It remains to be seen if her large readership will follow her onto this more challenging path, and if she will avoid another flight of the sort she attempted in *Fool's Sanctuary*.

Notes

1 All eight of these were first published by Hamish Hamilton, London: *The Captains and the Kings* (1972), *The Gates* (1973), *How Many Miles to Babylon?* (1974), *Shadows on Our Skin* (1977), *The Old Jest* (1979), *The Christmas Tree* (1981), *The Railway Station Man* (1984) and *Fool's Sanctuary* (1987).

2 McMahon, "Anglo-Irish Attitudes"; Donnelly; Mortimer; Benstock; Deane, "Jennifer Johnston"; Lubbers, "Irish Fiction"; Imhof; Burleigh; Kosok; Connolly.

3 The capital letter here ("Woman") is Benstock's, and is a useful way of designating a specific genre of writing.

4 Jennifer Johnston offered this information in an informal public gathering at the Canadian Irish Studies Association Meeting in Montreal, Quebec, March 1988.

5 This theory of bourgeois aesthetics is developed by Robinson, "Working/Women/Writing" 226.

6 See 468–9. For a very different view of Jane Austen's "world", see Williams 113–15.

7 "The 'real' Irish (the peasant Catholic Irish) seem only to enter this world – and thus Molly Keane/Farrell's faithful rendering – as a sub-species, good for opening gates and giving amusing, barely subservient lip service, the words and rhythms of which were recounted as hilarious anecdotes with broguish emphasis on the Oirishness of it all" (Devlin).

8 In *The Railway Station Man* and, to a lesser extent in *The Christmas Tree*, Johnston makes multiple opportunities to show how men of all the classes – fathers, husbands, sons, even the male companion of a son – expect as a kind of birthright, service from the attendant women of their class, or the service of servants. The only men who resist this behaviour are those like Damian Sweeney and Roger Hawthorne (*The Railway Station Man*) or Jacob Weinberg (*The Christmas Tree*) who challenge a number of social orthodoxies.

9 It is interesting to note that Constance's sister, Bibi, converts to Catholicism in order to marry a wealthy Catholic lawyer, and that this hitherto unthinkable betrayal is treated as a mere social convenience that provides Bibi with the same sort of life as that lived by their Anglican mother.

10 Throughout all her novels, one finds an almost obsessive use of bird imagery, most particularly in the moments of extreme stress, as the swans, rooks or larks simply pull themselves above the scene of human suffering.

11 Seamus Deane traces very convincingly the 400-year-old history of such Irish cultural oppositions and their terrible capacity to "govern our responses and limit our imaginations" ("Civilians and Barbarians" 42).

8

Tropes and traps: Aspects of "Woman" and nationality in twentieth-century Irish drama

David Cairns and Shaun Richards

Seamus Deane has asserted that in the present moment "The cultural machinery of Romantic Ireland has . . . taken over in the North . . ." with the consequence that the issues which dominated in the politics of Ireland in the late nineteenth- and earlier twentieth-century struggles have re-emerged; Deane's view is that: "The dissolution of that mystique [of Romantic Ireland] is an urgent necessity . . . Everything, including our politics and our literature, has to be rewritten – i.e. re-read" ("Heroic Styles: The Tradition of an Idea" 58). In this chapter, we take Deane's position as the starting point for a reconsideration of some aspects of the use of images of "woman" in cultural-political struggles in early and late twentieth-century Ireland. We begin, therefore, with a consideration of the reasons Deane advances for his opposition to a perceived cultural reprise, focusing upon the form of a particular element in the Revival's cultural machinery – the trope of the "Poor Old Woman" or "Shan Van Vocht" (Sean Bhean Bhoct) as exemplified in Yeats's play *Cathleen Ní Houlihan* and Maud Gonne MacBride's tableau "Dawn". These comments then form the basis for an examination of two current dramatic engagements with Revival tropes, Tom Murphy's *Bailegangaire* and Stewart Parker's *Lost Belongings*, and for some further observations on the implications of the use of such metonymies in the earlier and the contemporary moments.

Deane's concern that the forms of the late nineteenth- and early twentieth-century Revival are being recycled derives from his belief that the current struggles in the North are informed, on the Nationalist side, by concepts of an eternal, immanent, national identity. Clearly, given the disparity in material power between that available to metropolitan Britain and Irish separatism in the early twentieth-century struggle, some form of enabling myth was essential to the task of convincing nationalists that theirs was a struggle predestined to succeed – but more than that, as Hayden White has argued, "A given culture is only as strong as its power to convince its least dedicated members that its fictions are truths" (6). Hence in the earlier Revival, the elaboration of ideological materials, including plays, was of vital importance, first, in convincing Irish readers and audiences of the inevitable success of separatism by countering contemporary Unionist assertions of an Anglo-Saxon or Teuton Imperial destiny in which the Irish should merge, and second, as a part of what Conor Cruise O'Brien, writing in *The Observer* in 1985, termed a "rhetorical competition [taking place between contending groups of nationalists] involving the glorification of past insurrections etc. . . . and which was about being able to take the credit and the power" for bringing about independence.

In plays of the Revival the presentation of "Ireland" as the "Poor Old Woman" or "Shan Van Vocht" had obvious advantages for dramatists, stemming from the popularity of the trope in ballads and Irish language poems, and its familiarity to audiences whose reading of it was unambiguously nationalist. In what is now its best known literary form, Yeats's play *Cathleen Ní Houlihan*, the unlooked-for arrival of the "Poor Old Woman" in a household preparing for the marriage of the eldest son, and her easily understood metaphorical account of her/Ireland's tribulation over the generations from "Too many strangers in the house", induces the bridegroom to abandon his wedding to join a rebellion (*Variorum Plays* 222). The Old Woman promises those who serve her that "They shall be remembered for ever" and a choice between serving narrow, personal, ends, or self-sacrifice on behalf of the Mother/Nation – with consequent immortality for those who heed the call, and rejuvenation for the Mother/Nation. After the bridegroom has gone to fight, his younger brother announces that national sovereignty, in the female form of Cathleen Ní Houlihan has, vampire-like, been rejuvenated. Rather than the Poor Old Woman who left the room: "I saw a young girl, and she had the walk of a queen" (231).

The lasting impact of *Cathleen Ní Houlihan* on contemporary audiences is as difficult to assess now as it was for Yeats in 1938, when in "The Man and the Echo" he asked "Did that play of mine send out / Certain men the English Shot?" (*Collected Poems* 393), though Norman Jeffares notes that the parliamentary Nationalist MP Stephen Gwynn wrote afterwards that he "went home asking . . . if such plays should be produced unless one was prepared for people to go out to shoot and be shot" (*A Commentary on the Collected Poems of W.B. Yeats* 512). Similarly, Hogan and Kilroy's observation that Yeats's play immediately inspired a number of imitations suggests some additional measure of its capacity to produce intense nationalist emotion. One of these imitations, and in their opinion the most significant, was Maud Gonne MacBride's "Dawn" (Hogan and Kilroy 51).

"Dawn" dramatizes the dispossession of the leading figure in the community, the widowed Bride, by an interloper, a "stranger" who has evicted many families in the district. Bride has visionary powers and the play commences with an announcement by one of the characters of a prophecy that the "stranger" is soon to be driven from the land he has seized. This play, too, concludes with the sacrifice of a young man's life in the interests of Mother Ireland, only this time with the added piquancy that it is the life of the son of the widowed Bride, seeking atonement for joining the British Army which has killed his father and enforced his Mother's dispossession. "Mother, forgive me", he begs, "Let me, too, die for you . . . I have vengeance to take for all that you have suffered"(84). The "Dawn" of the title is revealed as "the red sun that rises with our luck" as the men go out to make "Bride of the Sorrows Bride of the Victories" (85).

Both Yeats's and Maud Gonne MacBride's plays display the more significant elements of this major trope of the Revival: an idealized *persona* suffering historic wrongs; the sacrifice of a few in each generation to maintain this entity; recurrent heroic failures to eject the invader, which will culminate finally in regained independence. In such a form the linear presentation – from historic dispossession to the defeat of the interloper – becomes in itself a guarantee of the ultimate success of insurgency.

Whereas for some writers, "Cathleen Ní Houlihan" or the "Shan Van Vocht" was no more than a convenient representational form, there is clear evidence that many others, including among them two of the leaders of the Easter Rising, Patrick Pearse and Joseph Mary Plunkett, believed in "Mother Ireland" and "Roisin Dubh" as real personalities. Their charged rhetoric in poetry and prose was augmented by the nature of their deaths, which with liturgical solemnity translated their works from the status of polemic to founding truths. Thus endorsed, the notion of an Ireland, symbolically represented as "woman", whose destiny was to be independent and united, passed into the educational and cultural formation of two generations of Irish men and women. Subsequent endorsements of the notion of a temporally transcendent, immanent nationality, served to bracket together essential "Irishness" and "the Gael", itself a stereotype of "hypermasculinity" (Nandy, *Intimate Enemy* 50–2). In its origin, as we have shown elsewhere, the category of "the Gael" emerged in the later nineteenth century as writers and political activists such as D.P. Moran and Michael Cusack sought to negate the Anglo-Saxonist anti-Irish stereotype of the "Celt", in which the political subordination of the Irish was underpinned by the femininity of their race and by the masculinity of the Anglo-Saxons (Cairns and Richards, "Woman in the Discourse of Celticism" 46). The need to ensure the stability of the Gael's hypermasculinity, through maintenance of Irish women's dependence, may explain why many nationalist groups, including the parliamentarians and the Ancient Order of Hibernians, were determined to resist the enfranchisement of women – despite the congruence, as Cliona Murphy notes, that contemporaries detected in the cases then being advanced for national and women's emancipation (164–95). In political terms, this resistance was grounded in the needs of the parliamentarians to garner support from the majority of Irish electors – the tenant farmers – and in the dictates of the contemporary realities of rural Ireland's familist economy, an especially stringent form of patriarchy (Cairns and Richards, *Writing Ireland* 42–3; 58–63). Together, these interdependent cultural and material constraints ensured that while "those women who put nationalism before [emancipation] . . . almost immediately acquired a revered place in the sphere of folk history as heroines" (*Cliona Murphy* 1), Cathleen Ní Houlihan's corporeal sisters were marginalized within the political process of the decolonizing of Ireland. This marginalization was a direct consequence, Margaret Ward and Cliona Murphy suggest, of decisions within the womens' nationalist group *Cumann na mBan* to give absolute priority to the independence struggle over the achievement of emancipation, lest the nationalist movement, which after 1916 was under the umbrella of Sinn Féin, should be split (Ward 249–54; Cliona Murphy 200–3). In relation to women, therefore, post-colonial nationalism in Ireland continued to develop on the basis of discourses which themselves had derived from negating, rather than deconstructing, colonialist discourses (Chatterjee 30). This included the idealization of woman in public and private culture through the cult of the Virgin, the poetry and dramas of the Revival, and the subordination of women domestically and politically – later to be confirmed by the 1937 Constitution, *Bunreacht na hÉireann* (Scannell 124–7).

Notwithstanding the impact of the Rising in endorsing the trope of the "Poor Old Woman", reactions to its inherently disabling qualities were to be observed almost from the moment of its consolidation. Thus, as the trope was triumphantly mobilizing the forces of the Rising, Eoin MacNeill could say: "We have to remember that what we call our country is not a poetical abstraction. There is no such person as Caitlin ni Uallachain or Rosin Dubh or the Sean-bhean Bhocht, who is calling on us to serve her. What we call our country is the Irish nation, which is a concrete and visible reality" (Dalton 352). The reaction to the power of the image has been particularly powerfully expressed in literature: from *Ulysses* where the old milk woman is described as a "lowly form of an immortal", one whose "Old shrunken paps" (12) promise no sustenance, through Beckett's deliberately provocative description of Miss Counihan in *Murphy*: "Standing in profile against the blazing corridor, with her high buttocks and her low breasts she looked not merely queenly, but on for anything" (123), to Paul

Muldoon's contemporary poetic evocation of "Anorexia" in a savage inversion of the traditional *aisling* (*Quoof* 39).

In drama, the work of Synge and O'Casey – particularly the latter's
Dublin Trilogy – contrast the dominant demands of sacrifice for an
idealized Ireland, while the lot of the flesh and blood woman is denied; in
Synge the denial of sexuality, in O'Casey the denial of material need.
"Ireland", swears Jack Clitheroe in *The Plough and the Stars*, is "greater than
a wife" (178), and he condemns himself to death in the Easter Rising and
his wife to the delivery of a still born child and consequent insanity. The
need to break free of the constraining trope of the "Old Woman" and the
grip of the past was forcefully articulated by Sean O'Faolain in his first
editorial in *The Bell* in 1940: the time was ripe for the abandonment of the
"old symbolic words. They are", he said, "as dead as . . . the Shan Van
Vocht . . . Roisin Dubh . . . Cathleen Ní Houlihan . . ." (McMahon 13).

Clearly then, this trope of the "Poor Old Woman" and the practice of
using "woman" as a symbol of sovereignty was widely understood and (in
some quarters at least) subject to deconstruction. This is not to say, of
course, that this was the only, or even the major, trope of the pre-Rising
Revival: in terms of impact there can be no doubt that the trope of Ireland,
and those who fought for Ireland, as Christ Crucified/Christ Risen was far
more significant – culturally and politically. Pearse's plays, stories and
poems are redolent with these images, and we should not misread the
warning from Deane that we have focused upon, to imply that only the
imagery of *Cathleen Ní Houlihan*, the Abbey Theatre and its precursors and
imitators, is being currently recycled. To read Bobby Sands's poetry, prose
and polemics is to realize that he recycles the images of Pearse – and those
of the Young Irelanders who inspired Pearse. In Sands's poetry and prose,
Pearse's images are translated to the situation of the "H Blocks" and the
"Dirty Protest", linking the Volunteer to the suffering Christ, as for example in "The Torture Mill – H Block":

> Blessed is the man who stands
> Before his God in pain,
> And on his back a cross of woe
> His wounds a gaping shame,
> For this man is a son of God
> And hallowed be his name (*Skylark* 75)

But elsewhere, for example in "Ghosts in my Tomb" (120–1), Ireland is
"Roísin Dubh", which in "The Sleeping Rose" will only bloom again
when Munster men rise (148), a clear echo of Plunkett's poem "The Little
Black Rose Shall be Red at Last" and Mangan's "Dark Rosaleen" (Cairns
and Richards, *Writing Ireland* 103). There is, then, ample justification for the
warning note struck by Seamus Deane in his 1984 article, "Remembering
the Irish Future".

Here, Deane adopted the terminology of the American philosopher and psychologist William James, which the latter had used to describe the opposed and dominant temperaments to which most people were assigned – the Tough Minded and The Tender Minded. In the case of the Tender-Minded there is a preference for a single point of view: "They would give their assent, even devotion, to concepts like race, nationality, faith and they would respect the past". Opposed to this position is that of the Tough-Minded, who "Would be inclined towards innovation, change, an escape from traditional pieties which they would see as restrictive and binding". As Deane surveyed the preceding decades of economic expansion, he concluded that "we have not escaped from history into prosperity after all. The siren-call of the Tender-Minded has become audible again. Just as the scar-tissue of material advancement had begun to form, the old wounds opened again – Identity, National Character, Historical Destiny" ("Remembering" 81). "The dissolution of that mystique is an urgent necessity", he subsequently argued, demanding that: "Everything, including our politics and our literature, has to be rewritten – i.e. re-read" ("Heroic Styles" 58).

Re-writing and re-reading was (and is) urgent, according to Deane, because of the need to ensure that materials and mechanisms touted as having been centrally important to Ireland's early twentieth-century struggle (such as the materials recycled by Sands) were not allowed to be mobilized in the North without challenge, and implicit in his call to action is a desire to avoid any repetition of the outcome of the earlier struggle. Central to this task on the cultural field is what Gayatri Spivak has termed "tropological deconstruction" (225), and it is on two recent dramatic manifestations of this tendency to deconstruction – Stewart Parker's six-part television drama serial *Lost Belongings*, shown on British television in the spring of 1987, and Tom Murphy's play *Bailegangaire*, first performed by the Druid Theatre Company, Galway, in December 1985, and subsequently transferred to London's Donmar Warehouse theatre in 1986 – that the remainder of this chapter focuses.

Parker's "play" can be most usefully approached from the standpoint which Richard Kearney adopted in his analysis of Joyce's *Ulysses* within the context of "Myth and Motherland", which, with Deane's "Civilians and Barbarians", appeared in the first Field Day pamphlet series in 1983. "Joyce", suggests Kearney, "revolts against the use of myth to sacrifice the creative individual to tribal cults. By demythologizing the fetishized myths of the Motherland, he hoped to emancipate the self from the constraints of the past" (Kearney 73). As the name of the female protagonist, and the title of the opening part of Parker's *Lost Belongings* series, informs its audience, this is the story of Deirdre, and Parker, in his prefatory comments to the published script, confirms that his intention was to create a latter-day version of the Deirdre myth. His commentary on his source concludes: "Although a modern audience would be unaware of the source, I'm convinced that stories as timeless as this one contain a universal resonance, which lends them infinitely more value than a merely anecdotal narrative" (Parker 4). Parker's "play" is a six-part television serial and this, inevitably, poses problems of both reception and retention of the complex plot strand, most crucially in the nature of what Parker, after Marshall McLuhan, recognizes to be a "cool medium" in which the serial is sandwiched between comedy and sport, its dramatic intensity punctuated by advertisements. Moreover, as Claudia Harris has noted in "A Living Mythology", the train of narrative can be easily lost, as even when a missed screening can be taped it is sometimes not viewed in time to re-establish continuity. Parker, however, recognized the inherent problems and his decision to present *Lost Belongings* as a television serial is a testimony to his belief in the importance of the medium and, moreover, his belief that the centrality of the issues he wished to dramatize required that they be transmitted through the culturally central means of communication and entertainment. As Parker himself observed:

> I don't understand how any serious playwright in this day and age can fail to rise to the challenge of it. It is not merely the great popular medium of the time, it is part of the fabric of people's lives to a degree which is unprecedented. It is not merely the real national theatre, but the multinational one to boot. (Harris 15)

While there were recognized limitations in the medium, however, the present intention is to address problems inherent in the adoption of a mythic narrative to a contemporary situation.

In the final part of the series the contemporary Deirdre, daughter of a scandalous cross-sectarian love affair, escapes from imprisonment by her hard-line Unionist uncle – a situation which has clearly deranged her – and, pregnant by her Catholic boyfriend, crosses a nightmarish townscape of modern-day Belfast, and is finally picked up by an RUC patrol car. The viewer's access to the state of Deirdre's mind is purely through the television images. The final seven sequences are as follows:

Deirdre sits in the back of the police car, cradling the doll. Looking down at the doll, she sees a bloodstain slowly blooming through the material of her maternity dress, between her legs. She has begun to miscarry. She digs her nails into the flesh of her forehead, drags them down across her cheeks to her mouth, leaving a trail of weals, then thrusts her fingers into her mouth to stifle herself (Parker 296).

The next sequence is a Goyaesque street scene; a wounded carthorse struggling to lift itself upright within the shafts of a junk cart, the burning contents of which are strewn across the street, while the driver lies in the road calling for help.

The police car arrives, the RUC men exit into a hail of gunfire. The camera focuses on Deirdre: "with her fingers still jammed in her mouth". She clutches the doll, claws at the handle, gets the door open, pushes her way out, leaving a circle of blood on the seat upholstery.

The next sequence sees her dragging herself along the railings of a church "with a huge, ugly fluorescent cross on the side of it". The soundtrack is made up of the crackling of a burning vehicle and the sound of gunfire. "She lies, writhing and moaning, clutching the doll" (297).

There follow two sequences, one in the hospital where her boyfriend Niall is incapacitated as a result of the two broken legs inflicted on him by Deirdre's uncle, and one at a concert in the Ulster Hall. The concert has been one of a "James Galway" style escapee from Ulster into the prosperity of the international concert circuit but, as the audience applauds and he prepares for an encore, "He deliberately launches into a savagely discordant, atonal piece". This music continues over what is the final sequence: "Deirdre dying under the neon cross." The final directions are central to Parker's purpose: "She raises her head, looks straight at us. The face is wracked and lacerated. The gaze is steady and lacerating. It is a death of youth, love, hope and vision – staring us unforgivingly in the face" (299). The intention of the serial was, as Parker expressed it, "to provoke shame and rage, that she should be let die" (7).

The focus on the woman – Deirdre – particularly as she miscarries and dies in mute but "unforgiving" (Parker's word) anger, reveals the intention of "tropological deconstruction". Whereas the classic trope saw death as redeeming and transforming – the old woman becoming the young girl with the walk of a queen – Parker inverts the sequence to show the degeneration of youth and beauty, with death, rather than life, being the outcome of rigid adherence to the modes of thought inherited from the past. Deirdre is both character and symbol. She is grounded in contemporary reality so as to be representative of a generation scarred by conflict yet, through the mythic underpinning, and – albeit, inversion of – the trope, she is also symbol of an Ireland whose beauty degenerates into a condition which is truly terrible. Parker has been explicit as to the intention behind his adaptation of the myth, seeing it as the job of the artist to construct a model of wholeness for Northern Ireland. As he argued in his John Malone Memorial Lecture in 1986: "Alternative versions of the historical myths sacred to each of the communities have been staged: not in a spirit of mockery but in a spirit of realism and out of a desire to substitute vibrant and authentic myths for the false and destructive ones on which we have been weaned" (Harris 16).

In this series it is Parker's use of the Deirdre myth itself which raises questions as to the clarity of his achievement, for while the narrative replays the destructive outcome of the original, Parker's intention, in statement if not technique, is decidedly Brechtian. As Brecht argued in "A Short Organum for the Theatre", the major social problem was that "The same attitude as men once showed in the face of unpredictable natural catastrophes they now adopt to their own undertakings" (185). "We need a type of theatre", he went on, "which not only releases the feelings, insights and impulses possible within the particular field of human relations in which the action takes place, but employs and encourages those thoughts and feelings which help transform the field itself' (190). What Parker intends is that the audience will be sufficiently aroused by this destructive reprise to act – and so alter the next run of the narrative. The problem is that the very oppressive nature of an "inherited" narrative carries with it intimations of inevitability.

In part, Parker's intention may have been that of Shaw – to make the audience feel like guilty creatures, but the linear narrative, whose outcome is determined by that of the received version of the myth – acting as a "Fate" in this context – and the TV "thriller" format, impose constraints on the drama which has itself no "space" for audience reflection in which the possibility of alternatives may be perceived. "How many times must the death of Deirdre Connell be re-enacted" asks Parker in his comments on the play (8). The answer is, "when the narrative is ended": the theme and dramatic substance of Murphy's *Bailegangaire*.

This play is set in "the country kitchen . . . of the traditional three-room thatched house" (Thomas Murphy 9) but elements of the set – the radio and the electric light, and later references to a Japanese computer factory which is on the verge of closure (45) – confirm that the set is symbolic of the condition which Murphy intends to dramatize – and, indeed, exorcize – the extension of modes of the past into the consequent restricted life of the present. The set, along with the central focus on an old woman, evokes plays of "peasant quality" and central images of Ireland as the Shan Van Vocht. The release from the past and the demythologizing of the dominant trope is central to Murphy's objective, his cultural prescription that articulated in the play by Mary: "And she never finishes it – Why doesn't she finish it? And have done with it. For God's sake" (19). The Old Woman – Mommo – is, like Ireland we might infer, locked into a narrative, the conclusion and implications of which she is incapable of finishing and facing. It is a situation into which the descendants of the old woman are bound, moreover, until Mary, one of the granddaughters, recognizes that only by finishing the narrative and exorcizing the memory of bleakness and death which has scarred the past, will harmony and the hope of a future return. Mary herself enters the story, imitating and prompting Mommo to the release of finally taking the tale to its conclusion, and to admitting the knowledge of the death of her grandson in a paraffin fire into present consciousness. As Mary observes: "I can't do anything the way things are" (46), and the movement of the drama, overlaying the finally linear movement of Mommo's narrative, is towards the point where Mommo can finish the tale and, as her acknowledgement of Mary by name implies, come at last to a recognition of the present. As articulated by Mary, her strategy is to "Live out the story – finish it, move on to a place where, perhaps, we could make some kind of new start" (61).

Murphy's play – indeed all his work – is central to this recognition of the need for "tropological deconstruction" as his career has, in the words of Fintan O'Toole, run parallel with the period in which "Ireland was gradually ceasing to think of herself as the Island of Saints and Scholars whose greatest export was missionaries to the Black Babies, and to try on the image of what the Industrial Development Authority's advertisements in *Time* and *Newsweek* would soon be calling 'The Most Profitable Industrual Location in Europe' " (O'Toole 29).

Parker's consideration of the Deirdre myth as having "universal resonance" and "timelessness' and his presentation of the woman Deirdre as the object of violence (presumably also timeless?) indicate how urgently the deconstruction of the trope of idealized woman as suffering Ireland is needed. In this respect, Murphy's play, with its advocated abandonment of the old story and its reprises, represents a powerful dramatic support to the demands of women such as Joanna McMinn (in "It Ain't What You Do") that they receive less adoration and more material support, demands which themselves indicate a concerned awareness that some at least of the tropes of the earlier Revival are being recycled for contemporary duty.

Contemporary textual evidence, then, supports the contention that identity formed in a narrative of the past, informed by tropes whose vital moment is over, is incomplete; is indeed, as Parker's play suggests, destructive or, as in Murphy's, inhibiting. As Margaret Ward shows, the trap sprung upon Irish women in post-Independence Ireland led to the prioritization and "liberation" of an abstraction, rather than action to remedy the economic, social and political disadvantages of the living (and emigrating) women of Ireland (Lee 374–86). In this, Ward's account clearly undercuts McKillen's more optimistic conclusion that the activities of *Cumann na mBan* gave rise to a heightening of feminist consciousness and achievement. (Ward 252; McKillen 66–7; Cliona Murphy 5, 200). In this particular respect "the dissolution of [the] mystique [of Romantic Ireland] is an urgent necessity' (Deane, "Heroic Styles" 58).

As E.F. O'Doherty put the case in 1963, before the present resurgence of old modes of thought and feeling:

> One cannot change the economic underpinning of our way of life, our self-image as a nation, and our role in international affairs without accepting as a necessary concomitant, radical and far reaching consequences in the structure and culture of our society . . . The fear that we may be lost as a cultural or political entity in the world of the future is only too well grounded if our thinking is that we must resist or resent change and merely preserve the past. That way is impossible and that way lies stagnation and death. (134)

Twenty years later Deane has made the point even more succinctly: "We should start from actualities not from abstractions . . . Identity is here and now, not elsewhere and at another time" ("Remembering" 91).

Works cited

Andrews, Elmer. *The Poetry of Seamus Heaney*. London: Macmillan, 1988.

Anon. "Elise in Search of a Blouse". *Sinn Féin* (1 December 1906): 1.

Ardener, Shirley, ed. *Perceiving Women*. London: Dent, 1975.

Arnold, Matthew. *On the Study of Celtic Literature and Other Essays*. London: Dent, 1976.

Auerbach, Nina. "Engorging the Patriarchy". In Shari Benstock, ed., *Feminist Issues in Literary Scholarship*. Bloomington: Indiana UP, 1987, 150–60.

—— *Woman and the Demon*. Cambridge, Mass.: Harvard UP, 1982.

Austen, Jane. *Letters to Her Sister Cassandra and Others*, edited by R.W. Chapman (2nd edn). London: Oxford UP, 1952.

Bair, Deirdre. *Samuel Beckett, A Biography*. London: Cape, 1978.

"Banba". "Irish Dress Materials". *Sinn Féin* (21 July 1906): 1.

Barker, Francis *et al.*, eds. *Literature, Politics and Theory*. London: Methuen, 1986.

Beale, Jenny. *Women in Ireland: Voices of Change*. Indiana: Indiana UP, 1987.

"Beartin Fraoch". "Coláiste Connacht". *Sinn Féin* (21 July 1906): 3.

Beckett, Samuel. *All That Fall*. London: Faber and Faber, 1957.

—— *Happy Days*. London: Faber and Faber, 1963.

—— *Murphy*. London: Picador, 1973.

—— *Not I*. In *Collected Shorter Plays*. London: Faber and Faber, 1984, 213–23.

Belsey, Catherine. "Constructing the Subject: Deconstructing the Text". In Judith Newton and Deborah Rosenfelt, eds, *Feminist Criticism and Social Change*. Bloomington: Indiana UP, 1985, 45–64.

Benstock, Shari. "The Masculine World of Jennifer Johnston". In Thomas Staley, ed., *Twentieth Century Women Novelists*. London: Macmillan, 1982, 191–217.

Benton, John F. "Clio and Venus: An Historical View of Medieval Love". In F.X. Newman, ed., *The Meaning of Courtly Love*. Albany: State U of New York Press, 1968, 19–42.

Berger, Pamela. *The Goddess Obscured: Transformation of the Grain Protectress from Goddess to Saint.* Boston: Beacon Press, 1985.

Bhabha, Homi K. "The Other Question: Difference, Discrimination and the Discourse of Colonialism". In Francis Barker *et al.*, eds, *Literature, Politics and Theory.* London: Methuen, 1986, 148–72.

Binchy, D.A. *Celtic and Anglo-Saxon Kingship.* Oxford: Clarendon, 1970.

Blackstock, Charity. "Jennifer Johnston". *Books and Bookmen* 19.7 (April 1974): 93.

Blythe, Ronald. "Starving Differently". *The Listener* (28 February 1974): 281.

Boland, Eavan. "A Kind of Scar: The Woman Poet in a National Tradition". *Lip.* Dublin: Attic Press, 1989.

Breatnach, Liam. "Canon Law and Secular Law in Early Ireland. The Significance of *Bretha Nemed*". *Peritia* 3 (1984): 439–59.

Brecht, Bertolt. "A Short Organum for the Theatre". In *Brecht on Theatre.* London: Methuen, 1964, 185–90.

Broadbent, J.B. *Poetic Love.* London: Chatto & Windus, 1964.

Brown, Penelope, and Lydia Jordanova. "Oppressive Dichotomies: The Nature–Culture Debate". In Cambridge Women's Studies Group, eds, *Women in Society.* London: Virago, 1981, 224–41.

Burleigh David. "Dead and Gone: The Fiction of Jennifer Johnston and Julia O'Faolain". In Masaru Sekine, ed., *Irish Writers and Society at Large.* Gerrards Cross: Colin Smythe, 1985, 1–15.

Butler, Mary E. *Irishwomen and the Home Language.* Dublin: Gaelic League, n.d. (1900?).

Butler Cullingford, Elizabeth. "Labor and Memory in the Love Poetry of W. B. Yeats". In Susan Dick *et al.*, eds, *Essays for Richard Ellmann.* Belfast: McGill: Queens UP, 1989; Gerrards Cross: Colin Smythe, 1989, 204–19.

—— " 'Thinking of her . . . as . . . Ireland': Yeats, Pearse and Heaney". *Textual Practice* 4. 1 (1990): 1–21.

—— *Yeats, Ireland and Fascism.* London: Macmillan, 1981.

Cairns, David and Shaun Richards. "Reading a riot: the reading formation of Synge's Abbey audience". *Literature and History* 13.2 (1987): 219–37.

—— "Woman in the Discourse of Celticism: A Reading of *The Shadow of the Glen*". *Canadian Journal of Irish Studies* 13.1 (1987): 43–60.

—— *Writing Ireland: Colonialism, Nationalism and Culture.* Manchester: Manchester UP, 1988.

Callaghan, Mary Rose. "Jennifer Johnston". In Robert Hogan, ed., *Dictionary of Irish Literature.* Westport, Conn.: Greenwood Press, 1979, 315–16.

Cambridge Women's Studies Group, eds. *Women in Society.* London: Virago, 1981, 224–41.

Cameron, Deborah. *Feminism and Linguistic Theory.* N.Y.: St Martin's Press, 1985.

Campbell, Joseph. *The Hero with a Thousand Faces.* London: Sphere, 1975.

Carey, John. "Notes on the Irish War-Goddess". *Eigse* 19 (1983): 263–75.

Castle, Terry. "Lab'ring Bards: Birth Topoi and English Poetics 1660–1820". *JEGP* 78 (1979): 193–208.

Chatterjee, Partha. *Nationalist Thought and the Colonial World: A Derivative Discourse.* London: Zed Books, 1986.

Cixous, Hélène. "Sorties". In Hélène Cixous, *The Newly Born Woman*, trans. Betsey Wing. Minneapolis: U of Minnesota P, 1986, 63–132.

Coates, Jennifer. *Women, Men and Language*. London: Longman, 1986.

Cole, William. "Trade Winds". *Saturday Review* 3/4 (1978): 33.

Connolly, Joseph. "Legend and Lyric in the Selected Fiction of Jennifer Johnston". *Éire-Ireland* 21.3 (1986): 119–24.

Corcoran, Clodagh. "Pornography: The New Terrorism". *Lip*. Dublin: Attic Press, 1989.

Corcoran, Neil. *Seamus Heaney*. London: Faber and Faber, 1986.

Cosgrave, Art, ed. *Marriage in Ireland*. Dublin: College Press, 1985.

Coward, Rosalind. *Patriarchal Precedents*. London: Routledge, 1983.

Cullen, Mary. "Telling it Our Way". In Liz Steiner Scott, ed., *Personally Speaking*. Dublin: Attic Press 254–66.

Curnow, D.H. "Language and Theatre in Beckett's 'English' Plays". *Mosaic* 2 (1969): 54–65.

Curtin, Chris, Pauline Jackson and Barbara O'Connor, eds, *Gender in Irish Society*. Galway: Galway UP, 1987.

Dalton, G.F. "The Tradition of Blood Sacrifice to the Goddess Eire". *Studies*, Dublin, LXIII (1974): 343–54.

Daly, Mary. *Beyond God the Father*. London: The Women's Press, 1986.

Dante. *The Comedy of Dante Alighieri, Cantica 1: Hell*, trans. Dorothy L. Sayers, Harmondsworth: Penguin, 1949.

Davis, Richard. *Arthur Griffith and Non-Violent Sinn Féin*. Dublin: Gill and Macmillan, 1974.

De Buidleir, Maire. "Our Irish Homes". *Sinn Féin*, 17 November 1906, 1.

Deane, Seamus. *A Short History of Irish Literature*. London: Hutchinson, 1986.

—— "Civilians and Barbarians". In Field Day Theatre Company, *Ireland's Field Day*. London: Hutchinson, 1985, 33–42.

—— "Heroic Styles: The Tradition of an Idea". In Field Day Theatre Company. *Ireland's Field Day*. London: Hutchinson, 1985, 45–58.

—— "Jennifer Johnston". *Bulletin of Foreign Affairs* 1015, Dublin (February 1985): 4–6.

—— "Remembering the Irish Future". *The Crane Bag*, 8.1 (1984): 81–92.

Devlin, Polly. "Introduction". In M. J. Farrell, *The Rising Tide*. London: Virago Press, 1984, v–xvi.

Dijkstra, Bram. *Idols of Perversity*. New York: Oxford UP, 1986.

Dillon, Myles. "The Archaism of Irish Tradition". *Proceedings of the British Academy* 33 (1947 [1951]): 245–64.

Dinnerstein, Dorothy. *The Mermaid and the Minotaur: Sexual Arrangements and Human Malaise*. New York: Harper and Row, 1976.

Donnelly, Brian. "The Big House in the Recent Novel". *Studies*, 54 (1985), 133–42.

Dooley, Ann. "The Heroic Word: The Reading of Early Irish Sagas". In Robert O'Driscoll, ed., *The Celtic Consciousness*. Dublin: Dolmen; Edinburgh: Canongate, 1982, 155–9.

Dronke, Peter. *Medieval Latin and the Rise of the European Love Lyric* (2 vols). Oxford: Clarendon, 1965.

Dudley, E. and M.E. Novak, eds. *The Wild Man Within: An Image in Western Thought from the Renaissance to Romanticism*. Pittsburgh: Pittsburgh UP, 1972.

Dumézil, Georges. *The Destiny of a King*, trans. Alf Hiltebeitel. Chicago and London: U of Chicago P, 1973.

—— *The Destiny of the Warrior*, trans. Alf Hiltebeitel. Chicago and London: U of Chicago P, 1970.

Dunn, Douglas. "Strait Gate". *New Statesman* (28 January 1972): 119.

"E.B." "Herself". *Sinn Féin* (3 November 1906): 3.

Ecker, Gisela, ed. *Feminist Aesthetics*, trans. Harriet Anderson. London: The Women's Press, 1985.

Edgeworth, Maria. *Castle Rackrent* (reprint). New York: Oxford UP, 1980.

Edwards, Ruth Dudley. *Patrick Pearse: The Triumph of Failure*. London: Gollancz, 1977.

"Eibhlin". "Letters to Nora". *Sinn Féin* (5 May 1906): 4; (19 May 1906): 4; (2 June 1906): 3; (16 June 1906): 3.

Eliade, Mircea. *Patterns in Comparative Religion*. London: Sheed and Ward, 1958.

Ellmann, Mary. *Thinking about Women*. New York: Harcourt, 1968.

Empson, William. *Seven Types of Ambiguity*. Harmondsworth: Penguin, 1977.

Engels, Friedrich. "The Origin of the Family, Private Property, and the State". In Robert Tucker, ed., *The Marx-Engels Reader* (2nd edn). New York: Norton, 1978, 734–59.

Evans, Mary, ed. *The Woman Question*. London: Fontana, 1982.

Field Day Theatre Company. *Ireland's Field Day*. London: Hutchinson, 1985.

FitzGerald, Mary, ed. *Selected Plays of Lady Gregory*. Gerrards Cross: Colin Smythe, 1983.

Foster, Hal. *The Anti-Aesthetic: Essays on Postmodern Culture*. Washington: Bay Press, 1983.

Foster, John Wilson, ed. "Critical Forum: Feminism North and South, 15 Years On". *The Honest Ulsterman* 83 (Summer 1987): 39–70.

—— *Fictions of the Irish Literary Revival: A Changeling Art*. New York: Syracuse UP; Dublin: Gill and Macmillan, 1988.

Foucault, Michel. *The History of Sexuality*, trans. Robert Hurley. New York: Vintage, 1980.

Freud, Sigmund. "Fetishism". In *On Sexuality*. Harmondsworth: Penguin, 1981, 351–7.

Friedman, Susan Stamford. "Creativity and the Childbirth Metaphor: Gender Difference in Literary Discourse". *Feminist Studies* 13.1 (1987): 49–82.

Furman, Nelly. "The politics of language: beyond the gender principle". In G. Greene and C. Kahn, eds, *Making a Difference*. London: Methuen, 1985, 59–79.

Gallagher, Seán, ed. *Woman in Irish Legend, Life and Literature*. Gerrards Cross: Colin Smythe, 1983.

Gantz, Jeffrey, trans. "The Exile of the Sons of Uisliu". In *Early Irish Myths and Sagas*. Harmondsworth: Penguin, 1981, 257–67.

Genet, Jacqueline. "Heaney et l'homme des tourbieres". In Jacqueline Genet, ed., *Studies on Seamus Heaney*. Caen: Centre de Publications de l'Université de Caen, 1987, 123–47.

Gilbert, Sandra and Gubar, Susan. *No Man's Land: The Place of the Woman Writer in the Twentieth Century* (2 vols). New Haven, Conn. and London: Yale UP, 1988–9.

—— *The Madwoman in the Attic.* New Haven, Conn.: Yale UP, 1979.

Glob, P.V. *The Bog People,* trans. Rupert Bruce-Mitford. London: Paladin, 1971.

Gontarski, S.E. *Beckett's Happy Days: A Manuscript Study.* Columbus: Ohio State University Libraries, 1977.

Goodby, John. "Inner Emigrés: A Study of Seven Irish Poets (1955–1985)". Unpublished PhD thesis, University of Leeds, 1987.

—— "Ocean's Love to Ireland": Some Aspects of Stereotyping, Gender and Sexuality in Contemporary Irish poetry". Unpublished paper, n.d.

Gose, Elliott B., Jr. *The World of the Irish Wonder Tale.* Toronto: Toronto UP, 1985.

Graves, Robert. *The White Goddess.* Harmondsworth: Penguin, 1949.

Gray, John. "Field Day Five Years On". *Linenhall Review* 2.2 (1985): 4–10.

Greene, David, and Fergus Kelly, eds and trans. *The Irish Adam and Eve Story from Saltair na Rann,* Vol. 1: Text and Translation. Dublin: Dublin Institute for Advanced Studies, 1976.

Greene, G. and C. Kahn, eds. *Making a Difference: Feminist Literary Criticism.* London: Methuen, 1985.

Gregory, Lady Augusta. *Our Irish Theatre.* Gerrards Cross: Colin Smythe, 1972.

—— *Poets and Dreamers.* Gerrards Cross: Colin Smythe, 1974.

Grossman, Allen. *Poetic Knowledge in the Early Yeats.* Charlottesville: UP of Virginia, 1969.

Hadfield Paul, and Lynda Henderson. "Field Day: The Magical Mystery". *Theatre Ireland* 2 (January–May 1983), 63–9.

Hall, Michael, and Mark Langhammer, eds. *The Third Force.* Belfast: Hand To Mouth Press, 1986.

Harris, Claudia W. "A Living Mythology". *Theatre Ireland* 13 (1987): 15–16.

Hawkins, Maureen. "The Dramatic Treatment of Robert Emmet and Sarah Curran". In Seán Gallagher, ed. *Woman in Irish Legend, Life and Literature.* Gerrards Cross: Colin Smythe, 1983, 125–36.

Heaney, Seamus. "A Field Day for the Irish". *The Times* (5 December 1988): 18.

—— *Death of a Naturalist.* London: Faber and Faber, 1966.

—— *Door into the Dark.* London: Faber and Faber, 1969.

—— *Field Work.* London: Faber and Faber, 1979.

—— *North.* London: Faber and Faber, 1975.

—— *Preoccupations: Selected Prose 1968–1978.* London: Faber and Faber, 1980.

—— *Station Island.* London: Faber and Faber, 1984.

—— *The Haw Lantern.* London: Faber and Faber, 1988.

—— *Wintering Out.* London: Faber and Faber, 1972.

Heath, Stephen. "Difference". *Screen* 19.3 (1978): 51–112.

—— *The Sexual Fix.* London: Macmillan, 1982.

Heilbrun, Carolyn. *Toward a Recognition of Androgyny.* New York: Norton, 1982.

Herrick, Robert. *Poetical Works* edited by L.C. Martin. Oxford: Clarendon, 1956.

Hogan, Robert and J. Kilroy, eds. *Lost Plays of the Irish Renaissance.* New York: Proscenium Press, 1970.

Hull, Eleanor. "The Story of Deirdre in its Bearing on the Social Development of the Folk-Tale". *Folk-Lore* XV (1904): 224–39.

Hull, Vernam, ed. and trans. *Longas mac nUislenn. The exile of the sons of Uisliu*. New York: The Modern Language Association of America, 1949.

Humm, Maggie. *Feminist Criticism*. Brighton: Harvester Press, 1986.

Hutcheon, Linda. *The Politics of Postmodernism*. London: Routledge, 1989.

Hyde, Douglas. *A Literary History of Ireland*. London: Benn, 1967.

—— *The Irish Language and Irish Intermediate Education 6: Dr. Hyde's Reply to Dr. Atkinson*. Dublin: Gaelic League, n.d (1899?).

Imhof, Rüdiger. " 'A Little Bit of Ivory, Two Inches Wide': The Small World of Jennifer Johnston's Fiction". *Études Irlandaises* 10 (December 1985): 129–44.

Ingoldby, Grace. "Spook Time". *New Statesman*. (26 October 1984): 32.

Irigaray, Luce. *Speculum of the Other Woman*, trans. Gillian C. Gill. Ithaca, NY: Cornell UP, 1985.

Jackson, Kenneth Hurlstone. *The Oldest Irish Tradition: A Window on the Iron Age*. Cambridge: Cambridge UP, 1964.

Jeffares, A. Norman. *A Commentary on the Collected Poems of W.B. Yeats*. London: Macmillan, 1968.

Jeffares, A.N. and A.S. Knowland. *A Commentary on the Collected Plays of W.B. Yeats*. London: Macmillan, 1975.

Johnson, Toni O'Brien. "An Ante-text for Samuel Beckett's *Happy Days*". *Irish University Review* 19.2 (Autumn 1989): 302–9.

—— "Making Strange to See Afresh: Re-visionary Techniques in Some Contemporary Irish Poetry". *SPELL: Swiss Papers in English Language and Literature* 5, edited by Margaret Bridges. Tübingen: Gunter Narr Verlag, 1990, 141–58.

Johnston, Jennifer. *Fool's Sanctuary*. London: Hamish Hamilton, 1987.

—— *How Many Miles to Babylon?* London: Hamish Hamilton, 1974.

—— "Q and A" (interview with Michael Kenneally). *Irish Literary Supplement* 3.2 (1984): 25–7.

—— *Shadows on Our Skin*. London: Hamish Hamilton, 1977.

—— *The Captains and the Kings*. London: Hamish Hamilton, 1972.

—— *The Christmas Tree*. London: Hamish Hamilton, 1981.

—— *The Gates*. London: Hamish Hamilton, 1973.

—— *The Old Jest*. London: Hamish Hamilton, 1979.

—— *The Railway Station Man*. London: Hamish Hamilton, 1984.

Joyce, James. *A Portrait of the Artist as A Young Man*. Frogmore: Granada, 1977.

—— *Ulysses: The Corrected Text*. Harmondsworth: Penguin, 1986.

Kearney, Richard. "Myth and Motherland". In Field Day Theatre Company, *Ireland's Field Day*. London: Hutchinson, 1985, 61–80.

Kiberd, Declan. *Men and Feminism*. London: Macmillan, 1985.

—— *Synge and the Irish Language*. London: Macmillan, 1979.

Kirk, G.S. *Myth: Its Meaning and Functions in Ancient and Other Cultures*. Cambridge: Cambridge UP; Berkeley: U of California P, 1971.

Knowlson, James, ed. *A Bilingual Edition of Happy Days/Oh Les Beaux Jours*. London: Faber and Faber, 1978.

Knowlson, James, and John Pilling. *Frescoes of the Skull, The Later Prose and Drama of Samuel Beckett*. New York: Grove Press, 1980.

Kosok, Heinz. "The Novels of Jennifer Johnston". In Maria Diedrich and Christoph Schöneich, eds, *Studien zur englischen und amerikanischen Prosa nach dem Ersten Weltkrieg*. Darmstadt: Wissenschaftliche Buchgesellschaft, 1986, 98–111.

Kristeva, Julia. *Desire in Language*, trans. Thomas Gora, Alice Jardine and Leon Roudiez. Oxford: Blackwell, 1981.

—— *Étrangers à nous mêmes*. Paris: Fayard, 1988.

—— *Revolution in Poetic Language*, trans. Margaret Waller. New York: Columbia UP, 1984.

—— *The Kristeva Reader*, edited by Toril Moi. Oxford: Blackwell, 1986.

Lacan, Jacques. *Écrits*. Paris: Editions du Seuil, 1966.

—— *Le Séminaire*, XX. Paris: Éditions du Seuil, 1975.

Laity, Cassandra. "W. B. Yeats and Florence Farr: The Influence of the 'New Woman' Actress on Yeats's Changing Images of Women". *Modern Drama* 28 (1985): 621–37.

Lee, Joseph J. *Ireland 1912–1985. Politics and Society*. Cambridge: Cambridge UP, 1989.

Leerssen, Joseph. *Mere Irish & Fíor-Ghael: Studies in the Idea of Nationality, its Development and Literary Expression Prior to the Nineteenth Century*. Utrecht Publications in General & Comparative Literature, 22. Amsterdam and Philadelphia: John Benjamins, 1986.

Lenk, Elisabeth. "The Self-reflecting woman". In Gisela Ecker, ed., *Feminist Aesthetics*. London: The Women's Press, 1985, 51–8.

Levi-Strauss, Claude. *Structural Anthropology*. New York: Anchor Books, 1967.

Lewis, C.S. *The Allegory of Love* (2nd edn). New York: Oxford UP, 1958.

Lincoln, Bruce. *Myth, Cosmos, and Society: Indo-European Themes of Creation and Destruction*. Cambridge, Mass. and London: Harvard UP, 1986.

Littleton, C. Scott. *The New Comparative Mythology: An Anthropological Assessment of the Theories of Georges Dumézil* (3rd edn). Berkeley and Los Angeles: U of California P, 1982.

Longley, Edna. "From Cathleen to Anorexia: the breakdown of Irelands". *Lip*. Dublin: Attic Press, 1990.

—— "Including the North". *Text & Context* 3 (Autumn 1988): 17–24.

—— *Poetry in the Wars*. Newcastle upon Tyne: Bloodaxe Books, 1986.

Lubbers, Klaus. "Irish Fiction: A Mirror for Specifics". *Éire-Ireland* (Summer, 1985): 20–2.

Lynch, David. *Yeats: The Poetics of the Self*. Chicago: U of Chicago P, 1979.

Mac Cana, Proinsiais. "Aspects of the Theme of King and Goddess in Irish Literature". *Études Celtiques* 7 (1955–6): 76–114, 356–413; 8 (1958–9): 59–65.

—— *Celtic Mythology*. London: Hamlyn, 1970.

—— "Women in Irish Mythology". *The Crane Bag* 4.1 (1980): 7–11.

MacBride, Maud Gonne. *A Servant of the Queen*. London: Gollancz, 1938.

—— "Dawn" (n.d.). In Robert Hogan and James Kilroy, eds, *Lost Plays of the Irish Renaissance*. New York: Proscenium Press, 1970, 73–84.

MacCormack, Carol and Marilyn Strathern, eds. *Nature, Culture and Gender*. Cambridge: Cambridge UP, 1980.

Mackey, William F. "Yeats's Debt to Ronsard on a *Carpe Diem* Theme". *Comparative Literature Studies* 5.19 (1946): 4–7.

McMahon, Seán. "Anglo-Irish Attitudes: The Novels of Jennifer Johnston". *Éire-Ireland* 10 (1975): 137–41.

—— ed. *The Best From the Bell*. Dublin: O'Brien Press, 1978.

Marcus, Jane. *Art and Anger: Reading Like a Woman*. Columbus: Ohio State UP, 1988.

Mathieu, Nicole-Claude. "Man–Culture and Woman–Nature?" trans D.M. Leonard Barker. *Women's Studies International Quarterly* 1 (1978): 55–65.

McGivern, Marie Therese. "Families Under Siege" in Liz Steiner Scott, ed., *Personally Speaking*. Dublin: Attic Press, 1985, 59–73.

McKillen, Beth. "Irish Feminism and Nationalist Separation". *Eire-Ireland* 17.3 (1982): 52–67.

McMinn, Joanna. "It Ain't What You Do – Its the Way That You Do It". In Michael Hall and Mark Langhammer, eds, *The Third Force*. Belfast: Hand to Mouth Press, 1986, 26–7.

—— and Margaret Ward. "Belfast Women: Against All Odds". In Liz Steiner Scott, ed., *Personally Speaking*. Dublin: Attic Press, 1985, 189–200.

Millett, Kate. *Sexual Politics* (2nd edn). London: Virago, 1977.

Mills, Patricia Jagentowicz. *Women, Nature and Psyche*. New Haven, Conn. and London: Yale UP, 1987.

Montague, John. *A Slow Dance*. Dublin: Dolmen Press, 1972.

—— *Mount Eagle*. Oldcastle, Co. Meath: Gallery Books, 1988.

—— *Poisoned Lands*. Dublin: Dolmen Press, 1977.

—— *The Dead Kingdom*. Dublin: Dolmen Press, 1984.

—— *The Great Cloak*. Dublin: Dolmen Press, 1978.

—— *The Rough Field*. Dublin: Dolmen Press, 1972.

Moore, Virginia. *The Unicorn*. New York: Macmillan, 1954.

Morrison, Blake. *Seamus Heaney*. London: Methuen, 1982.

Mortimer, Mark. "The World of Jennifer Johnston". *Crane Bag* 4.1 (1980): 88–94.

Muldoon, Paul. *Quoof*. London: Faber and Faber, 1983.

—— *Selected Poems, 1968–1983* London: Faber and Faber, 1986.

Mueller, John P. and William J. Richardson. *Lacan and Language; A Guide to* Écrits. New York: International Universities Press, 1982.

Mulvey, Laura. "Visual Pleasure and Narrative Cinema". *Screen* 16 (1978): 6–18.

Murdoch, Brian O. *The Irish Adam and Eve Story from Saltair na Rann*. Vol. 2: Commentary. Dublin: Dublin Institute for Advanced Studies. 1976.

Murphy, Cliona. *The Women's Suffrage Movement and Irish Society in the Early Twentieth Century*. Hemel Hempstead: Harvester Wheatsheaf, 1989.

Murphy, Gerard, ed. *Early Irish Lyrics: Eighth to Twelfth Century*. Oxford: Clarendon, 1970.

—— "Notes on Aisling Poetry". *Éigse* 1.1 (1939): 40–50.

Murphy, Thomas. *Bailegangaire: The Story of Bailegangaire and How It Came by Its Appellation*. Dublin: Gallery Books, 1986.

Murphy, William Martin. *Prodigal Father*. Ithaca, NY: Cornell UP, 1978.

Nandy, Ashis. *At the Edge of Psychology*. Delhi: Oxford UP, 1980.

—— *The Intimate Enemy: Loss and Recovery of Self under Colonialism*. Oxford: Oxford UP, 1983.

Newton, Judith and Deborah Rosenfelt. "Introduction". In Newton and Rosenfelt, eds, *Feminist Criticism and Social Change*. Bloomington: Indiana UP, 1985. xv–xxxix.

Ní Bhrolcháin, Muireann. "Women in Early Irish Myths and Sagas". In Christine Nulty, ed., *The Crane Bag Book of Irish Studies*. Dublin: Blackwater Press, 1982, 525–32.

Ní Chuilleanáin, Eiléan, ed. *Irish Women: Image and Achievement*. Dublin: Arlen House, 1985.

Nulty, Christine, ed. "Images of the Irish Woman". *The Crane Bag Book of Irish Studies*. Dublin: Blackwater Press, 1982, 517–630.

O'Brien, Conor Cruise. "Willie and Augusta". *The Observer* (19 May 1985): 27.

O'Casey Sean. *Three Plays*. London: Macmillan, 1963.

O'Conaire, Brendan, ed. *The Love Songs of Connacht*. Dublin: Irish Academic Press, 1987.

Ó Corráin, Donnchadh. "Marriage in early Ireland". In Art Cosgrave, ed, *Marriage in Ireland*. Dublin: College Press, 1985.

O'Doherty, E. "Society, Identity and Change". *Studies*, Dublin 52 (1963): 123–35.

O Dowd, Liam. "Church, State and Women: the Aftermath of Partition". In Chris Curtin, Pauline Jackson and Barbara O'Connor, eds, *Gender in Irish Society*. Galway: Galway UP, 1987, 3–36.

O'Keeffe, J.G., ed. and trans. *Buile Suibhne*. London: Irish Texts Society, 1913.

O'Loughlin, Michael. *Stalingrad: The Street Directory*. Dublin: Raven Arts Press, 1980.

O'Toole, Fintan. *The Politics of Magic: The Work and Times of Tom Murphy*. Dublin: Raven Arts Press, 1987.

Olney, James. *The Rhizome and the Flower*. Berkeley: U of California P, 1980.

Ong, Walter J. *Orality and Literacy: The Technologizing of the Word*. London and New York: Methuen, 1982.

Ortner, Sherry. "Is Female to Male as Nature is to Culture?" In M. Rosaldo and L. Lamphere, eds, *Woman, Culture and Society*. Stanford, Calif.: Stanford UP, 1974, 67–88.

Owens, Rosemary. *Smashing Times: A History of the Irish Women's Suffrage Movement*. Dublin: Attic Press, 1984.

Pagels, Elaine. *Adam, Eve, and the Serpent*. London: Weidenfeld and Nicolson, 1988.

—— "What Became of God the Mother?" In Elizabeth Abel and Emily K. Abel, eds, *The Signs Reader: Women, Gender and Scholarship*. Chicago: U of Chicago P, 1983, 97–107.

Parker, Stewart. *Lost Belongings*. London: Euston Films/Thames Television PLC, 1987.

Parkin, Andrew. "Women in the Plays of W. B. Yeats". In Seán Gallagher, ed., *Woman in Irish Legend, Life and Literature*. Gerrards Cross: Colin Smythe, 1983, 38–57.

Pomeroy, Sarah. *Goddesses, Whores, Wives, and Slaves*. New York: Schocken, 1975.

Pountney, Rosemary. *Theatre of Shadows: Samuel Beckett's Drama 1956–76*. Gerrards Cross: Colin Smythe; Totowa, NJ: Barnes & Noble, 1988.

Praz, Mario. *The Romantic Agony*. 1933. London: Collins, 1960.

Quin, E.G. "Longas Mac n-Uisnig". In Myles Dillon, ed., *Irish Sagas*. Cork: Mercier, 1968, 53–66.

Rees, Alwyn and Rees, Brinley. *Celtic Heritage*. London: Thames and Hudson, 1961.

Renan, Ernest. *The Poetry of the Celtic Races*. London: Scott, n.d.

Rich, Adrienne. *On Lies, Secrets, and Silence*. New York: Norton, 1979.

Robertson, D.W. "The Concept of Courtly Love as an Impediment to the Understanding of Medieval Texts". In F.X. Newman, ed., *The Meaning of Courtly Love*. Albany: State U of New York P, 1968, 1–18.

Robinson, Lillian S. "Dwelling in Decencies". In *Sex, Class, and Culture*. Bloomington: Indiana UP, 1978, 3–10.

—— "Working/Women/Writing". In Judith Newton and Deborah Rosenfelt, eds, *Feminist Criticism and Social Change*. Bloomington: Indiana UP, 1985, 223–53.

Roe, Nicholas. "Wordsworth at the Flax-Dam: An Early Poem by Seamus Heaney". In Michael Allen and Angela Wilcox, eds, *Critical Approaches to Anglo-Irish Literature*. Gerrards Cross, Colin Smythe, 1989, 166–70.

Ronsard, Pierre de. *Oeuvres*, edited by Isidore Silver (7 vols). Chicago: U of Chicago P, 1966.

Rosaldo, Michelle Z. and Louise Lamphere, eds. *Woman, Culture and Society*. Stanford, Calif.: Stanford UP, 1974.

Ruether, Rosemary Radford. *Sexism and God-Talk: Towards a Feminist Theology*. London: SCM, 1983.

Saddlemyer, Ann. ed, *J.M. Synge: Collected Works III and IV: Plays Book I and II*. London: Oxford UP, 1968.

—— "Synge and the Nature of Woman." In Seán Gallagher ed., *Woman in Irish Legend, Life and Literature*. Gerrards Cross: Colin Smythe, 1983, 58–73.

Said, Edward. "Opponents, Audiences Constituencies and Communities". In Hal Foster, ed., *The Anti-Aesthetic: Essays on Postmodern Culture*. Washington: Bay Press, 1983, 135–59.

—— *The World, the Text, and the Critic*. London: Faber and Faber, 1983.

Sanday, Peggy Reeves. *Female Power and Male Dominance: On the origins of sexual inequality*. Cambridge: Cambridge UP, 1987.

Sands, Bobby. *One Day in My Life*. London: Pluto, 1983.

—— *Skylark Sing Your Lonely Song: An Anthology of the Writings of Bobby Sands*. Cork: Mercier Press, 1981.

Scannell, Yvonne. "The Constitution and the Role of Women". In Brian Farrell, ed. *De Valera's Constitution and Ours*. Dublin: Gill and Macmillan, 1988, 123–36.

Scrutator. "Private Theatricals in Excelsis". *Sinn Féin* (27 April 1907): 3.

Segal, Naomi. *Narcissus and Echo: Women in the French récit*. Manchester: Manchester UP, 1988.

Showalter, Elaine, ed. *The New Feminist Criticism*. New York: Pantheon, 1985.

Sjoestedt, Marie-Louise. *Gods and Heroes of the Celts*, trans. Myles Dillon. 1949. Berkeley, Calif.: Turtle Island Foundation, 1982.

Smyth, Ailbhe. "The Floozie in the Jacuzzi". *The Irish Review* 6 (Spring 1989): 7–24.

—— "Women and Power in Ireland: Problems, Progress, Practice". *Women's Studies International Forum* 8.4 (1985): 255–62.

—— *Women's Rights in Ireland*. Dublin: Ward River Press, 1983.

Spivak, Gayatri. "Imperialism and Sexual Difference". *Oxford Literary Review* 1/2 (1986): 225.

Stallworthy, Jon, ed. *The Penguin Anthology of Love Poetry*. Harmondsworth: Penguin, 1976.

Steiner Scott, Liz. ed. *Personally Speaking*. Dublin: Attic Press, 1985.

Stoker, Bram. *Dracula*. Oxford: Oxford UP, 1983.

Tuohy, Frank. "Destroyer's Derry". *Times Literary Supplement* (15 April 1977): 451.

Turner, Victor. "Social Dramas and Stories about Them". In W.J.T. Mitchell, ed., *On Narrative*. Chicago and London: U of Chicago P, 1981, 137–64.

Tymoczko, Maria. "Animal Imagery in *Loinges Mac nUislenn*". *Studia Celtica* 20/21 (1985–86): 145–66.

Viney, Ethna. "Ancient Wars: Sex and Sexuality". *Lip*. Dublin: Attic Press, 1989.

Waller, Edmund. *Poems*, edited by G. Thorn Drury. New York: Greenwood, 1968.

Ward, Margaret. *Unmanageable Revolutionaries: Women and Irish Nationalism*. London: Pluto, 1983.

Watson, George J. *Irish Identity and the Literary Revival*. London: Croom Helm, 1979.

Waugh, Auberon. "The Ireland We Know and Love". *The Spectator* (13 January 1973): 44.

Webster, Brenda. *Yeats: A Psychoanalytic Study*. London: Macmillan, 1974.

White, Hayden. "The Forms of Wildness: Archaeology of an Idea". In E. Dudley and M.E. Novak, eds, *The Wild Man Within*. Pittsburgh: Pittsburgh UP, 1972, 3–38.

Williams, Raymond. *The Country and the City*. London: Chatto & Windus, 1973.

Wills, Clair. "The Perfect Mother: Authority in the Poetry of Medbh McGuckian". *Text and Context* 3 (Autumn 1988): 91–111.

Yeats, William Butler. *Autobiographies*. London: Macmillan, 1955.

—— *Collected Plays*. London: Macmillan, 1963.

—— *Essays and Introductions*. London: Macmillan, 1961.

—— *Letters*, edited by Allan Wade. London: Hart Davis, 1954.

—— *Memoirs*, edited by Denis Donoghue. London: Macmillan, 1972.

—— *Mythologies*. New York: Macmillan, 1959.

—— *Poems*, edited by Richard Finneran. New York: Macmillan, 1983.

—— *The Collected Poems of W.B. Yeats*. London: Macmillan, 1973.

—— *The Variorum Edition of the Plays of W.B. Yeats*. London: Macmillan, 1966.

—— *The Variorum Edition of the Poems of W.B. Yeats*, edited by Peter Allt and Russell Alspach. New York: Macmillan, 1957.

—— *Uncollected Prose*, edited by J.P. Frayne (2 vols). New York: Columbia UP, 1970.

Younger, Calton. *Gills Irish. Lives Arthur Griffith*. Dublin: Gill and Macmillan, 1981.

Index